FURNITURE DESIGNED BY ARCHITECTS

FURNITURE
DESIGNED BY ARCHITECTS
BY MARIAN PAGE

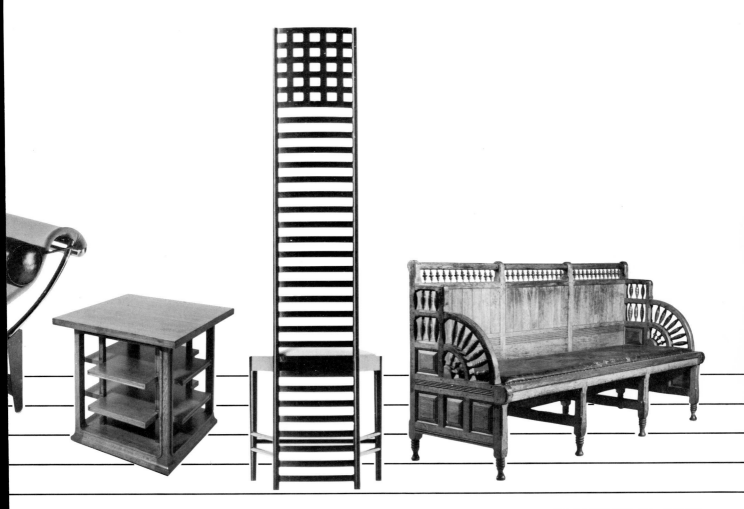

WHITNEY LIBRARY OF DESIGN

an imprint of Watson-Guptill Publications/New York

THE ARCHITECTURAL PRESS LTD./LONDON

First published 1980 in the United States and Canada by Whitney Library of Design,
an imprint of Watson-Guptill Publications,
a division of Billboard Publications, Inc.,
1515 Broadway, New York, N.Y. 10036

Library of Congress Cataloging in Publication Data
Page, Marian, 1918-
    Furniture designed by architects.
    Bibliography: p.
    Includes index.
    1. Furniture design.   2.   Architects.   I.   Title.
TT196.P33   749.2   79-27961
ISBN 0-8230-7180-4

Published in Great Britain by The Architectural Press Ltd.,
9 Queen Anne's Gate, London SW1H 9BY
ISBN 0-85139-235-0

Manufactured in U.S.A.

First Printing, 1980

Edited by Sharon Lee Ryder and Susan Davis
Designed by Bob Fillie
Graphic production by Ellen Greene

CONTENTS

ACKNOWLEDGMENTS

A great deal has been written about the architects discussed in this book and, to a lesser degree, about the furniture they designed. No one could write a book like this without being indebted to these sources and I have tried to list most of them in the Selected Bibliography.

I am also indebted to many individuals who have given me invaluable assistance and would especially like to express my appreciation to Susan E. Meyer, Editorial Director, for her suggestion that my article "Rediscovering the Furniture of Six American Architects" in *American Art & Antiques* of July–August 1978 be expanded into a book; to Marjorie Folsom Leighey and Herbert Jacobs for so courteously and eloquently answering my questions about what it was like to live with Frank Lloyd Wright's furniture; and last but by no means least to Susan Colgan for her indispensable and untiring efforts in collecting the photographs.

INTRODUCTION

Why do architects design furniture? There are many reasons ranging from the egotistical to the philanthropic, from a wish to unify the arts to a desire to counteract the effects of industrialism. They may be rebelling against the incongruities of machine-made furniture, or reacting, as Henry David Thoreau did, to the clutter he found in Concord houses: "Furniture! Thank God, I can sit and I can stand without the aid of a furniture warehouse." They may believe they are enhancing the lives of those who live and work in their buildings. Peter Blake suggests in *The Master Builders* that the reason modern architects like Le Corbusier, Mies van der Rohe, Marcel Breuer, and Alvar Aalto devoted so much time to designing furniture was because "the inside and outside of a modern structure are regarded as one thanks to the technological development of building with large sheets of glass, and the aesthetic development of sensing objects simultaneously from many vantage points." But whatever the reason, architects have been providing furniture for their buildings ever since the 17th century.

The 18th-century English architect Robert Adam, however, seems to have been the first to include the furniture and other furnishings in his architectural scheme. In an Adam interior the carpet on the floor repeats the pattern of the stuccoed ceiling, and even the wine coolers are architect-designed. What started with Adam was carried on by Samuel McIntire and a few others in America through the early years of the 19th century. Then things began to get out of hand. By the end of the 1830s the fine traditions of handcraftsmanship were almost forgotten while the machine was beginning to exert its baleful influence on furniture and much else. Not long after the middle of the century drawing rooms were overflowing with an astonishing array of furniture and knickknacks as if to proclaim the miracle of mass production. A reaction was inevitable and it came during the last 30 years of the century when a group of English architects spurred on by William Morris revolted against the ornate vulgarity of popular taste. Morris blamed all the ornamental excess of the Victorians on the industrial revolution and called for a return to the honesty and simplicity of medieval times. His emphasis on handcraftsmanship set off a debate between the hand and the machine that has never been completely silenced. His plea for honesty and simplicity, however, had a more realistic and valuable influence on the architects who followed him.

These architects, perhaps more than anything else, were rebelling against the inhumanity of industrialism just as Ruskin, Carlyle, Whistler, and the Pre-Raphaelites had. Designing furniture may seem an odd way of rebelling against a world of such harsh realities as technology and mass production, but then furniture is an important symbol of life in the Western world. It is more intimately connected with people's existence than any other household article. We live with it day and night. Furniture is certainly as important to our well-being as architecture. For that reason it has a talismanic importance, which the Anglo-Irish writer Elizabeth Bowen thoroughly understood. "After inside upheavals," she writes in *The Death of the Heart*, "it is important to fix on imperturbable *things*. Their imperturbableness, and air that nothing has happened renews our guarantee." And furniture takes an important place among those imperturbable things which "are what we mean by civilisation." In that sense, she adds, "the destruction of buildings and furniture is more palpably dreadful to the human spirit than the destruction of human life." And when the Woolf's London house was bombed during World War II, Elizabeth Bowen wrote to Virginia Woolf: "All my life I have said, 'Whatever happens there will always be tables and chairs'—and what a mistake."

Furniture, moreover, no less than windows, doors, and decorative details, can destroy the quality of an interior if it is badly proportioned, out of scale, or so intrusive that it detracts from the architecture. However, furniture can lend an interior scale and poetic enrichment as well as provide for the functions of living and working. Baillie Scott, one of Morris's followers, said much the same thing in 1895: "It is difficult for the architect to draw a fixed line between the architecture of a house and the furniture. The conception of an interior must necessarily include the furniture which is to be used in it, and this naturally leads to the conclusion that the architect should design chairs and tables as well as the house itself. Every architect who loves his work must have had his enthusiasm dampened by a prophetic vision of the hideous furniture with which his client may fill his rooms, and looks all the more incongruous as the rooms themselves are architecturally beautiful." It can be argued, of course, that most people prefer to select their own furniture and personal objects. They especially want the interiors of their houses to have the imprint of their own personalities. The Viennese architect Adolf Loos was aware of this when he wrote his parable of the Poor Rich Man who tried to add little objects to his house. "Don't you know," says the architect, "you are complete."

There is no doubt that architects sometimes see themselves as molding and shaping the lives of those who live and work in their buildings. There is, in fact, something utopian in the thinking of most architects who have designed furniture from Morris and Wright to Gaudi and Le Corbusier. Not only did they consider it both their right and their duty to design every part of their buildings inside and out, they believed they were making the world a better place by doing it. But, as Oscar Wilde put it: "A map of the world that does not include Utopia is not worth even glancing at, for it leaves out the one country at which Humanity is always landing."

The architects of the modern movement didn't reject industrial society so much as they espoused it. It was in their nature to design everything from a chair to a skyscraper entirely independent of the past. "All I ask," Le Corbusier wrote in 1925, "is that we build modern mass-produced furniture and not affectations of royal styles." No one can deny that they did lead

furniture makers out of the morass they had fallen into, but they were less successful in building mass-produced furniture. Marcel Breuer and Alvar Aalto were among the exceptions. Italian furniture builder Dino Gavina, whom Breuer once called "the most emotional and impulsive of all furniture builders in the world," was quoted in the October 1979 *Skyline* as saying neither Mies's Barcelona chair nor Le Corbusier's chairs were designed for mass production. Mies, Gavina believes, designed the Barcelona chair expressly for the Barcelona Pavilion because he "felt the need for a chair which would not disturb the purity of the space" but had no idea of it as a mass-produced object. Le Corbusier's chairs, he surmises, were also designed for a particular space and never intended to be mass produced. However, he says Breuer's chairs were "specifically geared to mass distribution and meant to be fabricated in a large series, an industrial product belonging to our time, and simultaneously in harmony with our culture, our materials, and the contemporary technology." And while Aalto designed his furniture for particular spaces he also designed it to be mass produced albeit in comparatively small quantities. Nevertheless it was the post-World War II architects Charles Eames and Eero Saarinen who were probably the first to completely come to terms with modern technology and mass production. In the hands of Eames and Saarinen the machine was no longer a threat—nor an incentive as it had been for the architects of the modern movement—but an obedient servant, even a partner, of design.

Today architecture has become so complex and technologically involved that it is almost impossible for an architect to design a building, let alone its furnishings. The answer, of course, has been teamwork. But the teamwork of today is not the teamwork of yesterday when builder and cabinetmaker shared common ideals and cared more for craftsmanship than personal recognition. Too often today's team members are after personal fame and fortune, which is not to condemn them so much as the industrialized society that brought them into being. One can hardly compare the satisfaction of creating a beautiful chair by hand to the dubious satisfaction of ordering one from a factory which is spewing out the same chair by the millions. In that sense Morris was right when he condemned the machine and lauded "the joy of the maker." It is ironical, or perhaps inevitable, that there has been a return to Morris's way of thinking in our post-modern era, and technology is again suspect.

It is a long and sometimes circuitous route from the beautifully crafted chair of a Robert Adam or Samuel McIntire to the bicycle-inspired chairs of Breuer or Saarinen's pedestal chair, but the elegance of the modern chairs might never have come into being without Morris. In spite of his hatred of the machine, it was his poetic philosophy that helped spur the later architects "to dominate the work of the contrivance" their genius had created, to use Wright's words. Whether these architects were impelled by idealism, rebellion, vanity, or even arrogance, there can be little doubt that they changed people's way of looking at a chair just as Picasso changed their way of looking at a painting. But something was lost, too, by the architectural takeover of furniture. Tubular steel—even gently bent plywood—can hardly replace that "furniture with its time-stained patina," those "objects lovingly worked by generations of cabinetmakers, potters, and goldsmiths," which Professor Mario Praz has bemoaned the loss of. Or, as the family retainer put it in Bowen's *The Death of the Heart*: "Oh, furniture like we've got is too much for some that would rather not have the past." It was an elite that adorned their drawing rooms with those "objects lovingly worked by generations of cabinetmakers," and it was another kind of elite—an intellectual elite—that embraced the functional simplicity and machine esthetic of the modern movement.

Of course many more architects have designed furniture for their buildings than those mentioned in these pages. It was not the author's intention to write a history of furniture designed by architects, but to focus on some of the important architects who designed furniture as an integral part of their architecture and to trace the forces that impelled them to do so. Nor did the practice end with Eames and Saarinen as the book does. The stage moved from America, however, where one might have expected it to have found its natural home, to Italy. Gio Ponti, Joe Colombo, Marco Zanuso, Gae Aulenti, and other Italian architects have continued the interest in furniture design that, in this century at least, started with the Arts and Crafts architects who were disciples of Morris. Describing their work with the word "art," however, might be challenged by some, including Ada Louise Huxtable who calls modern Italian furniture "molded polyurethane marvels of 'anti-design.'" But while the furniture designed by the Italian architects may be innovative, it seemed to the author to be but a continuation of the fusion of art and technology that was so well achieved by Eames.

18TH-CENTURY ENGLAND AND FEDERAL AMERICA

Lord Burlington's protégé William Kent was probably the first English architect to design furniture for its particular setting, and Robert Adam went even further in making furniture an integral part of his interior schemes. Although it was not unusual for 18th-century architects to take an interest in furniture, they usually left its design to the cabinetmaker. In a letter written in 1724 by Sir John Vanbrugh, the architect of Blenheim Palace, to the Earl of Carlisle at Castle Howard, he says: "I believe four doors will give both Light and View sufficient, without Windows, and then there will be Space enough for Chairs; the Table I think (as I mentioned formerly) shou'd stand always fix'd in the Middle of the Room."

In the 19th century, however, it was almost considered bad manners for an architect to concern himself with furniture—a mere accessory only fit for lesser beings to bother about. England's early 19th-century architect Sir John Soane, for instance, admired Robert Adam's achievement but considered his commitment to furniture design something of an aberration. ". . . it is to the activity of Messrs. Adam that we are more particularly indebted for breaking the talismanic charm which the fashion of the day had imposed," he told a Royal Academy audience. "However Mr. Adam," he added, "may occasionally, in his flights of fancy have descended to a Sedan Chair, or to the Keyhole of a Lady's Escritoire, let us, in candour and justice to departed merit, remember that in the preceding age, the great . . . Kent . . . was likewise consulted for State Coaches, City Barges and Children's Cradles." And therein we glimpse the beginning of the self-conscious architect who sometimes places himself too far above the users of his buildings, the sitters on chairs, the sleepers in beds, the diners at tables, the writers at desks, and so on.

The 18th century was a decorous and elegant age. The 19th was not. The furniture and interiors of Kent and Adam were an expression of a society that cultivated the graces of life—"the natural outcome of the ethos of the age, parts of a process of supply and demand," as the historian G. M. Trevelyan put it. "And the same may be said of the literary world of Gray, Goldsmith, Cowper, Johnson, Boswell, and Burke." He could have added the art world of Thomas Gainsborough and Sir Joshua Reynolds. "In its quiet, settled unity of aim and thought it was a classical age," says Trevelyan, "unlike the vexed Victorian, when most of the great men—Carlyle, Ruskin, Matthew Arnold, the Pre-Raphaelites, William Morris, Whistler, Browning, and Meredith—were in a state of revolt against the debased ideals of their time . . ." And, as we shall see, that state of revolt again led numerous architects not only to look at furniture once more but to design it. The 18th century was still a time when maker and purchaser of goods thought in terms of handicraft. The artist and the manufacturer were not yet going their own very different ways. "Life and art were still human, not mechanical, and quality still counted for more than quantity," in the words of Trevelyan.

In America more or less the same ethos ruled the ways of life, but those ways were usually on a smaller and simpler scale. And since Americans, even after the Revolution, followed England's lead when it came to architecture and furniture design, there was a time lag as well. Thus Samuel McIntire, who was the most effective translator of the Adam style into American terms, created most of his masterpieces in the two decades after Adam's death in 1792.

WILLIAM KENT 1684-1748

. . . the Taste is not to conform to the Art, but the Art to the Taste. JOSEPH ADDISON

Two adjectives generally attributed to William Kent—versatile and genial—could hardly be more apt. Sir John Summerson expressed his versatility when he pointed out that to assess Kent properly "one must take account not only of his decorative painting and his classical architecture, but of his illustrations for the *Faerie Queene* and Gay's *Fables*, his occasional essays in a very personal kind of Gothic, his furniture, and, above all, his landscape gardening." And almost all contemporary reports point to his geniality as well as his spirit of fun. He was, according to one account, large, voluble, and merry. Although he was of humble birth, uneducated, and sometimes "gross in habits," to use James Lees-Milne's phrase, his familiarity with and importance to his many noble patrons indicate both talent and geniality. In fact we have it straight from Horace Walpole, that acute observer of 18th-century life and art, that Kent's "oracle was so much consulted by all who affected taste, that nothing was thought complete without his assistance. He was not only consulted for furniture, as frames of pictures, glasses, tables, chairs, etc., but for plate, for a barge, for a cradle." He even designed ladies' dresses, as did many architect-designers including William Morris, Hector Guimard, and Frank Lloyd Wright. Perhaps it is, as the fashion historian James Laver said, "Woman is the mould into which the spirit of the age pours itself."

William Kent's talents and personality first attracted the attention of members of the gentry in his native Yorkshire, who sent him to Rome to study painting and to collect art objects for them. While in Italy he met and impressed many well-born Englishmen who were making the Grand Tour and who were later to commission him for one thing or another. Among these were Lord Burlington who brought Kent back to London in 1719 and became his patron and friend—an arrangement that lasted throughout Kent's life and had far-reaching consequences for the arts. It was under Burlington's aegis that Kent became an architect and furniture designer. It was Burlington who brought out his "magniloquent decorative sense," as it has been aptly termed. His first furniture was undoubtedly designed for Chiswick house, Lord Burlington's style-setting Palladian villa on the Thames.

Kent's furniture, which was as flamboyant as his personality, seemed to contradict the austerity of the Palladian exterior. In fact it expressed his own ebullience just as the Augustan formality and simplicity of Palladian architecture expressed the character of the 18th-century English aristocrat. Kent, as James Lees-Milne notes, had all the imagination, fire, and genius which most of his noble patrons and friends lacked. He admits, however, that without their guidance and companionship he never would have achieved his successes. In a sense, he says, Kent was "their product and crowning fulfillment." And it is certainly true that it took both Kent's imagination and Sir Robert Walpole's nobility to bring about such a fabulous piece of furniture as the state bed at Houghton Hall. The trimmings alone cost £1,219/3*s*/11*d*!

But with all his imagination and extroverted furniture, it should be remembered that when Kent designed an entire building such as Holkham Hall, which he did for the Earl of Leicester, he, too, put up a stark Palladian front. Inside, however, all is opulence. It was plainly in

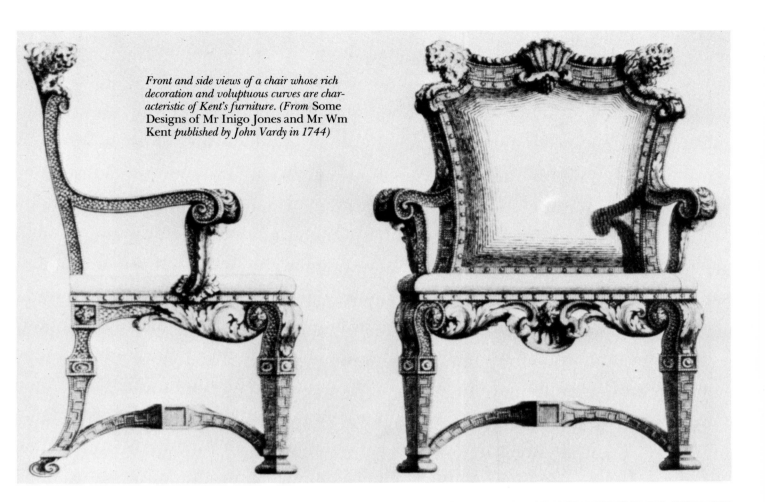

Front and side views of a chair whose rich decoration and voluptuous curves are characteristic of Kent's furniture. (From Some Designs of Mr Inigo Jones and Mr Wm Kent *published by John Vardy in 1744*)

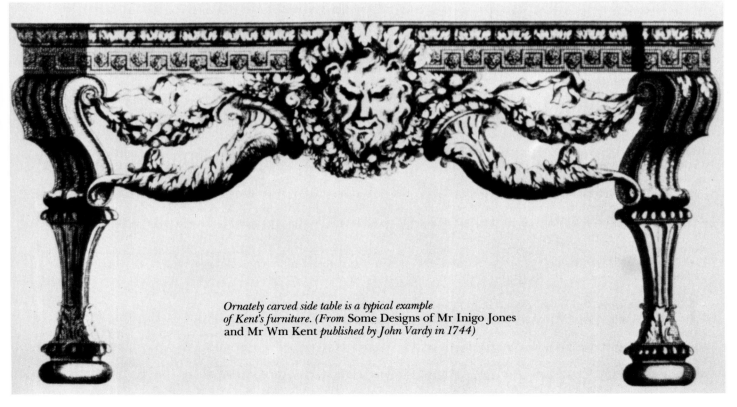

Ornately carved side table is a typical example of Kent's furniture. (From Some Designs of Mr Inigo Jones and Mr Wm Kent *published by John Vardy in 1744*)

his furniture and his gardens that Kent gave his own fantasy full play. It was there that he instilled imaginative life into Palladian austerity or, as Rudolph Wittkower put it, "gave Burlington's solemn Palladian building its gay and festive quality." And since Kent designed his furniture for men who were arbiters of taste, one can only surmise that there was more to those dignified and discriminating 18th-century Palladians than meets the eye. Kent's furniture, as an early 19th-century writer expressed it, was "audacious, splendid, sumptuous and of finished technique, and as these qualities were in demand, Kent was supreme in his own generation." Even William Hogarth, who disliked the man, couldn't have depicted his furniture more lovingly than he did in his painting, "Assembly at Wanstead House."

The furniture style that Kent popularized for Palladian interiors was often architectural in character, which is not surprising for one who was probably the first English architect to design furniture in direct relation to its architectural setting. This is particularly notice-

able in the large bookcases and mahogany cabinets which he framed between columns or pilasters and surmounted with entablatures and pediments. These pieces were intended to remain in the house for which they were designed and to contribute directly to an interior effect. These large wall pieces, along with the carved and gilt wood chairs, settees, and stools he designed to harmonize with them, all complemented the elaborate doors, windows, chimneypieces, and cornices of the rooms. The chairs and settees often had backs surmounted by a cresting of heavily scrolled acanthus and the space beneath the seat rail filled with large acanthus scrolls or swags of fruit centering a mask or a double shell. The scroll-shaped legs were frequently topped by masks—female or lion masks were Kent's favorites.

Kent's furniture, like Frank Lloyd Wright's furniture, is so much a part of its architectural setting that it can't be appreciated out of its context where it only seems massive, overdone, and often of eccentric proportions. Even Horace Walpole who was certainly familiar with it (Kent designed the furniture for his father Sir Robert

Above: The opulent saloon at Holkham Hall in Norfolk is almost exactly as Kent designed it. The original Genoese velvet is still on its walls as well as on Kent's gilt suite of armchairs, and the paintings by Rubens, Vandyke, etc., are the "many capital pictures standing there to be put up" that Mrs. Lybbe Powys noted when she visited the just finished room in 1756.

Opposite page: "The Assembly at Wanstead House" by William Hogarth depicts furniture attributed to Kent including a heavily carved and gilded table on the right with an elaborately carved elbow chair beside it. A typical Kent chimneypiece can be seen above the table, and the back of a heavy gilt chair with scroll feet is visible under the chandelier. The painting was commissioned in 1727 and probably finished in the 1740s.

Walpole at Houghton Hall) didn't refrain from calling the architect's hand "immeasurably ponderous." Fortunately it can still be seen in its original setting at Houghton and Holkham. Particularly at Holkham one can understand Allan Cunningham's appreciation of Kent's talents as he described them in his *Lives of the Most Eminent Painters, etc.* of 1820: "He could plan bookcases, cabinets, and chimney pieces, hang curtains with grace; and in short do all and more than all the upholsterer aspires to now."

While Kent's furniture designs were highly influential among the small privileged class for which they were provided, his influence ended when he died in 1748. Even during his lifetime there were a few members of that 18th-century aristocracy who preferred the outdated styles of Wren. Horace Walpole was never overly enthusiastic, and when Lord Oxford visited Raynham Hall, he commented rather acidly that the "rooms are fitted up by Mr. Kent and consequently there is a great deal of gilding; very clumsy over-charged chimney pieces to the great waste of fine marble." Kent did, however, make an impression on the young Adam.

ROBERT ADAM 1728–1792

. . . it is in the great rooms where walls, ceilings, carpets, curtains, furniture are designed as a whole that we marvel at Adam's ability to devise displays of amazing originality. TERENCE DAVIS

No one could have been more concerned about furniture than the Scottish-born architect Robert Adam who considered that his responsibility as master designer extended to every detail of the interior from the ceiling decoration to the carpet pattern. He designed furniture to be an essential part of his decorating schemes and he placed each piece in its correct position. Only in that way, he felt, could a truly harmonious result be achieved. He might employ the painter Angelica Kauffmann to decorate his ceilings, the landscape gardener "Capability" Brown to lay out the gardens, an Italian craftsman to execute the stucco work, Thomas Moore to weave the carpet, a cabinetmaker to carry out his furniture designs, but Adam was the designer and planner.

William Kent had been dead a decade when Adam returned from three years of study in Italy and lost no time in putting the ideas he had gleaned from antiquity into practice. It was as if, in rebellion against Kent's somewhat heavy style, Adam brought 18th-century interiors more into conformity with their neoclassic exteriors. Kent was supreme in his own generation, but his heavy architectural interiors hardly outlasted him. The light and delicate character of Adam's furniture, however, not only inspired Chippendale, Sheraton, and Hepplewhite, but also the cabinetmakers and designers of Federal America. Adam may have derived his ideas from Diocletian's Palace at Spalatro, from Hadrian's villa at Tivoli, from the new discoveries of Herculaneum and Pompeii, among other antique sites, but he fused them into his own extremely personal style.

Robert Adam embarked on his career as a furniture designer in 1762. In 1773 when the first volume of the *Works in Architecture of Robert and James Adam* was published, the brothers could justly boast: ". . . we have not only met with the approbation of our employers, but even with the imitation of other artists, to such a degree, as in some measure to have brought about, in this country, a kind of evolution . . . within these few years . . . in the decoration of the inside, an almost total change." Robert (for it was chiefly his doing) had become the unchallenged arbiter of taste. And we have the 19th-century words of Sir John Soane to his Royal Academy students to show us that Adam's importance was appreciated by at least one architect of the following generation: "To Mr. Adam's taste in the Ornament of his Buildings, and Furniture, we stand indebted, inasmuch as Manufacturers of every kind felt, as it were, the electric power of this Revolution in Art."

George III had acceded to the throne in 1760 and, as patron of the arts, much was expected of him. Change was in the air and Adam was there to implement it. "If there are any talents among us," as Horace Walpole put it, "this seems the crisis for their appearance: The Throne itself is now the altar of the graces, and whoever sacrifices to them becomingly, is sure that his offer-

A doorway flanked by candlestands in the drawing room of Northumberland House, c. 1773–1774. Candlestands were often used in drawing rooms, according to Sheraton's Cabinet-Maker and Upholsterer's Drawing Book *of 1792, "for the convenience of affording additional light to such parts of the room where it neither be ornamental nor easy to introduce any other kind."*

ing will be smiled upon." And Adam's offering was surely smiled upon.

Robert was the second of ten Adam children who were descended, as he put it, from "two of the ancientist families in Scotland." Their father, William Adam, was himself a distinguished architect, and after his death Robert and his older brother carried on his architectural practice in Scotland. Then, at the end of 1754, Robert set off on a Grand Tour that was to bring him the friendship and influence of the French architect and draughtsman Clérisseau (whose followers also included Thomas Jefferson) and the Venetian Piranesi. Upon the completion of his Grand Tour in 1758, Adam set up his practice in London, and apparently conscious of being an artist and innovator from the beginning, it didn't take him too long to achieve what he set out to do.

Although Adam was an architect, he hardly built any houses during the first decade of his practice. He did, however, complete several which had been started by other architects and he remodeled others within their existing shells. It is, in any case, as an interior architect that he is remembered. The Adam conception of exterior design, as Sir John Summerson noted, never became as free or as felicitous as his management of interiors. While Adam's furniture and interior decoration were related as Kent's had been earlier in the century, they were totally different in character. Kent's furniture and interiors were marked by a lusty grandeur, Adam's by a delicate gaiety. Horace Walpole may have regretted that "From Kent's mahogany we are dwindled to Adam's filigree. Grandeur and simplicity are not yet fashion," but everyone else seemed to be delighted with the change.

Osterly Park, for which Adam designed all the interiors for the banker Robert Child between 1761 and 1780 along with a complete range of furniture, still retains most of its contents and is especially interesting since it represents his early as well as his mature style. The house actually retains all the furniture that is listed in a 1782 inventory. When the sometimes capricious Horace Walpole visited Osterly in 1773, he found it "the palace of palaces!—and yet a place sans crown sans coronet, but such expense, such taste. . . . There is a hall, library, breakfast-room, eating-room, all chefs-d'oeuvre of Adam, a gallery one hundred and thirty feet long and a drawing room worthy of Eve before the Fall. . . . Mr. Child's dressing room is full of pictures, gold, filigree, china and japan. So is all the house; the chairs are taken from antique lyres, and make charming harmony. . . ."

Walpole, however, didn't think much of the Park: "the ugliest spot of ground in the universe—and so I returned comforted to Strawberry." (He was referring, of course, to Strawberry Hill, his Gothicized mansion which

Above: Drawing of a section of the drawing room for Northumberland House, c. 1773– 1774, shows how precisely Adam designed and placed his furniture to be part of the overall composition of a room.

Opposite page: Drawing of an oval-backed armchair for Sir Abraham Hume in 1779.

Above: "The chairs are taken from antique lyres, and make charming harmony," said Horace Walpole of Adam's lyre-back chairs for the eating room at Osterly Park in Middlesex of 1761–1780. Their delicate and graceful carving is beautifully integrated with the room's plaster panels.

Opposite page, top: The furniture in the Tapestry Room at Osterly Park is placed to relate to the patterns of the wall tapestries.

Opposite page, bottom: This view of the Osterly Park eating room shows the handsome sideboard table on the right flanked by urns–a feature of several Adam dining rooms. In the middle is a lyre-back chair shown above. On the left is one of a pair of pier tables beneath corresponding mirrors which stand against the piers for which Adam designed them.

set the whole Gothic revival madness in motion.) When Walpole returned for a second visit to Osterly in 1778, the Etruscan room, the state bedroom, and the tapestry room had been completed, and he was not impressed: "The last chamber after these two proud rooms, chills you: it is called the Etruscan, and is painted all over like Wedgwood's ware, with black and yellow small grotesques. Even the chairs are of painted wood. It would be a pretty waiting-room in a garden. I never saw such a profound tumble into the Bathos. It is going out of a palace into a potter's field. . . ." He disclaimed the green velvet bedchamber with its ornate bedstead as "too theatric, and too like a modern head-dress, for round the outside of the dome are festoons of artificial flowers. What," he asked, "would Vitruvius think of a dome decorated by a milliner?" Our own contemporary Ian Nairn, however, finds the state bed at Osterly "exactly balanced between a sense of occasion and a sense of humor."

Adam's revolutionary furniture was slight and streamlined. His wall furniture including tables, commodes, mirrors, girandoles was almost always considered part of the architectural treatment of a room and thus of his design as an architect, while movable pieces were occasionally designed by others. Adam's semicircular commodes create a vastly different impression than Kent's massive rectangular ones. His tables have slender tapered legs. Usually his furniture is either gilded or painted with soft pastel colors which blend with ceiling and wall colors. Marquetry is not often used in Adam furniture as it was by professional cabinetmakers. His ornaments are either painted directly onto the piece or are executed in metal or composition. The lyre-back armchairs which he designed for Osterly and which made such "charming harmony" for Horace Walpole were copied about a year or so later by Chippendale but without the delicacy of Adam's chair. Chippendale, in fact, often designed furniture in the Adam style. Sometimes both Chippendale (or another cabinetmaker) and Adam provided furniture designs for a particular house. When the execution of Adam's designs was included in one of his commissions (it wasn't always), he was responsible for choosing the cabinetmaker, supervising and approving the work.

If anything, Adam furniture is even more a part of the architectural scheme than Kent's. Tables, bookcases, consoles, even chairs were designed as decorative accents for a particular place. Recently the Department of Furniture and Woodwork of the Victorian and Albert Museum (administrators of Osterly Park) did considerable research to discover Adam's original placement of furniture and came to the conclusion that chairs and sofas, even dining room

Demilune commode designed for the drawing room at Osterly Park is one of a pair. Veneered with satinwood, a medium peculiarly suited to Adam's designs, it is enriched with inlaid medallions of classical figures mounted in chased and gilt bronze.

Above: Detail of decoration above the fireplace in the Etruscan Room at Osterly Park.

Opposite page: The chairs and painted decoration in the Etruscan dressing room at Osterly Park are closely related in both design and color. The lacquer commode with the pier glass above it probably served as the dressing table in this room, which seemed to Horace Walpole "a cold bath next to the bed chamber."

chairs, were placed in symmetrical arrangements against the wall when not in use, thus leaving the center of the room clear. In this way the viewer gets the full impact of a chair's carving and upholstery while its largely undecorated back is hidden. The Victoria and Albert study, moreover, has brought out how certain chairs, settees, and sofas complete a wall composition and how their decoration is consonant with the decoration of the rest of the room. Actually there is quite a lot of evidence in memoirs and diaries to indicate that it was the fashion during most of the 18th century to place furniture against the wall when not in use. Francis Watson tells us the story of Madame de Maintenon who, when she pulled a chair from the wall where it normally stood, was reprimanded by Louis XIV for "spoiling the architecture." And an early 19th-century French visitor to Osterly records his dismayed impression of the then-arrangement of the furniture in his *Journal of a Tour and Residence in Great Britain during the Years 1810 and 1811*: "... tables, sofas, and chairs, were studiously *dérangés* about the fireplaces, and in the middle of the rooms, as if the family had just left them although the house had not been inhabited for several years. Such is the modern fashion of placing of furniture carried to an extreme, as fashions always are, that the apartments of a fashionable house look like an upholsterer's or cabinetmaker's shop."

Confirmation of the customary wall arrangement of furniture is also to be found in a passage in the *Housekeeping Book* by Susanna Whatman published in the middle of the 18th century: "One of the most useful directions [for a new servant] next to carrying a candle upright is that of putting away chairs, tables, and anything that goes next to a wall, with the hand behind it. For want of this trifling attention, great pieces are frequently knocked out of the stucco and the backs of the chairs, if bending, sloping backwards, leave a mark on the wall." The Victoria and Albert research also serves to remind us that even when the original furniture still exists in an 18th-century house, it has obviously not remained in its original place. Subsequent generations have had their own ideas of furniture arrangement. And this is just as true of a 19th- and even 20th-century house.

Adam played a central role in the first phase of English neoclassicism, and it was Adam who influenced America's Federal style which was also essentially an interior architecture. Samuel McIntire, one of the chief and most sensitive propagators of the Adam style in Federal America, matched the sheer virtuosity of Adam in harmonious, albeit simpler interiors that he suited to the Puritan tastes of the wealthy merchants of New England.

SAMUEL McINTIRE 1757–1811

. . . if one style may be called typical of the complex Federal era, it is not the Romanism of Jefferson and Ramée, not the Grecian note struck by Latrobe, but the cautious yet splendid manner evolved by the Salem carver Samuel McIntire. WAYNE ANDREWS

Salem's splendid foursquare houses—more elegant than those in many early New England towns because of the prosperity and worldliness brought on by the far-reaching clipper ships—were largely the work of Samuel McIntire. Following Robert Adam's lead in his own way, McIntire designed many of that little seafaring city's late 18th- and early 19th-century houses, and he carved the chimneypieces and furniture that went into them. "Not only could he conceive the whole," as Dean A. Fales, former director of Salem's Essex Institute, put it, "but he could execute the particular." Thus he achieved the harmonious results that Robert Adam believed were only possible if the architect was responsible for the design of every aspect of the interior. But McIntire, unlike Adam, probably didn't have any theories about design. He was merely continuing old craft traditions, and because of his innate artistic sense, he achieved those harmonious results instinctively, much as the builders of the clipper ships did whose designs grew inevitably out of the nature of the materials and the structure. McIntire was a direct descendant of the American house carpenters who were often the furniture makers as well, and if not, house builder and cabinetmaker were essentially craftsmen and thought alike. They were motivated by the same cultural forces and couldn't help but create a homogeneous style. Perhaps the American Shakers, who built their houses and their furniture anonymously, present the most striking example of this natural rapport between builder and cabinetmaker. The communal culture of the Shakers, their belief in functional simplicity, and their exquisite craftsmanship all combined to endow everything they created with a simple elegance.

Thomas Merton, in his introduction to Faith and Edward Deming Andrews' *Religion in Wood*, observed that the "peculiar grace of a Shaker chair is due to the fact that it was made by someone capable of believing that an angel might come and sit on it." McIntire probably didn't expect any angels to sit on his chairs since he designed them for the wealthy and worldly merchants of Salem, but the same kind of rapport that existed among the Shakers existed among those New England craftsmen. Their art was communal, a clear response to a common environment, a common history.

McIntire was born in Salem, learned woodcarving from his father, and taught himself architecture. He never traveled and never saw an Adam interior. He acquired his style from architectural handbooks which he refined through his own impeccable artistic sense to fit the Puritan tastes of his clientele. McIntire's style was chaste and simple whereas Adam's was rich and extravagant, but both were marked by a rhythmic harmony of the parts and a sure sense of proportion.

McIntire, according to his friend and famous Salem diarist, the Reverend William Bentley, was "descended of a family of carpenters who had no claims on public favor and was educated at a branch of that business." But he adds, "By attention he soon gained a superiority to all of his occupation & the Present Court House, the North & South Meeting houses, and indeed all the improvements of Salem for nearly 30 years past have been done to his eye." It is certainly true that he couldn't claim the background, education, and sophistication of a Robert Adam or, for that matter, his fellow American Thomas Jefferson, who, incidentally, was building the

Side chair from a drawing by McIntire.

Left: The design and carving of this great chest-on-chest for Madam Elizabeth Derby, c. 1796, is attributed to McIntire. It was made by William Lemon.

Below: Detail of McIntire's cornucopia carving on the sides of the Madam Elizabeth Derby chest-on-chest, shown at left.

second version of Monticello when McIntire was building some of his graceful Salem houses. He could, however, claim to be their equals in artistry and a remarkable sense of rightness.

Actually the first intimation of the new Adamesque furniture styles appeared in America as early as 1776 in a small desk made by the Philadelphia cabinetmaker Benjamin Randolph probably from Jefferson's design. This little desk, on which Jefferson wrote the Declaration of Independence, boasts a line inlay of lighter wood that anticipated a major decorative element of the furniture that was later to achieve popularity through the work of McIntire and others. It seems inevitable that Jefferson, the most versatile genius in an age of virtuosity, should have designed furniture. In fact he probably designed many more pieces for Monticello than anyone realizes since most of that furniture was dispersed after his death. We do know, however, that Jefferson's furniture, like Monticello itself, was peculiarly his own creation designed for his own purposes. He designed whatever he needed from hen coops for his farm to dumb waiters for his dining room. Monticello's overseer credited James Dinsmore, one of Jefferson's master builders, with making "a great deal of nice mahogany furniture," much of which was probably of Jefferson's design. There is no doubt that furniture interested Jefferson. He made measurements of pieces he saw in France and elsewhere. Among his drawings are furniture designs although no pieces made from those drawings are known to have survived.

Both Jefferson and McIntire entered the competition for the design of the new Capitol in Washington, which is perhaps indicative of the culture of the time—McIntire, the self-taught architect who had never left his native Salem, and the learned, widely traveled Jefferson for whom architecture was one of many concerns. When McIntire submitted his drawings, Senator George Cabot explained in a letter that "Mr. McIntire's circumstances in Life have confined him to labor in a small sphere, his genius has been denied those aids to which Nature seems to have given him some claims."

One reason that McIntire's genius came to be recognized well beyond the borders of his native Salem was because not long after he set up shop in partnership with his two brothers he came under the patronage of Elias Hasket Derby, the

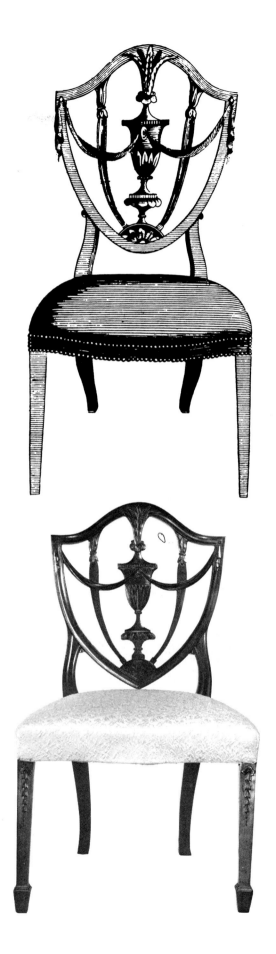

Right, top: Plate 2 of Hepplewhite's Guide *of 1788 from which the design of the chair below was taken.*

Right, bottom: Shield-back chair probably carved for Elias Hasket Derby by McIntire has been called one of the finest American chairs. Its design—taken from Plate 2 of Hepplewhite's Guide *of 1788—is beautifully enriched with carved beading, grapes, and grape leaves.*

This richly carved sofa believed to have been made for Elias Hasket Derby and carved by McIntire has all the delicacy and grace that Robert Adam sought. Carved crossed cornucopias tied by a ribbon in the center closely relate to the cornucopias on the great chest-on-chest shown on page 28.

greatest of Salem's merchant princes whose wife, Elizabeth Crowninshield, loved to build and furnish ever more sumptuous and fashionable houses. The last of Mrs. Derby's houses was, according to contemporary reports, "more like a palace than the dwelling of an American merchant," and the interiors of that mansion gained much of their splendor from McIntire's carvings. The Derby mansion boasted an elegant Adam ceiling designed by McIntire and executed by stucco-worker Daniel Raynard as well as magnificent furniture carved by McIntire.

But even without the Derbys there is no doubt that McIntire would have been recognized because, as Fiske Kimball put it, his "contribution to the artistic character of the buildings was . . . not limited to the giving of general designs, but included the carving of the rich ornaments to which so much of their beauty is due." As his reputation grew, he carved more and more furniture, some of it on pieces made in his own shop and some on pieces by other cabinetmakers. The age of specialization had arrived by the end of the 18th century, as Fales pointed out in the commemorative record of the McIntire Bicentennial in 1957, "and instead of one man making an entire piece of furniture, there were turners, carvers, inlay workers, and varnishers, all of whom frequently combined their skills on a single piece of furniture." In this McIntire was not entirely unlike such later architects as Henry Hobson Richardson, Frank Lloyd Wright, and many others who designed furniture but gave it to a cabinetmaker to execute. Even when McIntire didn't design the form of a particular piece, it was his carving that gave it a special poetry. It was the exquisitely carved mantels of a McIntire living room so harmoniously attuned to the carving on the back of a sofa or the moldings of a cornice that gave those Salem interiors their singing oneness. McIntire matched the sheer virtuosity of Adam in interiors that were on a less dazzling scale, but they were no less symphonic. They suited the tastes of the wealthy merchants of New England just as Adam's suited those of the aristocratic gentry of England.

Furniture was an important element in the creation of a coherent, decisive whole in both an Adam interior and a McIntire interior. It is therefore sad that we can't view a McIntire interior with the furniture he carved especially for it. The furniture in an Adam room might have been disarranged or removed to the attic, but it usually still exists. While 18th- and early 19th-century New Englanders may have been puritanical, they were more concerned with following the latest fashion than they were with posterity. Nevertheless no one can look at a McIntire interior without remembering Adam—not that the New Englander copied Adam's designs, but he was infected by their lightness and gaiety. And while he seems to have bowed to New England Calvinism with his austere exteriors, the interiors dared their own type of gaiety—less pretentious, perhaps, but no less felicitous than Adam's.

Top: Detail of the mantel in the Pingree House parlor (below) shows some of McIntire's incomparable carving, including a sheaf of wheat and basket of fruit and flowers which were among his favorite motifs.

Bottom: Front and back parlors of the Pingree House in Salem designed by McIntire are a fine example of a Federal interpretation of Adam's style.

TWO GOTHIC REVIVAL ARCHITECTS

Not long after the felicitous age of Adam and McIntire, the 19th century saw the rise of the builder to the status of architect who then came to think of furniture as beneath his attention. In America as in Europe architecture and furniture went their separate ways. Architects thought of furniture as merely utilitarian while machine-happy cabinetmakers turned out ever more extravagant pieces whose styles ranged from Rococo to Renaissance and always with a strong Victorian accent. "Every room is a masquerade," as British author Mary Russell Mitford saw it in the 1830s, "the library Egyptian, all covered with hieroglyphics, and swarming with furniture crocodiles and sphynxes. They sleep in Turkish tents and dine in a Gothic chapel." No wonder such exotic clutter called forth rebels who wanted to return to an architecture that was harmonious inside and out, who wanted to create a personal style which required their attention to interior design just as much as to exterior elevations. To do this, of course, they had to design furniture too. Hence Alexander Jackson Davis; William Morris; Henry Hobson Richardson; the Prairie School, Art Nouveau, and Bauhaus designers. As Frank Lloyd Wright put it: "Furnishings should be consistent in design and construction, and used with style as an extension in the sense of the building which they 'furnish.' " That the Gothic revival architects were taken over by the exotica of 19th-century building doesn't mean they didn't see the point of harmony inside and out.

The Gothic revival was a literary as well as an architectural movement marked by a romantic nostalgia for the Middle Ages when machines were as unthinkable as specialization. It was helped along on both sides of the Atlantic by the romanticism of novelists like Sir Walter Scott and Horace Walpole. It was Scott's romantic writings along with his baronial castle Abbotsford on the River Tweed in Scotland that influenced many Gothic revival buildings in England as well as in America. And it was Walpole who gave Gothic its renewed distinction among the avant-garde when he turned a quite ordinary house into the neo-Gothic Strawberry Hill which he himself called his toy castle. Peter Collins has even suggested (in *Changing Ideas in Modern Architecture*) that the Gothic revival villa was inspired by a nostalgia to continue the romantic life of gloom and mystery portrayed in the Gothic novel.

In any case the high priest of the movement was the English architect Augustus Welby Pugin who designed Gothic-inspired houses, furniture, churches, and so on with a fervor that has rarely been matched. "In pure architecture," Pugin believed, "the smallest details should have a meaning or serve a purpose." And for him that meaning and purpose were to influence people to a Christian way of life. There are, in fact, moral and religious overtones and undercurrents in the revival of Gothic that sometimes cloud the issue. Gothic revivalists are also inclined to be eccentric, which may help explain why there are such extremes in furniture they designed, ranging from the truly simple to the truly absurd. Many who advocated medieval design for its simplicity seem to have reserved that simplicity for their writings and lectures on the subject. Not until William Morris came along in the 1860s did design come anywhere near the much-flaunted simplicity of the verbalizers.

At the age of 15 the precocious Pugin began designing Gothic furniture for the additions made by Wyatville to Windsor Castle, and even he was later to deride his achievements there. He says in *The Principles and Revival of Christian Architecture*: ". . . upholsterers seem to think that nothing can be Gothic unless it is found in some church. Hence your modern man designs a sofa or occasional table from details culled out of Britton's Cathedrals, and all the ordinary articles of furniture, which require to be simple and convenient, are made not only very expensive but very uneasy. We find diminutive flying buttresses about an armchair; every thing is crocketed with angular projections, innumerable mitres, sharp ornaments, and turreted extremeties. A man who remains any length of time in a Gothic room, and escapes without being wounded by some of its minutiae, may consider himself extremely fortunate. There are often as many pinnacles and gablets about a pier-glass frame as are to be found in an ordinary church, and not infrequently the whole canopy of a tomb has been transferred for the purpose, as at Strawberry Hill. I have perpetrated many of these enormities in the furniture I designed some years ago for Windsor Castle. At that time I had not the least idea of the principles I am now explaining; all my knowledge of Pointed Architecture was confined to a tolerably good notion of details in the abstract; but these I employed with so little judgment or propriety, that, although the parts were correct and exceedingly well executed, collectively they appeared a complete burlesque of pointed design."

After his youthful aberrations at Windsor, however, Pugin designed many pieces of Gothic furniture for his own as well as other houses, castles, and churches presumably with judgment and propriety. As he himself said, "I seek *antiquity* and not *novelty*. I strive to *revive* not *invent*...." In any case he was continually attacking the incongruities of Victorian Gothic furniture with ardor as well as humor: "The fender is a sort of embattled parapet, with a lodge-gate at each end; at the end of the poker is a sharp-pointed finial, at the summit of the tongs is a saint."

While Pugin was serious in his pursuit of a Gothic that had "meaning or serves a purpose," Horace Walpole's Gothic might be said to have been romantic playacting. As he himself said of the rooms in his Gothicized villa, "every true Goth must perceive that they are more the works of fancy than imitation." He didn't mean, he explains in the preface to his *Description of Strawberry Hill*, to make his house so Gothic as to exclude convenience and modern refinements of luxury. The poet Thomas Gray, who helped him with furnishings for Strawberry, agreed with this premise, "for it is mere pedantry of Gothicism to stick to nothing but altars and tombs, and there is no end to it, if we are to sit upon nothing but Coronation chairs."

Even so the bookcases in Strawberry Hill's library were copied from the arched choir doors of Old St. Paul's, and a mantelpiece in the little parlor is an adaptation of the Bishop of Durham's tomb in Westminster Abbey. "I do not mean to defend by argument a small capricious house," wrote Walpole. "It was built to please my own taste, and in some degree to realize my own visions." Nevertheless Walpole, who was an acknowledged arbiter of taste and a man of influence, made the Gothic revival fashionable in England as well as in America with his little neo-Gothic villa and his nightmarish novel, *The Castle of Otranto*. There was nothing capricious about the neo-Gothic furniture created by Pugin who, unlike most of his contemporaries, really captured the spirit of medieval design rather than assembling its parts for ornamental effect.

The difficulty most Gothic revival architects had was finding something to revive. They only had chests and cupboards, hard benches, and Coronation chairs to go on, and as Alan Gowans put it, if they "pieced out furniture designs with crockets and colonnets from chimney pieces, trefoils and tendrils from illuminated borders," who could blame them? In fact they superimposed those Gothic finials, crockets, and colonnets on what were basically 18th-century prototypes.

Even the American horticulturist and moralist Andrew Jackson Downing, who was Alexander Jackson Davis's ally in the propagation of Gothic revival architecture on American shores, didn't quite see his way clear to adopting the style for furniture. "The radical objection to Gothic furniture as generally seen," he says in *The Architecture of Country Houses*, "is, that it is too elaborately Gothic—with the same high-pointed arches, crockets, and carving usually seen in the front of some cathedral. Elaborate exhibition of style gives it too ostentatious and stately a character." Thus understandably there were reservations about Gothic furniture, but what could a Gothic revival architect do? Gothic castles needed Gothic furniture just as Gothic novels need gloom and suspense.

ALEXANDER JACKSON DAVIS 1803–1892

As a smile or a glance, in familiar conversation, often reveals to us more of the real character of a professional man than a long study of him at the pulpit or the bar, so a table or a chair will sometimes give us the key to the intimate tastes of those who might be inscrutable in the hieroglyphics of white walls and plain ceilings. A. J. DOWNING

Alexander Jackson Davis, America's strongest champion of the Gothic revival, designed large and small Gothic revival villas which made no pretense of growing out of the nature of materials or structure, let alone the American soil. But at least he stuck to Gothic inside and out. Gothic castles had little affinity with the American countryside, Gothic furniture had little affinity with American housekeeping, but they may have had something to do with the American dream getting a little out of hand. Although the Gothic revival, like the Greek revival, was thought to be symbolic of American values, one might well ask as Mr. Effingham does in James Fenimore Cooper's *Home as Found*, "Are you quite sure that yonder castellated roof, for instance, is quite suited to the deep snows of these mountains?" He was referring to the old family house which had been Gothicized or, as Aristabulus put it, "We consider it denationalized . . . there being nothing like it, west of Albany at least."

When it came to Gothic Furniture for his Gothic revival villas, Davis paid little heed to Downing's distrust of it. For all his important Gothic revival houses, he seems to have designed furniture with details freely borrowed from Strawberry Hill or from Pugin's furniture designs. If not that, he turned to the Gothic revival furniture in his 1835 copy of Loudon's *An Encyclopedia of Cottage, Farm, and Villa Architecture* on whose flyleaf he had made an index. In any case he must have designed a great deal of Gothic furniture. His diary records that for the 1838 Gothic revival mansion on the Hudson for William Paulding, he produced "Fifty designs for furniture." And when he enlarged the mansion in 1864 for George Merritt, who named it Lyndhurst, he designed more furniture "in the rich flamboyant Gothic of the period" particularly for the dining room where a suite of carved furniture complements the opulent Gothic revival decorative details of ceiling, walls, and marble mantel.

Davis was apparently a Gothicist from an early age. Even as a boy, he wrote in a biographical sketch of himself for Dunlap's *History of the Arts of Design in the United States* of 1834, he puzzled for hours "over the plan of some ancient castle of romance, arranging the trap doors, subterranean passages and drawbridges, as pictorial embellishments was the least of his care, invention all his aim." Not surprisingly this romantic youth had stage aspirations, but it was as an artist that he began his professional life. The many views of buildings he made during the 1820s and 1830s, in fact, have proved valuable records of the time. He started producing them in 1823 while attending the Antique School in New York City (later called the National Academy of Design), which had been formed by the painter John Trumbull. It was Trumbull who advised Davis "to devote himself to architecture, as a branch of art most likely to meet with encouragement, and one for which, by the particular bent of his mind, he appeared to be well fitted." His views of buildings also brought him into contact with the New York architect Ithiel Town who asked Davis to go into partnership with him in 1829. While with Town,

First floor hallway at Lyndhurst showing several pieces of Gothic revival furniture including the two wheelback chairs (see following page) and pedestal table designed by Davis in 1841.

Davis worked on many Greek revival buildings, including the New York Customs House. But as he wrote in his *Rural Residences* of 1837, "The Greek temple form, perfect in itself, and well adapted as it is to public edifices, and even to town mansions, is inappropriate for country residences. The English collegiate style is for many reasons to be preferred. It admits of greater variety both of plan and outline . . . its bay windows, oriels, turrets, and chimney shafts give a pictorial effect."

Davis's enthusiasm for the Gothic revival increased with the years. During the 1830s he designed many villas, college buildings, and churches in the style. In 1832 Robert Gilmor of Baltimore commissioned Town and Davis to design a baronial mansion for him in the style of Sir Walter Scott's Abbotsford. The result was Glen Ellen, said to have been the first Gothic revival house in the United States to be directly influenced by Abbotsford but not the last. It was fortunate for the young and romantic Gilmor that Davis was a member of the firm since Town never seems to have really had his heart in the Gothic style. Glen Ellen's convincing Gothic flavor was obviously Davis's doing. He designed the Gothic ornament and may have designed some Gothic furniture too, but that branch of his architectural career seems to have waited for the later Gothic revival villas he did on his own after he and Town parted in 1837.

In 1838 Downing asked Davis to collaborate with him and provide illustrations for "Rural Architecture," a section of his book on landscape gardening published in 1841. They collaborated for some ten years and between them—Davis as the master of the picturesque in architecture and Downing as its master in landscaping—formulated country house taste throughout the romantic decades of the 19th century.

D avis always called himself an "architectural composer," which not only implied that he was as much of a pictorial artist as a draftsman, but also that he needed to design the furniture for his houses to complete the pictorial composition. His belief that the interiors and furnishings should form a unity with the building was probably most effectively carried out in the Paulding House for which "Mr. Davis has designed every article of furniture," according to an 1843 article about it. Whether or not that is entirely true, the Paulding furniture does represent the earliest known group of American Gothic revival furniture, as Jane B. Davies pointed out in her article, "Gothic Revival Furniture Designs of Alexander J. Davis" published in *Antiques* in May 1977.

Davis stands close to the beginning of the deterioration of cabinetmaking as an art. He was one of the founders of the American Institute of Architects in 1857, which perhaps more than anything else raised the architect to professional

Above: The two neo-Gothic benches which now flank Lyndhurst's main entrance are attributed to Davis. The one on the right was designed in 1841 for William Paulding; the one on the left is probably of a later date. The finial of the latter is an elaboration of the finial on the side chair with a cane seat shown on the bottom right on page 44.

Opposite page, top: Preliminary study by Davis for the wheelback chairs designed for the Pauldings.

Opposite page, bottom: Close-up of one of the wheelback chairs designed for the Pauldings in 1841 and probably made by Byrne or Wright. Many have considered these chairs among the finest examples of Gothic revival furniture in America for their imaginative use of Gothic motifs.

Following page: The suite of carved Gothic revival furniture for George Merritt's dining room, c. 1865, at Lyndhurst includes the great extension table (see top page 44) and fourteen chairs which beautifully harmonize with the room's Gothic revival details. The simpler armchairs, of which there are twelve, are based on a design by Davis recorded in a rough sketch.

status and out of the ranks of artisans. This new status, as Alan Gowans put it, helped degrade craftsmen, and thus furniture making declined from a major art "to a minor one at best, and ultimately to an assembly-line-laborer's job." For architects, furniture became a "a kind of architectural detail, a form of decoration. . . ." The relationship of furniture maker to architect, at least during the first half of the century, is exemplified by the relationship between Davis and Richard Byrne, who executed some of his furniture designs along with other interior and exterior woodwork. In a biographical sketch of Byrne written by Davis's son and quoted in R. H. Newton's *Town and Davis Architects* published in 1942, he says: "Some of the original drawings remain as evidence of the combined skill of Davis as draftsman and Byrnes [sic] as woodworker." The relationship with Byrne, according to Davis's son, lasted about 30 years, and he "worked upon practically every important house by Town & Davis . . . and perhaps always upon the Gothic ones for which he had a peculiar talent as a wood-carver." Jane Davies tells us, however, that three cabinetmakers are mentioned in Davis's notes—Richard Byrne, Wright, and Burns. Burns and Byrne, she points out, have often been merged into "a fabricated composite, 'Richard H. Byrnes,'" as Davis's son obviously did. Richard Byrne and Ambrose Wright, according to Davies, "probably made the furniture that Davis designed in 1841 for the Pauldings." William Burns, who worked in partnership with Peter Trainque from 1842 to 1856, with his own brother from 1857 to 1859, and alone from 1860 to 1866, may have made the Paulding furniture of the later 1840s, says Davies, and "probably most of the furniture Davis subsequently de-

Opposite page: This oak Gothic revival bed at Lyndhurst was probably designed by Davis. A highly successful example of American Gothic revival furniture, it was used by Helen Gould Shepard, daughter of Jay Gould who bought Lyndhurst in 1880.

Above: Pencil drawing by Davis for the design of a Gothic revival bed similar to the one at Lyndhurst shown on the opposite page.

signed" until Burns' death in 1867. She also points out that in 1850 A. J. Downing (at Davis's suggestion) praised Burns and Trainque for "the most correct Gothic furniture that we have yet seen executed in this country."

But in spite of the fact that the quotation of Davis's son is probably apocryphal, R. H. Newton comes to the no less interesting conclusion that such an "outstanding example of successful cooperation between architect and cabinetmaker should make such contemporary artists and craftsmen of ours take heart and design furnishings for clients to harmonize with the house." He goes on to point out that in "all the great ages of building, the arts and crafts have flourished side by side—the architect, painter, sculptor, and cabinetmaker, working toward producing a harmonious ensemble." This seems to indicate that even in 1942 when Newton's book was published not everyone realized that the machine had made such collaboration economically unfeasible. Of course many architect-designers have tried to counteract that unfeasibility with furniture designed to be mass produced but rarely with success.

In England, Pugin had a similar association with J. G. Crace, which began with the building of furniture for Pugin's own house at Ramsgate. In Pugin's case, however, he designed wallpapers, rugs, fabrics, as well as furniture, and Crace managed the details and manufacture of them. In a letter Pugin wrote to John Crace in 1849, he says "I am anxious to introduce a sensible style of furniture of good oak and constructively put together that shall compete with the vile trash made and sold. These things are very simple and I am certain with a little patience can be made to pay." Almost all the tables, chairs, candelabra, rugs, and vestments designed by Pugin for innumerable Catholic churches throughout England were designed to be reproduced in quantity.

Davis, with the possible exception of James Renwick, may have been the first American architect to think of the furnishings as an important part of a building's architecture in a modern sense, but he was by no means the last. McIntire belonged to the handcraft past, Davis to the beginning of the technological present. While Davis didn't rethink the basic shape of furniture as Wright, Breuer, Mies, and Rietveld did, he showed great imagination in interpreting the Gothic revival style in American furniture. Davis's furniture designs, in the words of Jane Davies, "are among the most forceful and original examples of American nineteenth-century furniture." His romantic temperament seems to have been just right for developing a specifically American version of the Gothic revival style in furniture as well as in decorative details.

Top: Dining table probably designed by Davis (see also pages 40–41) is closely related to an octagon table designed by the English Gothic revivalist A.W. Pugin.

Bottom left: One of a pair of Gothic revival side chairs in the hallway at Lyndhurst.

Bottom, right: The imaginative design of this side chair attributed to Davis in 1841 relates to several of the architect's sketches.

JAMES RENWICK, JR. 1818-1895

. . . people once possessed of a three-legged stool soon contrive to make an easy chair. SIR WALTER SCOTT

James Renwick, Jr., who rivaled Davis as a Gothic enthusiast, may be best known for the Smithsonian's fanciful castle on the Mall in Washington, D.C. Although Downing had said the "castellated style never appears, completely at home except in wild and romantic scenery, or in situations where the neighboring mountains or wild passes, are sufficiently near to give that character to the landscape," Renwick built his Smithsonian in flat and unromantic Washington. His design, however, which won the award in open competition, couldn't have been better suited to fulfill Representative Robert Dale Owen's desire for a "large and showy building." Owen, the Scottish-born reformer who founded the ill-fated New Harmony community in Indiana, had been appointed by the Smithsonian's Board of Regents as a member of its building commission, and he was probably its most influential member.

After the Smithsonian was completed, not everyone was enchanted with the beturreted and betowered building. The English writer Anthony Trollope called it "bastard Gothic." And it startled the American sculptor Horatio Greenough when, as he put it, "Suddenly . . . the dark form of the Smithsonian palace rose between me and the white Capitol, and I stopped. Tower and battlement, and all that medieval confusion, stamped itself on the halls of Congress, as ink on paper! Dark on that whiteness—complication on that simplicity! It scared me. Was it a specter, or was I not another Rip Van Winkle who had slept too long? . . . I am not about to criticize the edifice. I have not quite recovered from my alarm. There is still a certain mystery about those towers and steep belfries that makes me uneasy. This is a practical land.

They must be for something. Is no *coup d'état* lurking there?"

The Gothic chairs and conference table Renwick designed for the Smithsonian's Regents Room were hardly less startling. The table and some of the 18 chairs were destroyed in a fire, but nine of the latter, of six different designs, are not only still intact but still in the Regents Room. Since Renwick graduated as an engineer from Columbia College in 1836 where he delivered a dissertation on "The Benefits Conferred upon Mankind by Philosophy," it is not surprising that the design of furniture interested him. A chair is as much an engineer's problem (and perhaps a philosophical one too) as it is a craftsman's.

Renwick was born in New York City to a socially prominent family. His father, an early Gothic revival enthusiast, had also graduated from Columbia as an engineer, although he later became a professor of natural philosophy. The younger Renwick began his professional career as a structural engineer with the Erie Railroad. Then at the age of 23 he won the competition for Grace Church in New York City with a design in the early Flamboyant Gothic style. When the church opened in 1845, the New York diarist Philip Hone noted: ". . . This is to be a fashionable church, and already its aisles are filled (especially on Sundays after the morning services in other churches) with gay parties of ladies in feathers and 'mousseline-delaine dresses,' and dandies with moustaches and high-heeled boots; the lofty arches resound with astute criticisms upon 'Gothic architecture' from fair ladies who have had the advantage of foreign travel, and scientific remarks upon 'accoustics' from elderly

One of a pair of walnut hall chairs attributed to Renwick. Originally in the house of John Taylor Johnston designed by Renwick in Plainfield, New Jersey, the chairs were made in New York, c. 1865.

The Renwick-designed Regents Room at the Smithsonian Institution as shown in an 1857 woodcut presumably showing some of the chairs which are still in the room.

millionaires who do not hear quite as well as formerly."

Such was the fashionable cachet of Gothic in the forties. Grace Church, moreover, proved the catalyst for Renwick's busy and lucrative career, which included the design of such landmarks as St. Patrick's Cathedral in New York, the Corcoran Gallery (now Renwick Gallery) in Washington, as well as private houses for many of the fashionable. Renwick's buildings were in a variety of styles besides Gothic. He designed three hotels in New York in the Italianate style, one of which was described by a reporter as "a rather outré and dreamy-looking building, six stories high."

Renwick undoubtedly designed furniture for his churches, and he probably designed many more pieces for his other buildings than is presently known. His specifications for the Smithsonian, for example, show that he did design furniture for several areas of that building, but the fire of 1865 took away most of the evidence. Of the surviving chairs in the Regents Room, the contract specifies: "Eighteen heavily carved arm Chairs, and one heavily carved table in the Norman style, will be carved for the Regents' room, from best black walnut, varnished 4 coats and polished. The whole to be carved according to the designs and directions of the Architect." The specifications also state that "the museum furniture will be arranged per plan and directions of its Architect. All the cases will be of the designs shown on the plans, and will be made of the best thoroughly seasoned clear white pine, handsomely carved turned and moulded, with caps and bases similar to those of Library, and most mouldings on the arches. . . ."

These pieces were probably executed by a cabinetmaker to Renwick's designs, as Davis's furniture was. In fact Jane B. Davies makes a tantalizing suggestion in her article, "Gothic Revival Furniture Designs of Alexander J. Davis" published in *Antiques* in May 1977, in which she quotes an 1848 entry in Davis's diary: ". . . met P. R. Paulding on wharf and Renwick—with carriage rode to Wright's—astonishing furniture." Wright, of course, was Ambrose Wright, the cabinetmaker who did work for Davis, and Jane Davies reasonably asks if the "astonishing furniture" could have been the Smithsonian's Regents chairs which Renwick designed in 1847?

Like most neo-Gothic enthusiasts, Renwick was something of an eccentric. In fact 19th-century Gothic revivalists seem to have shared many of the same idiosyncracies from childhood including a passion for all things Gothic in books as well as chairs. Gothic enthusiast William Morris read Scott's novels before he was seven and rode through Epping Forest in a toy suit of armor. By his own account, he was fascinated by "stories of knights and chivalry" when he was in his teens. The theater and the sea also seem to be among the shared passions of many Gothic devotees. Both Davis and Pugin designed stage sets. Although I have found no record of Davis's love of the sea, Renwick, who was at home in the most fashionable society, owned two steam yachts, one for northern and one for southern waters. Pugin's seagoing, and it was frequent and erratic, was done in sailboats. Before he was 20 he is supposed to have said, "There is nothing worth living for but Christian architecture and a boat." When he was working on the designs of the furniture and furnishings for the Houses of Parliament, he would vanish into the North Sea for months at a time, then suddenly emerge with dozens of exquisite working drawings for the panels, wallpapers, and chairs for the interiors of Sir Charles Barry's great neo-Gothic building. His last days, Kenneth Clark tells us, "were spent in designing inkpots and umbrella-stands."

Precociousness also seems to have been shared by the Gothic revivalists in question. Pugin designed the Windsor Castle furniture when he was 15. Renwick was only 23 when he won the competition to design New York's wealthy and fashionable Grace Church. He was 27 when he designed the Smithsonian and, in addition to Grace, had several New York City churches to his credit when he was summoned to Washington. At 26 Davis became a partner in the firm of Town and Davis, one of the first architectural partnerships in the country, and he had already acquired a reputation as an architectural illustrator. And Downing was only 36 when he died.

The Gothic revival period was a strange interlude for furniture as well as for buildings, and it is not surprising that their designers were strange and dedicated men. So dedicated was Pugin that he described his third wife as "a first-rate Gothic woman at last, who perfectly understands and delights in spires, churches, screens, stained windows, brasses and vestments." The strangeness of the furniture was even recognized by that contemporary advocate of the neo-Gothic, Downing. "There has been little attempt made at adapting furniture in this style to the more simple Gothic of our villas and country houses in America," he writes in *Country Houses*. "Yet," he adds, "we are confident this may be done in such a manner as to unite a simple and chaste Gothic style with forms adapted to and expressive of our modern domestic life." His confidence was not misplaced, but it had to wait for England's William Morris who cared nothing about the discomfort of a Gothic bench but greatly admired its simplicity.

Of course the 19th-century Gothic revivalists were not the first to Gothicize furniture. Thomas Chippendale had published Gothic designs for furniture in his *Gentleman and*

Three front and one back view of nine surviving chairs in the Regents Room of the Smithsonian Institution of 1847–1855, which were described in Renwick's specifications as "Eighteen heavily carved arm Chairs, and one heavily carved table in the Norman style, will be carved for the Regents Room, from best black walnut, varnished 4 coats and polished. The whole to be carved according to the designs and directions of the Architect." Of the original nine pairs of Gothic chairs, half were destroyed in the fire of 1865, as was the table.

Cabinet-Maker's Director of 1754. Robert Adam designed Gothic furniture for his interiors at Alnwick Castle (1777–1790), and William Kent dabbled in Gothic. But it wasn't until Scott's *Marmion* was published in 1808 that designers began to apply ornament from Gothic architecture to fashionable furniture forms, and the mania realized no bounds until well into the 19th century.

Although Renwick, Davis, and Downing, among other American contemporaries, believed "in theory at least," as George Bishop Tatum noted in his Ph.D. dissertation on *Andrew Jackson Downing, Arbiter of American Taste, 1815–1852*, that "the house was suited to its natural setting, the furnishings and interior decoration were a unit with the house, and all were expressive of, and in harmony with the unique person-

ality of its owner," it isn't all that obvious to someone who has experienced such Frank Lloyd Wright houses as Fallingwater or his two Taliesins. But one must remember that the Gothic revivalists were among the first to rebel against the disarray that occurred when the machine did away with the fine traditions of colonial craftsmanship, and architect and cabinetmaker went their separate ways. ". . . as taste had fallen to its lowest depth a favorable reaction commences" is the way Pugin put it in 1841. The Gothic revivalists' idea of unity inside and out may be neither the instinctive unity of a Samuel McIntire nor the discovered unity of a Frank Lloyd Wright, but it *was* unity.

They may have been fanatics who preached the Gothic gospel, but it has proven an alluring gospel. In the United States alone, a Gothic spirit has been revived every now and then since the beginning. One need only remember the Gothic temple Jefferson planned in his cemetery at Monticello, although it was never built, or observe the Gothic arches that rim the twin towers of the World Trade Center in New York City to realize the hardiness of the Gothic revival in America. Wayne Andrews may well have been right in saying that "but for his toy castle at Strawberry Hill we might never have witnessed the prairie-style houses of Frank Lloyd Wright, built from the inside out, or been confronted with the glass towers of Ludwig Mies van der Rohe." Perhaps if Davis, Renwick, Pugin, and so on had not given time and thought to redesigning furniture that would harmonize with their Gothic revival interiors, no one would have thought of giving a new form to the chair as Wright, Mies, Breuer, Rietveld, Aalto, and others did.

THE ARTS AND CRAFTS TRADITION

The last three decades of the 19th century comprised an era of paradox. On the one hand, there was an infatuation with the machine and all it meant for the material comfort and glory of man. On the other hand, there was fear of the machine and the significance it might have for the humanity of man. These two attitudes, as might be expected, had their effect on the arts. American tycoons and industrialists built houses that were evermore suggestive of old-world wealth just as their counterparts in England—"the filthy rich, God blast them!" to quote William Morris—built large and sometimes gaudy country houses. Then there were others who, dissatisfied with the increasingly mechanical quality of life, called for a return to the simplicities of an earlier age when houses and furniture were the unpretentious and harmonious works of handcraftsmen, when, in Morris's words, there was a union of the arts "mutually helpful and harmoniously subordinated one to another."

The Arts and Crafts movement grew out of the ideas of Morris and was particularly popular in England in the 1880s and 1890s. Its great popularity in the United States only began after the death of Morris in 1896, but its influence continued for many years on both sides of the Atlantic, eventually inspiring some of the most original furniture designs of the 20th century. The Arts and Crafts tradition, as H. Allen Brooks has pointed out, was an attitude rather than a style. It was an approach to a problem that demanded simplicity, elimination, and respect for materials. In furniture there was no style that could be identified as an Arts and Crafts chair as, say, one can identify a Queen Anne chair. Its diversity of expression ranged from richly inlaid pieces to the simplest rush-seated chair. It was both a revolt against the separation of the fine and decorative arts and a revolt against the extravagant clutter inspired by the machine. It is appropriate that the Arts and Crafts movement should have gotten its start in England. Not only was the industrial revolution born there, but in spite of those grandiose country houses, an Englishman's "unalterable preference is for the rural and rustic," as the German writer and critic Hermann Muthesius recognized when he spent several years in England at the end of the century. *Das Englische Haus*, published in Berlin in 1905, the book in which he reported his observations, greatly helped to spread Arts and Crafts ideas in Germany as well as on the rest of the Continent. In it he says: "The leading sector of the people in intellectual, spiritual matters is in particular given to the country life—precisely that sector which with us runs the greatest risk of falling prey to urban life. Great emphasis was placed upon untreated wooden surfaces. Primitive peasant forms were revived, construction details were always apparent, often in a most obtrusive fashion, and little heed was paid to comfort or refined modes of life. The thinking behind this was that one must go back and start at the beginning in order to get over the degenerate state of culture which the nineteenth century had brought about. The only room in the house to which the so-called artistic strivings of the time had not penetrated was the kitchen. So they went back to kitchen furniture: kitchen chairs gave them ideas for new forms of a chair, kitchen cupboards for new forms of cupboard. This new furniture differed from the genuine kitchen pieces in that it was ten times more expensive because it was produced under the economic conditions of works of art."

And therein lies contradiction. The furniture may have been simple and it may have been handcrafted, but producing it under the economic conditions of works of art made it only available to the wealthy. Morris—who once asked "What business have we with art at all unless we can share it?"—discovered that to his disgust when he realized he could only decorate houses for "the filthy rich."

The rooms of those English leaders in intellectual and spiritual matters, moreover, didn't always conform to the Arts and Crafts dictum of simplicity and elimination as we might understand those words. In his autobiography, Kenneth Clark recalled Myra Hess playing the piano in a room "furnished in a style identical with the rooms of Mr. Bernard Shaw and Miss Popham, headmistress of Cheltenham Ladies College: a heterogeneous collection of chintzes, many photographs, much modern brass of vaguely Indian character, although no doubt made in Birmingham, a procession of elephants carved in black

WILLIAM MORRIS
HENRY HOBSON RICHARDSON
FRANK FURNESS
CHARLES F. ANNESLEY VOYSEY
HARVEY ELLIS

wood, with white tusks." Since Mr. Bernard Shaw was not only on familiar terms with, but a admirer of, at least two of Morris's own houses, Lord Clark's recollections provide an interesting slant on simplicity and elimination.

Perhaps Reyner Banham best characterized the Arts and Crafts philosophy when he called it "an attitude in which the house becomes a shrine for objects of well-wrought functional art, and the inhabitants the devoted worshippers." And, he adds, "it is an attitude that differs from that of the highly caricaturable vulgar Victorian collector of awful works of expensive 'fine' art, precisely in that word *functional*. These were objects to be sat upon, eaten off of, to hang clothes in, to arrange flowers in . . . and ultimately to inhabit." It may be arguable how functional a procession of carved elephants could be, but it was what seemed to belong in the houses of those high-minded fanciers of function.

The craft movement in the United States might be called the swan song of the English tradition. The first American Society of Arts and Crafts was founded in Boston in 1897 and the second in Chicago a few months later. The early furniture of Henry Hobson Richardson and Frank Lloyd Wright belonged to the craft tradition as did that of other Prairie School architects and such craft-oriented California architects as the Greene brothers and Bernard Maybeck. Wright, however, was more interested in bringing the work of the hand and the machine together than were either Morris or the Greene brothers. In his autobiography Wright lists among his "main motives and inclinations": "To incorporate as organic architecture—so far as possible—furnishings, making them all one with the building, designing the equipment in simple terms of machine work."

Of course one good reason why architects of an Arts and Crafts persuasion found it necessary to design furniture for their buildings was because there was nothing on the market that answered their demand for simplicity "as to kind and manner of design," as Morris put it, nor that was compatible with the unadorned white-walled cottages that he advocated, though few but Voysey actually produced. While Morris would have preferred to totally banish the ma-

chine, most craft-oriented architects particularly in the United States were less adamant. Nor was the furniture of most craft-oriented architects inspired by kitchen chairs. For them the movement implied that they could not only be responsible for the design of the house but the furniture and furnishings that went into it and, whenever possible, the garden outside. It implied a bringing together of all the arts and it implied honesty of purpose, materials, and manufacture. And perhaps most of all the Arts and Crafts movement was an attempt to reform public taste particularly in the field of household furnishings. But beyond that it might be a plain Mission chair by Gustav Stickley or a richly carved bench by Richardson. It might be white-washed walls or embroidered panels.

Whether one listens to their words or looks at their interiors, however, the long-term achievements of the Arts and Crafts movement are not to be derided. On the surface it was a reaction, as Lewis Mumford put it in his introduction to *Form in Civilization* by Morris-disciple W. R. Lethaby, "for it invoked an idealized image of the mediaeval past, when art and craft and morality and religion were all in the service of common life. But at the bottom, these leaders aimed at something more central: the restoration of human initiative, the respect for form and quality, the projection of human ideals of workmanship and beauty. While mechanical invention sought to simplify the processes of production, the Arts and Crafts movement sought to simplify—and amplify the ends." The Arts and Crafts movement, he rightly concludes, "cleansed even the machine arts of their decorative debasements: it encouraged a taste for simplicity, directness, honesty, common sense, and in the end it discouraged historic imitations and empty formalism."

The Arts and Crafts movement marked an important stage in humanity's continuing efforts to come to terms with industrialization. It coexisted with High Victorian historicism; it was the child of the Gothic revival, the inspiration for Art Nouveau, which in turn led to the Modern Movement. As late as 1955, Alvar Aalto reminded an audience in Vienna that "it is still the architect's duty to attempt to humanize the age of machines."

WILLIAM MORRIS 1834–1896

The higher the art rises, the greater the simplicity. WILLIAM MORRIS

There can be little doubt that the real rebellion against machine-made furniture and 19th-century excess got underway when Morris couldn't find any proper furniture for the studio he shared with Edward Burne-Jones and set about designing it himself. Dante Gabriel Rossetti wrote to a friend in 1856: "Morris . . . is having some intensely mediaeval furniture made—tables and chairs like incubi and succubi. He and I have painted the back of a chair with figures and inscriptions in gules and vert and azure, and we are all three going to cover a cabinet with pictures." And when Morris married and moved into the famous Red House in Kent which he and Philip Webb designed, it was again necessary to design furniture to supplement the settle and so-called Chaucer wardrobe painted with scenes from Chaucer's "Prioress's Tale" that had been moved from the studio.

The Red House and its furnishings influenced the esthetic tastes of the avant-garde for some time to come as is indicated by the words of Morris-disciple Walter Crane: "Plain white or green paint for woodwork drove wood-graining and marbling to the public house. The simple old Buckingham elbow chair, with its rush-bottomed seat was substituted for the wavy-backed, curly-legged and stuffed chair of the period."

Webb was responsible for most of the Red House furniture as he was later to be responsible for the design of many pieces for Morris and Co., the firm that Morris started with several designers, architects, and painters in 1861 as Morris, Marshall, Faulkner & Co. to revive the artistic craftsmanship of the Middle Ages. Later Rossetti recalled: "One evening a lot of us were together, and we got talking about the way in which artists did all kinds of things in olden times, designed every kind of decoration and most kinds of furniture, and some one suggested—as a joke more than anything else . . . that we should each put down five pounds and form a company."

Morris never actually designed any furniture after his experiments for the Red Lion Square studio, but he supervised the production of Morris and Co.'s furniture and designed the firm's general schemes of decoration for 25 years. After 1858 Webb designed most of the furniture both for Morris's personal use and for the firm. It was, however, Morris's Red Lion Square furniture—those rough wood pieces painted "with figures and inscriptions in gules and vert and azure"—that inspired the early Morris and Co. pieces.

Morris was trained in the offices of Gothic revival architect George Edmund Street, but he never practiced architecture on his own. Nevertheless he belongs at the head of any list of late 19th- and 20th-century architects who designed furniture for their buildings. Morris was a craftsman, poet, artist, and social reformer, and he designed almost everything from fabrics and wallpaper to books and furniture. He lectured extensively on artistic and social questions and spent his entire life campaigning against the complete lack of feeling for the essential unity of architecture which had made the riot of hybrid styles possible. He blamed the industrial revolu-

Oak cabinet designed by architect J.P. Seddon for Morris to hold his drawings and made by the Morris firm in 1862 stands in the Green Room of 1867, designed by the Morris firm for the Victoria and Albert Museum. It is painted with stories of "King Rene's Honeymoon" by Madox Brown, Rossetti, and Burne-Jones.

The Green Room contains windows and
painted wall panels by Burne-Jones, an embroidered screen by Morris and his wife illustrating Chaucer's Illustrious Women, and
a grand piano with gesso work by Kate
Faulkner. The Saint George cabinet stands
under the window.

Opposite page, top: This cabinet on an oak
stand designed by Philip Webb in 1861 and
painted by William Morris with scenes from
the legend of Saint George seems to follow
Morris's dictum that luxury is permissible "if
it is done for beauty's sake, and not for show."

Opposite page, bottom: Close-up of one of the
Saint George cabinet panels. The female
figure was probably inspired by Morris's wife
Janey, who seems to have been the original
model for the femme fatale that was such an
important motif of the Art Nouveau period.

tion for the vulgarity of contemporary decorative objects and believed it had killed "the joy of the maker." He considered "the two virtues most needed in modern life" were "honesty and simplicity." So did Frank Lloyd Wright.

It was Morris's ideas that inspired the Arts and Crafts theme that was inherited by many architects in Europe and the United States who might never have designed furniture for their buildings if it had not been for his example. We owe it to Morris, as Nikolaus Pevsner reminds us, "that an ordinary man's dwelling-house has once more become a worthy object of the architect's thought, and a chair, a wallpaper, or a vase a worthy object of the artist's imagination." Perhaps the only difference between Morris and Wright and other 20th-century architects who designed furniture is that Morris wanted to abolish the machine while the others realized the necessity of dealing with it. "Genius must dominate the work of the contrivance it has created," as Wright put it in his famous 1901 lecture on "The Art and Craft of the Machine" at Chicago's Hull House.

In the Middle Ages, Morris believed, "all handicraftsmen were artists." He called architecture "one of the most important things man can turn his hand to," but, he added, "noble as the art is . . . it neither ever has existed nor ever can exist alive and progressive by itself, but must cherish and be cherished by all the crafts whereby men make the things which they intend . . . shall last beyond the passing day."

But Morris, as Pevsner says, looked backward not forward, his "revival of handicraft is constructive, the essence of his teaching is destructive. Pleading for handicraft alone means pleading for conditions of medieval primitiveness." And it was that medieval primitiveness which made at least one pre-Raphaelite descendant less than enthusiastic about the furniture that came out of Morris and Co. In her book, *Three Houses*, Edward Burne-Jones's granddaughter Angela Thirkell recalls the furniture in her grandparents' house as a "triumph of pre-Raphaelite discomfort." She particularly remembered "a small wooden table and two or three wooden chairs which were suited to no human body. They had been designed by my grandfather for the seats of the knights at the Round Table in the tapestry which William Morris made from his cartoons and the chairs had actually been translated into wood by a skilful carpentering friend so that my grandfather could draw them from life." Altogether, she sums up, "a more unsuitable set of dining-room chairs for a royal dining-room can hardly be imagined. If that is how Arthur's court was furnished, it is quite enough to explain the eagerness of the knights to leave their seats and follow the quest of the Holy Grail."

Nevertheless the ideals that produced that furniture have never entirely died out. Morris's followers include many architects and designers on both sides of the Atlantic who have pursued his quest for simplicity and the essential unity of architecture, even if mastery of the machine interested them more than medievalism. Even Morris and Co. eventually succumbed to producing machine-carved furniture in the 1870s when mass-produced furniture began to fill the showrooms and create an even wider gap between the work of the trade and the advanced taste of furniture designed by architects. Thus one might say that Morris was a prime example of that dichotomy between saying and doing often exhibited by the Gothic revival architects. But his feelings and sayings about furniture never changed: ". . . for us to set to work to imitate . . . the degraded and nightmare whims of the blasé and bankrupt aristocracy of Louis XV's time seems to me merely ridiculous. So I say our furniture should be good citizen's furniture, solid and wellmade and workmanlike and in design should have nothing about it that is not easily defensible, no monstrosities or extravagances, not even of beauty, lest we weary of it." This in a sense is the credo of the Arts and Crafts movement that was carried on by C.F.A. Voysey, C. R. Ashbee, Ernest Gimson, among other English architects; by the Art Nouveau designers; and by such Americans as Henry Hobson Richardson, Wright, Harvey Ellis, the Greene brothers, Bernard Maybeck, and on into the post-World War I era of Mies van der Rohe, Le Corbusier, and Marcel Breuer. Even such post-World War II architects as Charles Eames and Eero Saarinen took some of its ideas into machine production.

Morris's contribution to furniture design, then, was his practical example and even more than that the ideas he set forth in the art lectures he started giving in 1877. It has often been pointed out that Morris and Co. designed rooms that were as full of furniture and bric-a-brac as any Victorian interior while Morris himself propounded meagerness and simplicity. "Simplicity," he said in one of his lectures, "is the one thing needful in furnishing, of that I am certain; I mean first as to quantity, and secondly as to kind and manner of design." But like any other firm, Morris and Co. had to depend on the market and in that, perhaps, Morris was inconsistent. But not in many of the things he said, and that is where his long and continuing influence lies. The poet W. B. Yeats remembered Morris saying, "I decorate modern houses for people, but the house that would please me would be some great room where one talked to one's friends in one corner and ate in another and slept in another and worked in another." And toward the end of his life he told writer and socialist Edward Carpenter: "I have spent, I

Refreshment room designed by Morris and Philip Webb in 1867 for the Victoria and Albert Museum.

Above: Oak armchair with rush seat produced by the Morris firm.

Opposite page: One of the well-known rush-seated chairs adapted from models found in Sussex cottages and produced by the Morris firm from the 1870s onwards.

know, a vast amount of time designing furniture and wall-papers, carpets and curtains; but after all I am inclined to think that sort of thing is mostly rubbish, and I would prefer for my part to live with the plainest whitewashed walls and wooden chairs and tables." That great 19th-century American Henry David Thoreau, of whom Morris so often reminds one, said something very similar in *Walden*: "I sometimes dream of a larger and more populous house standing in a golden age, of enduring materials, and without gingerbread work, which shall still consist of only one room, a vast, rude, substantial, primitive hall, without ceiling or plastering, with bare rafters and purlins supporting a sort of lower heaven over one's head. . . . a cavernous house, wherein you must reach up a torch upon a pole to see the roof; where some may live in the fireplace, some in the recess of the window, and some on settles, some at one end of the hall, some at another . . . where you can see all the treasures of the house at one view, and everything hangs upon its peg that a man should use; at once kitchen, pantry, parlor, chamber, storehouse, and garret. . . . A house whose inside is as open and manifest as a bird's nest. . . ."

Morris's lasting reputation in the history of furniture design, as Paul Thompson pointed out in *The Work of William Morris*, is not because his furniture was handcrafted or even that much of it made an important contribution to the stylistic development of the period, but because "all his design has a fundamental integrity, a respect for material and a quality of workmanship, which conveyed more than any characteristic of style." Morris, as Thompson says, was an educated and wealthy man who could have been famous as a poet. Instead he "spent the greatest part of his energies in the furnishing crafts. His example gave dignity to these crafts, and encouraged younger architects to take up similar work. His call for simplicity sprang from this same integrity and has proved an equal inspiration."

HENRY HOBSON RICHARDSON 1838–1886

I'll plan anything a man wants from a cathedral to a chicken coop. HENRY HOBSON RICHARDSON

Richardson, one of the first great American architects to design furniture, believed as Morris did that no object in a building was too simple to engage his thought and like Morris he was rebelling against everything implied by mid-Victorian design. Richardson was born in 1838, only four years after Morris, and he died in 1886, ten years before him, so the influence was probably not so great as the timeliness of revolt and the similarities between the two men, not only in temperament and taste but also in appearance. Henry-Russell Hitchcock has suggested that there may have been more similarity of temperament between them than either shared with his ordinary associates. "It is a pity," says Hitchcock, "particularly for Morris, that they could not have collaborated." The two men actually did meet in 1882 when Richardson, four years before his death, went to England and spent some time with Morris.

Richardson was born on a Louisiana plantation only ten years after the death of Thomas Jefferson. But when he began to practice architecture after the Civil War, it might have been in a different world. When he was born, architects, carpenters, cabinetmakers were still building in homogeneous style. When he started to practice architecture in 1867, architects and cabinetmakers had little if anything to do with one another. Architects were turning out buildings in styles that ranged from Greek and Gothic, Elizabethan and Italianate, to Byzantine and Indian, singly or in combination. While cabinetmakers, in the interest of competition or perhaps individualism, followed their own exotic ideas. Furniture, as might be expected, rarely had any relation to architecture. If any affinity did exist, it was when architects like Alexander

Jackson Davis or James Renwick designed furniture for their own buildings.

Mechanization and overelaboration were what Morris abhorred and tried to counteract. Richardson, too, protested the crudities of industrialism, and it was his concern with every detail of his buildings that did much to restore a unity between architecture and furniture design. This was not the conformity, however, that had existed in an earlier America when cabinetmaker and builder were impelled by the same cultural forces. With Richardson, as Alan Gowans explains it, "masons, carpenters, woodworkers, found themselves equals again; not in independence, however, but in common dependence on a single controlling and directing mind." Richardson was that mind. He brought together the best painters and sculptors he could find—John La Farge, William Morris Hunt, Augustus Saint-Gaudens, the "modeller and carver" John Evans—and under his guidance a generation of craftsmen learned to build and carve in a fashion that had begun to die out. While Morris thought "machines can do everything—except make works of art," Richardson realized as Wright did that machines could create beauty if directed by artists. Mrs. Schuyler Van Rensselaer, Richardson's first biographer, tells us that he "knew that architecture as the mother and centre of all other arts and handicrafts should encourage them all for

Oak and mahogany cathedra with Gothic details designed for the Church of the Unity in Springfield, Massachusetts, of 1866–1869 was among the earliest furniture designed by Richardson. The Springfield church furniture was followed by Gothic-inspired pieces for Trinity Church in Boston of 1872–1877, which have been removed from their setting.

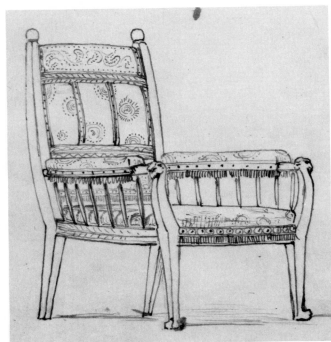

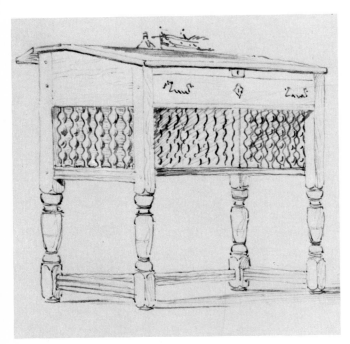

Top, left: Study for chair for the Senate Chamber in the New York State Capitol designed by Richardson in 1876–1881.

Top, right: Study for chair for the Senate Chamber in the New York State Capitol. The materials specified for the chair were mahogany and red leather stamped with brown.

Above: Study for desks for the Senate Chamber in the New York State Capitol.

Right: Sketch for wooden armchair for the Converse Memorial Library in Malden, Massachusetts, designed by Richardson in 1884–1885.

her own sake no less than for theirs. He was among the first American architects to preach and practice the fundamental precept that when walls and roof are standing a building is not finished, but still needs that its builder should concern himself with every detail of decoration, perfecting it himself or calling upon other artists to perfect it in a way harmonious with his results." Morris expressed the same idea when he told the Arts and Crafts Society in 1889: "A true architectural work is a building duly provided with all necessary furniture, decorated with all due ornament, according to the use, quality, and dignity of the building, from mere mouldings or abstract lines, to the great epical works of sculpture and painting, which, except as decorations of the nobler form of such buildings cannot be produced at all. As looked on, a work of architecture is a harmonious co-operative work of art, inclusive of all the serious arts, all those which are not engaged in the production of mere toys, or of ephemeral prettiness." It is only regrettable, as Henry-Russell Hitchcock has said, that Richardson was not more able than Morris to bring the arts together in a synthesis.

Richardson graduated from Harvard in 1859 and entered the École des Beaux-Arts in Paris in 1860. Returning to the United States after the Civil War, he practiced first in New York and then moved to Brookline, Massachusetts, in 1874. His first real opportunity came in 1866 when he was still in New York and won a competition for the Church of the Unity in Springfield, Massachusetts. An oak and mahogany cathedra with Gothic details which he designed for the Springfield church seems to have been the first of many pieces of furniture he was to design for his buildings. Like so many late 19th-century English and American architects he considered the design of the furniture, fixtures, and other interior elements part of the architect's job. The Prairie School architects carried this premise even further by using furniture as an architectural element to define space or act as a screen.

There was great variety in Richardson's furniture, ranging from pieces that were massive and straightforward like his Romanesque buildings to spindle-form benches and chairs not unrelated to the contemporary furniture made by Morris and his group. There were, however, a few pieces like the cathedra for the Springfield church which were influenced by Gothic revival design. Unfortunately, not much Richardson furniture remains in the setting of which it was such an integral part so we are inclined to see only the variety and not the homogeneity of furniture and architecture. Out of its intended context, the furniture loses much of its meaning.

While it is not certain whether all the furniture came directly from Richardson's hand, it all came out of the Richardson office and was designed under his supervision, just as the furniture that came out of Morris and Co. was supervised by Morris. Alan Gowans contends that Richardson furniture reveals even better than the architecture "how essentially new was the concept of art developing in his work." The furniture, Gowans claims, represents "the very antithesis of the classical ideal of self-contained forms; it is fundamentally alien to the Renaissance tradition. Nor does Richardson furniture revive medieval tradition, either. In form, it is, if anything, less 'Romanesque,' more eclectic, than Richardson architecture; its spirit is thoroughly picturesque, in the High Victorian manner. In a word, it is itself; it belongs to a 'tradition of its own.'"

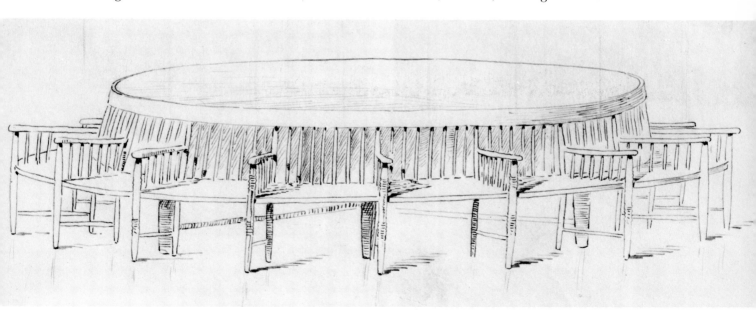

Sketch for annular settee, c. 1885, for the Billings Memorial Library, University of Vermont.

Some Richardson pieces are in collections, but a great many of them are only known through photographs and drawings. The drawings, however, such as those preserved in the Richardson collection at Harvard's Houghton Library add greatly to our picture of the buildings and to our understanding of the furniture as an important element of the architecture. They serve to remind us, moreover, as Mrs. Van Rensselaer said of a Richardson building: "We cannot dismember it in thought without hurting both what we leave and what we take away." In the Houghton collection, for example, are drawings for the original altar table, cathedra, apse chairs among other details which were removed from Boston's Trinity Church in 1938 plainly hurting what is left, but helping us to visualize the whole. While some of the furniture of the Billings Memorial Library at the University of Vermont has vanished, a series of seven drawings in the collection shows the spindle-backed benches and chairs with a variety of tables. The library has recently been restored, and with the aid of the drawings, much of the original Richardson furniture has been refinished, thus giving us a Richardson building less mutilated than most. In a few cases, such as a drawing of a spindle armchair and six-legged table for the Converse Memorial Library in Malden, Massachusetts, both drawings and objects have survived.

Some Richardson furniture is only known through photographic records. One such piece, as Richard H. Randall, Jr. pointed out in the catalog of an exhibition of Richardson furniture he organized at Boston's Museum of Fine Arts in 1962, is a sidechair with cartwheel arms which is related to the Woburn Library reading room benches. And he suggests this may have been designed for private use, "like another chair in a drawing labelled 'for Olly Ames—1 doz Chairs to be of St. Domingo Mahogany.'" But, as Randall concludes, the "variety seen in the existing examples, the drawings and photographs reveal the sanity, power and urbanity of the designs, and place Richardson among the masters of 19th-century furniture design."

Perhaps the Richardson monumental Romanesque style is best approximated in the rugged tables and spindle armchairs he designed for the chamber of the Albany Court of Appeals. The A. H. Davenport Company in Boston is known to have executed this furniture for Richardson as well as the furniture for other Richardson interiors, including the Billings Library in Vermont of 1883–1886, the Converse Memorial Library of 1883–1885 in Malden, Massachusetts, and the Glessner house in Chicago of 1885–1887. That the Davenport firm was one of the most prestigious furniture makers of the period can be gleaned by a glance at some of its clients, which included the White House in

Above: Old photograph of the Crane Memorial Library in Quincy, Massachusetts, of 1880–1882, showing the Morris-related chairs and reading table designed by Richardson.

Opposite page, top and bottom: The oak spindle-back armchairs, c. 1884, designed by Richardson for the Court of Appeals in the New York State Capitol are Byzantine in feeling as is the chamber itself. The ram's heads at the termination of the arms, the spiral turnings, and swirling bosses are similar to decoration in the Byzantine St. Mark's Cathedral in Venice. But in spite of the exotic origin of the decoration, Richardson has achieved a simplicity in keeping with the ideas of reform in furniture design.

Washington, Iolani Palace in Honolulu, as well as many of the merchant princes of New York and the wealthy residents of Boston's Back Bay. Francis H. Bacon who was with Davenport from 1885 until 1908, first as a designer and later as vice-president, worked in Richardson's office in 1884 and 1885, indicating the closeness that must have existed between the architectural firm and the furniture maker.

The loss of so many pieces of Richardson furniture only emphasizes how sad it is that furniture is so easily and so often removed or discarded. Richardson, like Robert Adam, Charles Rennie Mackintosh, and most of the architects discussed in this book, designed furniture as part of a particular interior, and without the furniture the interior is no more complete than a three-story house without a staircase or a book with most of its pages torn out. Alan Gowans put it well when he wrote: "Properly to appreciate the kind of benches, chairs, clocks, or fireplaces Richardson designed, we need not only to see them complete with original appointments—thick velvet cushions with fringes and tassels to soften their stark frames, deep red and green leather to enrich their golden oak, perhaps a large potted plant in some robust bowl to heighten textural contrasts—but even more to see them in the original setting of a Richardsonian library or church interior or parlor. There it is at once obvious how the structural lines and ornamental detail are designed in conjunction with hammerbeams and carved bookstalls and balustrades; and how similar to Richardsonian architecture in stylistic conception is the admixture within a generally medievalizing framework of vaguely Jacobean spindles, Queen Anne chair backs, William and Mary stretchers, and sweeping curves suggestive of the contemporary English Arts and Crafts movement."

Le style est l'homme is especially true in Richardson's case. In fact it is striking how many of his friends and contemporaries equate the man and his work. When Louis Sullivan's imag-

inary pupil in the *Kindergarten Chats* supposes Richardson's Marshall Field store in Chicago to be "a good piece of architecture," the Master explodes "No; I mean, here is a man for you to look at . . . a real man, a manly man; a virile force—broad, vigorous and with a whelm of energy—an entire male." That was Richardson, that was his architecture, and that was the furniture that went with it. Ralph Adams Cram in *My Life in Architecture* merely adds to the impression when he recalls that "for a space of time we were all Richardsonians . . . here was a real *man* at last." And Henry Adams, whom Richardson had known since they were Harvard classmates, wrote to a friend from Paris in 1899 when he was working on *Mont-Saint-Michel and Chartres*: "I am now all eleventh and twelfth century. . . . I caught the disease from dear old Richardson who was the only really big man I ever knew." Richardson, incidentally, may have been the author of at least some of the furniture for the house he designed for Henry Adams in Washington, D.C. Writing of the Adams's house in the *New Republic* of May 24, 1918, James Trus-

low Adams says: "This house built for him by his friend H. H. Richardson, was an odd home for such a fastidious man as Mr. Adams. The leather chairs which abounded, were all so low that they seemed to have been made for the host's own use."

Perhaps no other architect so well embodied his age as Richardson. He was as romantic as the paintings of the Hudson River School, as rational as the new industrialists. His gregarious and active self fit as well into that confident and ambitious age as his furniture fit into its surroundings. Richardson, as might be expected, didn't arrive at his architecture self-consciously as most architects do, but directly. And his furniture was part of that directness—well-constructed, large in scale, and made of oak.

Just as Jefferson was a man of the 18th century, Richardson was a man of the 19th. He designed railroad stations and railroad cars as well as churches, libraries, warehouses, and parlors for the new millionaire merchants and industrialists, and he once said he would like to design grain elevators and the interiors of steamboats.

Opposite page: Oak bench with leather seat of 1878 for the Winn Memorial Library in Woburn, Massachusetts, is suggestive of the exposed ceiling beams, paneling, and massive structural forms of a Richardson interior.

Right: Oak armchair with leather seat of 1878 for the reading room of the Winn Memorial Library in Woburn, Massachusetts, suggests something of Richardson's own sturdy and outgoing personality.

FRANK FURNESS 1839–1912

. . . something fresh and fair . . .
a human note as though someone
were talking. . . . LOUIS SULLIVAN of Furness's work

The Philadelphia architect Frank Furness who was an almost exact contemporary of Richardson was no less a colorful personality and no less a man of his time. He, too, designed the churches, libraries, and railroad stations that symbolized the age of expansion. And also like Richardson, he designed the furniture and fittings for his buildings particularly in the early years. Furness, however, didn't so much transcend his age as remain very much a part of it. He borrowed from the past with verve and imagination to come up with his own original designs. Richardson, however, looked to the future, particularly the American future and his influence on the next generation of architects was extensive both in the United States and in Europe. Even the young Eliel Saarinen in Finland was influenced by Richardson. But while Richardson was "the force that shifted the direction of American architecture away from the picturesque," in the words of James F. O'Gorman, the work of Furness "remained firmly within the bounds of the picturesque."

Furness's personality, however, was perhaps even more colorful than Richardson's. Although he was born of one of the most intellectually distinguished families of Philadelphia's upper class and his father was a Unitarian minister, many were impressed by his nonconformity and blasphemous language. Louis Sullivan, who had spent a year in Furness's office before he went to Chicago, recalled in his *Autobiography* the "loud plaids" he wore and the "marvelous red beard" which "depended fan-like" from his face. It was to the latter that Sullivan's "eyes were riveted, in infatuation" as he listened to "a string of oaths a mile long," but he was especially hypnotized when Furness "drew and swore at the same

time." Sullivan was probably right in thinking Furness a "curious character." He was certainly one of the eccentrics of American architecture. Bernard Maybeck and Harvey Ellis were others.

Furness was born in Philadelphia in 1839. His father, the Reverend William Henry Furness, was pastor of the First Congregational Unitarian Church and a lifelong friend of Ralph Waldo Emerson. The young Furness received his architectural training in the New York atelier of Richard Morris Hunt, who was the first American to graduate from the École des Beaux-Arts in Paris. After service in the Civil War for which he received the Congressional Medal of Honor, Furness returned to Hunt's office; then, in 1867 he set up his own office in Philadelphia and did almost all his subsequent work in and around that city. Sullivan described the atmosphere in Furness's office as "the free and easy one of a true workshop savoring of the guild where craftsmanship was paramount and personal."

There can be little doubt that Furness was rebelling against the genteel academism that had taken over his own cultured city as well as many others around the world. Sullivan admired Furness as one who "made buildings out of his head," and certainly they were a surprise to the citizenry of his Quaker city. While his Provident Life and Trust Company Bank of 1876–1879 was being built, a Philadelphia newspaper commented: "On this front, there seems to have been a new surprise every few mornings and there has been a constant strain in the public mind as to what might be coming. . . ." And some of his furniture, too, seems to have been "made out of his head."

These handsome chairs designed by Furness for the Rodef Shalom Synagogue in Philadelphia of 1869–1871 are among the earliest preserved examples of his work and show that from the beginning he was after what James O'Gorman calls "an electrifying surface effect of lines and shapes."

Frank Furness's love of ornament is given full play in this black walnut desk, c. 1875, designed for the Philadelphia house of his brother Horace. Many of the details that give the desk its strong architectonic quality can be found in the architect's buildings.

Furness, as was common at the time, apparently made a cult of ugliness. According to an 1869 issue of *The Builder*, the pursuit of ugliness was the result of competitions where "each man feels that his best chance of distinction is to put forth something more wild and startling than his neighbors have done." The "barbaric mania," claimed the writer, had even "spread to furniture design." Be that as it may, Furness "pushed ugliness to the point where it almost turned into beauty, or at least a brutal creativity," in the words of Lewis Mumford. Even architects of his own day called the bold decorations and details of Furness's buildings aberrations. But while some of the furniture he designed may seem the epitome of ugliness to us, it had great appeal for the taste-setters of Philadelphia. Almost all of Furness's clients were from the city's top social echelon, and probably the reason he did so many railroad stations was because the Pennsylvania Railroad was the monetary center of that elite—"an institution with a style and *allure* of its own, is not, even the world over, as other railroads are," observed Henry James when he visited Philadelphia in 1904.

Although much of Furness's furniture is lost, it is known that he designed the reading desks, pulpits, pews, and other fittings for all his churches. In fact the chairs he designed for the Rodef Shalom Synagogue in Philadelphia of 1869–1871 are among the earliest preserved examples of his furniture. Also preserved at the Philadelphia Museum of Art are a desk and chair he designed around 1875 for his brother Horace Howard Furness, a noted Shakespearian scholar. The desk is impressive for its daring massiveness of form not unlike that of his buildings. The desk also shows the love of ornament which is apparent in his buildings. This may not seem to conform to the tenets of the Arts and Crafts movement, but like Morris and his followers, Furness was reacting against the excesses of the midcentury revivals and the mechanically induced decline in the quality of ornament. The side chair that is thought to have gone with the desk is also architectural in conception. An early photograph of Horace Furness's library in the Philadelphia Museum of Art archives shows some of the furniture designed by Furness, including bookcases which echo the Moorish arch of the desk in a series of identical arches along their upper section. The furniture plainly contributes to the architectural unity of the room. In fact mantels and woodwork within most of Furness's domestic buildings formed transitional elements between the architecture and the furniture as it did with Richardson.

For many of Furness's domestic pieces he relied on such popular pattern books of the period as Charles Eastlake's *Hints on Household Taste* of 1868 or Bruce Talbert's *Gothic Forms Applied to*

Furniture of 1867. Even Eastlake, who was continually calling for simplicity and sincerity of design, recommended the use of marquetry, inlay, and shallow carving to achieve "an effect of greater richness." It was plainly difficult for many of those Arts and Crafts enthusiasts to completely renounce all the exuberances in their background. But as O'Gorman points out, Furness only derived the basic structural lines of his furniture from these sources, "which he then filled in with his own incised floral or animal patterns." His ornamental designs, which were invariably based on natural forms, might have surprised Morris, but they undoubtedly influenced Sullivan. It was, in fact, the uncompromising individualism of Furness's work that had originally attracted Sullivan and that individualism is to be found in his furniture as well as his architecture.

The furniture of Horace Furness's library was probably made in the Philadelphia cabinetmaking shop of German-born Daniel Pabst, one of the most prominent craftsmen of the late 19th century and one of the few who continued traditional craft techniques in the face of industrialization. He made only the finest furniture of the kind "that does not come out for the glue like your poor modern machine stuff," according to the Philadelphia *Evening Bulletin* of June 11, 1910. And his clientele, as might be expected, was also of the finest.

There is evidence that Pabst made many pieces of furniture from Furness's designs. The most notable commission which can be attributed to Furness and Pabst "with some certainty," according to David A. Hanks, was the furniture and interior woodwork in the house of Theodore Roosevelt, Sr. on West 57th Street in New York City. Hanks contends that the design of the dining room furniture as it appears in a contemporary photograph can be attributed to Furness "on the basis of very close similarity in style and the exact repetition of motifs, such as the pelican, used in other pieces by Furness." Horace Jayne, moreover, whose house Furness had designed in the 1890s, recalled in a letter to Calvin Hathaway of the Philadelphia Museum that a "German woodcarver" had done Furness's work. Other pieces of furniture executed by Pabst may well have been designed by Furness. It has even been speculated that Furness might have been a major influence in Pabst's style.

English designer Christopher Dresser, an adherent of Morris's ideas, was the author of *Principles of Decorative Design* and *Studies in Design* from which Furness derived some of his ornamental designs. They were also sources for Pabst's work. This may seem surprising after looking at the desk Furness designed for his brother and reading Dresser's dictum that furniture should have "simplicity of structure and truthfulness of construction." That, however, only underlines the fact that the 19th-century proponents of Arts and Crafts didn't always mean the same thing as we do by simplicity and truthfulness.

In any case eclecticism was the order of the day and Furness's furniture, as O'Gorman says, was as eclectically designed as his architecture to which it is closely related. Also eclectic was the den Furness built onto his own Philadelphia house with its "bewildering accumulation of guns, snowshoes, stuffed birds, a ram's head, nature prints, caricatures, Indian blankets, mugs, pipes, and rough-plank furniture that looked as if it were in the wilds of Montana. The author of *Artistic Houses* could only gasp 'it was absolutely unique,'" to quote O'Gorman again.

If Furness looked back to Ruskinian Gothic and Richardson ahead to the modern movement, they were both originals, and the work of both men reflects the robustness and vigor of an age that included Walt Whitman *and* the Pennsylvania Railroad.

Mahogany side chair, c. 1875, one of a pair designed by Furness for his brother Horace's Philadelphia house, has a compartment with a hinged lid contained in its crest rail.

CHARLES F. ANNESLEY VOYSEY 1857–1941

To be simple is the end, not the beginning of design. C. F. A. VOYSEY

The English architect C. F. A. Voysey gave a lot of thought to the furniture of his time and found it "a most depressing" subject. He wrote in the *Journal of the Royal Institute of Architects* in 1894: "Rich and poor alike are content to order their furniture from the upholsterer, as they do their funerals from the undertaker. The result is very similar, the bill being the most lasting impression made on their minds. What they have paid is the measure of their greatness." Later he adds, "The client never dreams that his architect's province is beyond drain-pipes and drawings, and has often himself received an excellent education in decoration and furnishing from periodicals and handbooks. Therefore he feels any interference on the architect's part, in the choice of furniture and fittings, is rather an impertinence. For this state of things, in a great measure, we have to thank the spirit of revivalism."

This, then, is what Voysey spent a lifetime trying to counteract. He was certainly a child of Morris in his respect for craftsmanship and the variety of things he designed for his houses—wallpapers, furniture, textiles, silverware, even toast-racks. But he was not a craftsman as Morris was. He was a designer. While Voysey agreed with many of Morris's ideas, he always kept him at arm's length, as David Gebhard put it, because he was afraid of merely becoming a minor imitator and follower as so many had. He even went further, says Gebhard, "and except for the rarest occasions, never wrote or spoke of him at all." In fact once when John Betjeman wanted to lend Voysey a book by Morris, he thanked him, saying he didn't feel he wanted to read him. "He was too much of an atheist for me." Nevertheless Voysey admitted in an interview published in the September 1896 *Builder's Journal & Architectural Record* that Morris "has done for me what I might not have been able to do for myself, made it possible for me to live."

Voysey was rebelling against the ornamental uninhibited ways of the Victorians just as Morris and Richardson were. Voysey, however, was his own man. While he was one of the leading English designers contemporary with Art Nouveau, he was certainly not a member of that movement. In fact he detested Art Nouveau and called it "mad eccentricity" while appreciating the reasoning behind it. Writing in the *Magazine of Art* in 1904, he said he thought "the condition which has made Art Nouveau possible is a distinctly healthy development, but at the same time the manifestation of it is distinctly unhealthy and revolting."

Unlike the Art Nouveau designers, Voysey was concerned with eliminating ornament, not adding to it. In a 1906 pamphlet entitled "Reason as a Basis of Art," he wrote: "The desire for gaudy richness and effect has produced the shams we find in the shops. The well-made solid, plain articles, such as the poor man, if he did not try to hide his poverty, would wish to have, are scarcely ever to be found. There is a universal desire (which is the outcome of insincerity) to make things look better than they are. The plain, solid oak furniture of bygone times is now replaced by stained and highly polished and decorated rubbish created by an endeavour to make something look better than it is. So-called ornament is lavishly used to hide workmanship and bad material. A general revolt against shams would surely check the supply."

The strikingly simple and elegant form of this oak writing desk with brass fittings of 1865 is typical of Voysey's work.

Needless to say Voysey's furniture was usually made of "plain, solid oak," never stained nor highly polished, and always well made.

Voysey was an individualist. He designed houses in the English cottage tradition, but always in a strongly individual style. And the furniture he designed for them was as bold, simple, and direct as the architecture. It was usually of unvarnished oak, often with cutout heart shapes as decoration, and large handles or hinges painted black. He always insisted, in the best Arts and Crafts tradition, on simple basic shapes and forms, and as David Gebhard puts it, "his 'jointery' of individual pieces of wood was as direct and uncomplicated as possible." But he gave it elegance and lightness by attenuating the uprights, elongating vertical pieces, and adding the cutouts and hardware for decoration. His furniture, like his houses, was rooted in tradition, albeit a very personal conception of tradition. He himself wrote in 1911: "I remain faithful to tradition but not its slave." And one can certainly echo what a writer wrote in *The Studio* in 1896: ". . . one thing is sure, that Mr. Voysey's furniture does not take kindly to its commercially produced relatives."

Voysey was born in Yorkshire, the son of a clergyman who was expelled from the Church of England for scorning belief in the existence of hell fire. The son, no less unorthodox than the father, didn't do well in school. In 1874, he was apprenticed to J. P. Seddon, who had been a London cabinetmaker before becoming an architect. Seddon designed furniture for his own buildings, and some of it was decorated by Rossetti and other members of the Morris group. Voysey later worked for about two years in the office of the architect George Devey and then, around 1882, opened his own office. While waiting for architectural commissions to come in, Voysey designed fabrics and wallpaper that were much admired in Europe as well as in England for their fresh and simple designs. "It was as if Spring had come all of a sudden" is the way Henri Van de Velde put it.

Voysey's stated reason for designing wallpapers is reason enough for his designing furniture: ". . . as most modern furniture is vulgar and bad in every way, elaborate papers of many colours help to disguise its ugliness." But H. Goodhart-Rendel points out another equally valid reason in *English Architecture Since the Regency*: The "disarming lack of pretension" of a Voysey house made it impossible to transfer furniture from the former homes of their occupants since it would often appear "extremely discordant, and even the farm-house antiques, or pretended antiques, then much sought after by tasteful suburbans, were apt to look rather guiltily experienced in surroundings so childishly artless."

Above: Staircase hall of "Garden Corner," Chelsea, for E.J. Horniman of 1906 is remarkably modern in feeling with its oak armchairs with heart-pierced splats and upholstered leather seats.

Opposite page, top: Voysey-designed chairs and folding table in the living room of "Hollymount" near Beaconsfield for C.T. Burke of 1905–1906—one house for which the architect was able to design everything inside and outside.

Opposite page, bottom: Three versions of a favorite Voysey chair design, c. 1896, distinguished by a broad splat pierced with a simple heart shape.

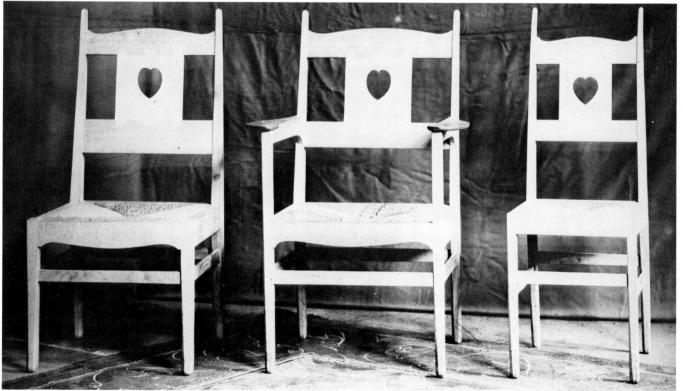

This high-backed oak armchair, c. 1907, has a leather seat and leather panel in the back embossed with ESI, the monogram of the firm for which Voysey designed it—the Essex and Suffolk Equitable Insurance Company.

It is worth noting that Voysey's early clients were often Quakers who, he himself said, encouraged his pursuit of simplicity. A large percentage of his later clients, as might be expected, were progressive artists and writers, including H. G. Wells for whom he designed a house in 1899.

Voysey has been called a pioneer of the modern movement although he lived long enough to be unhappy about modern architecture. He was associated with the Arts and Crafts movement which sought to simplify the processes of production. "It seems to me," he wrote in *The Studio* of September 1893, "that to produce any satisfactory work of art we must acquire a complete knowledge of our material and be thoroughly masters of the craft to be employed in its production . . . go to Nature direct for inspiration and guidance. Then we are at once relieved from restrictions of style or period, and can live and work in the present with laws revealing always fresh possibilities." But while Voysey belonged to the Arts and Crafts tradition, he was no enemy of the machine. In 1909 he said in a lecture he delivered in London: "When you design my tables and chairs you will think of the machine that is going to help in the making, and choose such shapes as are easily worked by machinery." And in another place: "The human quality in familiar objects has in many cases been driven out by the machine. Nevertheless the machine has come to liberate men's minds for more intellectual work."

He was, moreover, always concerned with utility. "Let every man judge furniture from the point of view of reason," he wrote in 1894. "Let us ask, Is it fit and thoroughly suited to the purpose for which it is intended? Is it as strong as, and no stronger than, it should be? And from the point of view of conscience ask, Is it true—is it all it pretends to be? Does it express qualities and feelings consistent with its owner and its surroundings? . . ."

And Voysey practiced what he preached. "Unlike some of his contemporaries who were concerned primarily with effect rather than utility," writes Elizabeth Aslin in *Nineteenth Century English Furniture*, "Voysey was prepared to adapt designs after experimental use. Thus one of his dining-chairs with the usual elegant, attenuated uprights, was put into production in a modified form because the high back proved to interfere with service at a dining-table." Voysey, as she says, had real feeling for his materials and was the "first thoroughly successful exponent of simplicity of form in interior decoration." This can be deduced from his own words: "Try the effect of a well-proportioned room, with white-washed walls, plain carpet and simple oak furniture, and nothing in it but necessary articles of use, and one pure ornament in the form of a simple vase of flowers, not a cosmopolitan crowd of sorts, but one or two sprays of one kind, and you will find reflection begin to dance in your brain." Or ". . . you must choose your hall furniture and ornaments as carefully as you choose the first words to a stranger on his arrival, if you would produce on him an effect of peaceful friendship and homely bliss." Almost all his words, in fact, denote the man and the designer. Simplicity, fitness, and harmony were the key words. "We must all be impressed by the utter want of harmony between the furniture and the architecture of today, except perhaps in jerry-built villas—there is a kind of harmony there. If artistic feeling always accompanied the architect's knowledge of materials and construction, he would in time, no doubt, be recognised as a fit person to design furniture. Then some sort of harmony might once more be seen. But, since the furniture has been taken out of the architect's hands and put into the upholsterer's, the tendency has been to make the architecture to fit the furniture."

Like Richardson, Voysey seems to have insinuated his own personality into his work. Richardson was exuberant, outgoing, and robust and so was his work. Voysey, the son of a parson, was neat, meticulous, and self-effacing. Not surprisingly most of Richardson's jobs were public buildings, most of Voysey's were houses. Voysey found Morris too sensual and he would probably have thought the same of Richardson.

When a reporter from *The Studio* wanted to interview Voysey in 1893, he says he only gained the architect's consent "by representing to him that *The Studio* was especially anxious to raise the appreciation of design, and to that end the maker of patterns must sacrifice himself for the good of his art." As a result of that interview we have a description of Voysey's "old-fashioned little house" in St. John's Wood where he lived in the 1890s. Although this was not a house he designed, it has been suggested that its plain white painted stucco exterior with wide eaves and low-pitched slate roof may have influenced his later style. In any case it was pure Voysey inside. Of its studio, the interviewer tells us, "one saw it was obviously not merely a work place but a living place, the reticence of its decoration, its furniture bearing the unmistakable impress of the owner's hand, showing that the creed of the artist was the creed he lived. . . ." Before leaving, the interviewer concludes, "my host took me into his house, and although it would be out of place to speak of the various pieces of furniture, the clever adaptation of use to beauty, one could not but feel that here was proof of comfort and entirely domestic requirements combined with art in a way that made it remarkable." Although we might regret the interviewer's reluctance to describe the furniture, what he does tell us rings

This settee of 1906 of unstained and unpolished oak was used by Voysey in several houses including "Garden Corner" for E.J. Horniman (see staircase hall on page 78).

true of the man who said, "Let us begin by discarding the mass of useless ornaments and banishing the millinery that degrades our furniture and fittings."

Voysey didn't seriously begin to design furniture until the 1890s, and his best designs were executed between 1895 and 1911 as were his most important houses. In 1899 he designed the Orchard at Chorleywood for himself, the first house for which he could complete every detail of the interior including the furniture, carpets, curtains, and wallcoverings. The Orchard was widely illustrated in architectural magazines in England and abroad and was soon followed by other houses for which he designed the furniture and furnishings.

Voysey believed a house should be designed to be lived in, and in order to carry out his ideas he wanted to design every part of it from planning it and fitting it into its setting to designing its furniture, fabrics, and silverware. We have the words of *The Studio* interviewer and photographs of his Chorleywood house to tell us how livable his own houses were. We also have a description of the rooms he lived in toward the

he specified in his drawings. His furniture was made by several craftsman's firms. One of the most important seems to have been F. D. Nielsen who worked with him from 1901 until the outbreak of World War I. He also worked with A. W. Simpson for whom he designed a house in 1909. The house, however, was furnished with pieces by Simpson, who was undoubtedly influenced by Voysey.

In addition to quality, good workmanship, and simple design, Voysey wanted his furniture to be comfortable and beautiful. Unlike Furness, he hated ugly things. "It is fatally easy to get accustomed to corrupting influences." Perhaps more than any other architect, Voysey was truly concerned that every detail of his clients' houses should be beautiful.

In 1904 Voysey delivered a lecture to the Royal Institute of British Architects in which he said: "I fear I am expected to say something much more practical about the design of furniture. I wish I could say something helpful, but I am myself groping in the dark, struggling to find out the true laws which govern fitness and beauty." He often spoke of "the divine law of fitness" which is not only Morrisanian and Bauhausian, it suggests Sullivan's "form follows function." Voysey's furniture, in fact, may well have influenced Wright and other Prairie school architects, but as David Gebhard has pointed out, Voysey conceived of furniture in a usable traditional sense while Wright conceived of it as "a small variation on an architectural theme."

When discussing either Voysey's furniture or his architecture, one should not neglect its Englishness. It preeminently reveals the Englishman's "unalterable preference" for the "rural and rustic" that impressed the German critic Hermann Muthesius. In a 1911 lecture entitled "Patriotism in Architecture," Voysey told his audience, "Each country has been given its own characteristics by its Creator and should work out its own salvation. The best architecture in the past has always been native to its own country and has grown out of a thorough knowledge of local requirements and conditions. Requirements including body, mind, and spirit. Conditions include Climate and National Character." Wright would have agreed with that.

The English architect Sir Edward Lutyens should have the last word about Voysey. In 1931 he wrote in the catalog of an exhibition of Voysey's works: "Simple, old-world forms, moulded to his own passion, as if an old testament had been rewrit in vivid print, bringing to light a renewed vision in turning of its pages, an old world made new, and with it, to younger men of whom I was one, the promise of a new, exhilarating sphere of invention. This was Voysey's achievement."

end of his life to complete the thesis. Robert Donat, who was married to Voysey's niece, broadcast his recollections of "Uncle Charles" shortly after the architect's death, in which he remembered when Voysey "drew apart from the world, like many a great artist before him, simply because he couldn't altogether cope with his work and with the world at the same time. . . . He had all he needed and more, and his rooms in St. James Street, though simple, were extremely comfortable and were filled with beautiful things of his own designing."

Every detail of Voysey's work, as John Brandon-Jones has noted, "was drawn from personal experience of building and the crafts." He himself said: "How often we see effectiveness in the place of genuine quality. What looks rich but is only brainless elaboration," and added, "Good craftsmanship, then, is the expression of good feeling, as good feeling leads to right and honest workmanship." The good craftsmanship as well as the good feeling were apparent in the design as well as the proportions of his furniture. They were apparent in the untreated oak "free from all stains and polish" as

HARVEY ELLIS 1852-1904

*Simple, structural plans, with
an absence of applied ornament,
are required from the construction
of things made by hands, whether
these things are greater or smaller:
the house to live in, the bed
to lie in, or the desk or table
at which to work.* HARVEY ELLIS

By all accounts Harvey Ellis was a poetic genius who cared nothing about personal fame. In any case he received little of it although many other architects seem to have prospered from his work. He has been called "a man of broad intellect and deep learning," "gifted but irresponsible," "a vagrant genius," "a link between the great romantic, Richardson, and the masters of the Prairie School." He drank heavily and may have been something of a mystic.

Ellis was born in Rochester, New York, in 1852 and later attended West Point. Most of the rest of his life is shrouded in mystery—a mystery that he seems to have done his best to foster. He began his professional career as a draftsman in Albany when Richardson was there as a member of the architectural commission working on the Albany City Hall and the New York State Capitol. Ellis worked as a draftsman and designer for Richardson whom he described at the time as "a magnificent big brute." He was equally impressed with Richardson's work, which remained an influence for a long time. In 1879 Ellis returned to Rochester where, for the next five years, he practiced architecture in partnership with his brother Charles. When he left Rochester he seems to have wandered around the midwest acting as a journeyman draftsman, and his name began to appear under the names of various architects. "The journeyman draftsmen," recalled Prairie school architect William Gray Purcell in the *Northwest Architect* of 1944, "were a jolly crowd, more often than not hard drinkers, drifting from one office to the next in a restless quest for romance and adventure, carrying with them the gossip of the building world and a homely philosophy of life which reached their architectural work only indirectly.

. . . Without question the most distinguished and capable of these journeyman draftsmen architects was Harvey Ellis. His name was known to everyone who read an architectural magazine from 1880 to well past 1900, for his remarkably fine pen drawings. . . . In men like . . . Ellis," Purcell continues, "the line between architect and draftsman disappears except for the fact that practically all of their work is credited to employing architects who were often men of little or no creative ability. . . ."

These journeyman draftsmen were actually wandering architects who augmented architectural staffs when a press of work made it necessary. Often they were given complete charge of a project from design through supervising the construction, and it was in that capacity that Ellis usually worked. Thus buildings all over the midwest bear the unmistakable stamp of Ellis although they are listed as the work of one or another architectural firm. Minnesota poet-architect Robert Ferguson has told how it gradually became apparent to him that some buildings in St. Joseph, Missouri, where he was brought up, "were particularly powerful in the mind." Later when he lived in St. Louis and in Minneapolis and St. Paul, he noticed that "the same personal design devices showed up familiarly on buildings, ostensibly by several different architects, which radiated the same intense and sometimes disturbing presence." The individuality and power of Ellis's buildings have struck others in a similar way. No one knows whether he designed furniture for any of these buildings, but it seems likely that he did, judging by the furniture he often put in his drawings and the furniture designs he executed later for Gustav Stickley.

Armchair designed by Ellis and executed by
Gustav Stickley's Craftsman Workshops,
Eastwood, New York, c. 1903–1904, of oak
with copper and pewter inlay. Ellis's stylized
inlaid motifs show a full awareness of the
work of Mackintosh and the Glasgow group.

Ellis returned to Rochester in the mid-1890s, and his designs began to reflect inspiration from the British Arts and Crafts movement. One of his projects in Rochester was a library and conservatory for the Joseph T. Cunningham house in 1900. His rendering of a section of it shows it to be clearly of the Arts and Crafts school, including plain wall surfaces and simple woodwork and furniture. In fact Ellis's work at this time shows the influence of such British architects as Voysey, Mackintosh, and H. Baillie Scott, whose work he was familiar with through his wide reading as well as his travels. He certainly knew of and undoubtedly admired Morris. It is a pity we can't have his own words on the subject. It is known, however, that he owned a copy of Ruskin's *Seven Lamps of Architecture* from which Morris derived many of his ideas.

Ellis's interest in the Arts and Crafts movement received wider expression when in 1902 he began to write for Gustav Stickley's magazine, *The Craftsman*, which he continued to do until his death in 1904. He also designed furniture for Stickley's workshop, which shows an elegance that is not usually associated with the "sturdy and primitive forms" of Stickley. Ellis used oak for his furniture as did many members of the Arts and Crafts movement and most of the Prairie school architects. "This native product," wrote Ellis in *The Craftsman* of January 1903, "the qualities of which are now receiving deserved attention, is, so to speak, the most human of woods, that is, the most amenable to the educative process: the literal drawing out of all that constitutes its value. Under the action of 'fuming' and of other chemical processes, which might be compared to the experiences and trials

of an individual, it discloses unsuspected qualities of beauty previously lying concealed within its heart."

Some of the Ellis pieces for Stickley incorporate inlays of contrasting wood, copper, brass, and pewter, which, as Ellis says in *The Craftsman* article, "contrast well with the gray-brown of the oak." He used ornament, Ellis explains, "to relieve and make interesting what otherwise would have been a too large area of plain, flat surface." In every case, he adds, it "emphasizes the structural lines; accenting in most cases the vertical elements, and so giving a certain slenderness of effect to a whole which was otherwise too solid and heavy." Ellis's sophisticated furniture designs were not long continued in the Stickley line of Craftsman Furniture, perhaps because the inlay made them too expensive. But, as someone put it, for a while Ellis made the craftsman movement poetic. Roger G. Kennedy, who has written about Minnesota architecture in general and Ellis in particular, rightly points out that in Ellis's hands the forms became slimmer, more graceful, delicately colored, with occasional inlays, but never weak. Ellis, he adds, "drew upon the ornamental motifs of the American Indian, and he wasn't afraid to draw, as well, upon the infinitely sophisticated Art Nouveau of the Glasgow School." During the few years he wrote for *The Craftsman*, as Rogers says, "he showed what American Arts and Crafts might be, in textiles, furniture, wall painting, and a few houses." He was, after all, an artist and his taste superb, as the articles and illustrations he did for *The Craftsman* make clear. In his article on "An Adirondack Camp" of July 1903, he wisely tells his readers that "nothing is safer than the old rule of decoration, formulated by

This watercolor rendering by Harvey Ellis of 1900 with its spindle-back chair is of a section of the library and conservatory for Joseph T. Cunningham in Rochester, New York, and evokes the Arts and Crafts tradition with clear English influence.

*Club chair designed by Ellis for Gustav
Stickley's Craftsman Workshops, Eastwood,
New York, in 1903 of oak inlaid with pewter,
copper, and various woods.*

Writing table designed by Ellis for Gustav Stickley in 1903 of oak with inlays of various woods, copper, and pewter. The inlays on the legs are conventionalized floral motifs with vignettes of Viking ships.

Owen Jones: 'When in doubt as to any detail of decoration, leave it out!' " But Ellis didn't need to be safe, his eye told him all he needed to know.

One small screen by Ellis, now in the Gamble House Museum in Pasadena, as Rogers points out, "shows how he, like the brothers Greene in California, almost led to a kind of relationship between the American architectural profession and its creative clients which, had history been kinder, might have made it less necessary for Frank Lloyd Wright to bully his way to greatness."

This "vagrant genius" died at the age of 52 virtually unknown except to a few architects and friends. In an appraisal of him in 1965, Purcell called him "a very great architect. . . . No man should be mentioned on any page about him." And yet, even today, few know his name. He did the work of many architects and influenced many, perhaps even the great Louis Sullivan. Writing of the Prairie school in the *Architectural Review* of April 1908, Thomas E. Tallmadge says: ". . . a pretty story could be written descriptive of the early struggles and aspirations and ultimate success of the little band of enthusiasts who had raised their standard of revolt against the disciplined ranks and array of custom. An ideal artistic atmosphere pervaded the colony in the old lofts of Steinway Hall. There was Perkins, Wright, Spencer, Myron Hunt, George Dean, Birch Long, and with them—associated in spirit if not in person—was the gifted but irresponsible genius Harvey Ellis, poet-architect, whose pencil Death stopped ere it had traced more than a few soft lines of his dream of beauty."

This man, so gifted and so admired by his contemporaries, is listed in *Who Was Who in America, 1897–1942* as follows: "Ellis, Harvey, artist; b. Rochester, N.Y. 1852; pupil of Edwin White, N.A. Exhibited at Paris Expn., 1900. Mem. New York Water Color Club; pres. Rochester Society of Arts and Crafts. Is also an architect. Home: Rochester, N.Y. Died 1904."

THREE ARCHITECTS OF THE PRAIRIE SCHOOL

"It is beginning to be more and more apparent that a number of the better architects of the West have a tendency consciously to break away from the time-honored European tradition to which their eastern brethren devotedly cleave," wrote Arthur C. David in *Architectural Record* of April 1904. He was speaking of the architects of the Prairie school who were just beginning to make their important contribution to the history of American architecture. The movement only lasted until 1915, but it was extraordinarily vigorous during those years, developing, perhaps, the first consciously original architecture America had ever had.

The Prairie school was, as H. Allen Brooks has said, "a regional manifestation of the international revolt and reform then occurring in the visual arts," but it was a purely American version of that revolt. It consisted of a group of Chicago architects who grew up around Frank Lloyd Wright and whose spiritual leader was Louis Sullivan. One of the important tenets of its philosophy was that a building and its furnishing were one, or as Wright put it, "It is quite impossible to consider the building one thing and its furnishings another, its setting and environment still another."

The Prairie school architects were close to the American Arts and Crafts movement which was centered in Chicago, and several of them, including Wright and George W. Maher, were charter members of the Chicago Arts and Crafts Society founded in 1897. There was, moreover, a close relationship between the Chicagoans and members of the English Arts and Crafts movement which had been founded by William Morris. Several members of the English movement visited Chicago, including Morris-follower C. R. Ashbee who paid his first visit there in 1900 when he and Wright became lasting friends. The *House Beautiful* magazine, which began publication in Chicago in 1896, also helped foster a connection between the English and Chicago architects. It featured the work of C. F. A. Voysey and Baillie Scott as well as the first published work of Frank Lloyd Wright. In an article about Wright's Oak Park studio in the December 1899 issue, we learn that "among the few books in Wright's library was one illustrating the work of Voysey and other English architects."

Although the Prairie architects' emphasis on unity of exterior and interior, their desire for simplicity, and their respect for natural materials, were largely derived from the English Arts and Crafts movement, there were differences between the American and English philosophies. Members of the English movement renounced the machine, while the Americans never did, as Wright made clear in his famous Hull House lecture on "The Art and Craft of the Machine" in which he calls the machine "the metamorphosis of ancient art and craft . . . the modern Sphinx—whose riddle the artist must solve if he would that art live—for his nature holds the key." The English movement, moreover, was interested in reviving the simplicities of the Middle Ages, but although the Prairie school architects were also interested in simplicity, they wanted to develop something entirely new. And so they did. The Prairie house was a completely new regional type of house, and for that reason if no other, it would have demanded a new type of furniture. It is not hard to imagine the shock to a Prairie school architect's sensibility to see such traditional 19th-century furniture as an ornately carved Belter chair or Louis XV loveseat in a simple rectilinear Prairie house living room. It has been suggested that the profusion of built-in furniture in the Prairie houses may have been calculated to soften that shock. As Wright put it in his *Autobiography*: "Very few of the houses were . . . anything but painful to me after the clients moved in and, helplessly, dragged the horrors of the old order along after them." Today one could find furniture that would be at least compatible with a Prairie house interior, but in the early decades of this century there was nothing with the sole exception of Mission furniture that wasn't totally incongruous. But Wright even turned up his nose at that. "Plainness was not necessarily simplicity," he says when describing how he evolved his Prairie houses in *The Natural House*. "Crude furniture of the Roycroft-Stickley-Mission style, which came along later, was offensively plain, plain as a barn door—but was never simple in a true sense. Nor, I found, were

FRANK LLOYD WRIGHT
GEORGE WASHINGTON MAHER
GEORGE GRANT ELMSLIE

merely machine-made things in themselves necessarily simple." (Nevertheless Stickley furniture was sometimes used in the secondary rooms of Wright's houses when the client couldn't afford his custom-designed furniture throughout. The Bradley House of 1900 in Kankakee, Illinois, is one such example. This was also apparently the case in George Grant Elmslie's houses since the secondary rooms in the Henry B. Babson house designed by Purcell, Feick and Elmslie in 1912 were also furnished with Stickley furniture.)

But the lack of appropriate furniture was not the only reason the Prairie school architects designed furniture. Prairie school furniture was as much a part of the architecture that gives it its name as its low hovering roof, its sophisticated spatial arrangements, its strong horizontality. The Prairie school philosophy embraced the idea that every facet of their buildings should contribute to the whole environment—from chairs and tables to lighting and landscaping. "There should be in any conception only one idea, one theme, one purpose," as George Grant Elmslie put it and Wright often expressed the same idea. Thus these architects designed a chair, a table, a bench, a desk, a cabinet, a light fixture, a rug as a very integral part of their architecture. Some of it may seem strange out of the architectural role it was designed to play, but in its proper place it becomes perfectly right and esthetically pleasing. In fact only when the furniture is seen in the context for which it was planned is its art and intent revealed.

Prairie school architects used built-in units to define space and sometimes act as visual blocks in the free-flowing spaces. Movable pieces were designed to act as screens. The high-backed chairs with their square vertical spindles found in several of Wright's Prairie house dining rooms serve to create a visual privacy around the dining table without blocking the flow of space. The Prairie school architects used furniture as Sir John Soane used mirror, semicircular arches, and sometimes even furniture to create spatial surprises—to mold without interrupting the "flowing oneness" of space.

The straight lines and rectilinear forms of Prairie school furniture give it an intimacy with its environment. Table and desk tops, like the spreading roof lines of the houses, extend beyond their upright supports. It is all of a piece with those low, ground-hugging houses that seem so right for the prairie. Prairie school furniture, as Donald Kalec has pointed out, was also in keeping with the living patterns of the early 1900s. "The very solidity and "rootedness' of the Prairie architecture and its concordant furniture," he says, "was a direct reflection of this stable way of life."

While all Prairie school furniture was in the spirit of the architecture, there was great variety in it. Each architect designed pieces to suit his particular architecture. A dining room chair for a Wright Prairie house might have a back of square spindles reaching from top to floor, a lyrical cut-out pattern might decorate the splat of an Elmslie dining chair, while a Maher dining room chair, like his architecture, was apt to be stockier, more solid than the others. It was all, however, based on straight lines and rectilinear forms.

In place of overstuffed chairs or sofas, the Prairie school architects used loose cushions on wood planks. Plain oak was the predominating material although birch and mahogany were sometimes used. "Who knows," as Donald Kalec asks, "but that oak, as the deciduous example of strength and durability, appealed to Mr. Wright and the other Prairie school architects for its symbolic qualities." That may be, but it also appealed for its color and graining. The oak they used for furniture, doors, window frames, trim, and floors might be lightly waxed, but no other finish was used. Prairie school architects appreciated the natural beauty of wood as the Scandinavians do. "Wood," said Wright in *In the Cause of Architecture*, "can never be wrought by the machine as it was lovingly wrought by hand into a violin for instance, except as a lifeless imitation. But the beautiful properties of wood may be released by the machine to the hand of the architect. His imagination must use it in true ways—worthy of its beauty. His *plastic* effects will refresh the life of wood, as well as the human-spirit that lost it—as inspiration—long since."

FRANK LLOYD WRIGHT 1867-1959

*I would rather sit on a pumpkin and
have it all to myself, than to be crowded
on a velvet cushion.*   HENRY DAVID THOREAU

If William Morris was the chief protagonist of the Arts and Crafts movement, Wright was the chief protagonist of the Prairie school. His ideas set much of the Prairie school philosophy that gave great importance to furniture design. In fact Wright's interest in furniture never diminished. Critics have derided it as the whim of a genius, but they are wrong. Wright was very serious about furniture. He probably designed his first pieces when he was in his early twenties and never stopped designing it. He was 88 in 1955 when he designed his first line of commercial furniture for sale to the public. Furniture was part and parcel of his concept of organic architecture. There probably wasn't a Wright house built from the 1890s through the 1950s that didn't have at least some Wright-designed furniture. Wright, moreover, certainly would not have said and written so much about furniture and its relation to architecture had it been merely a whim. And it should not be forgotten that he was the spokesman as well as the leader of the Prairie school architects.

Wright was as American as Emerson, Thoreau, and Jefferson. A British correspondent, in fact, called him "the most American American," and Siegfried Giedion thought "he sprang out of the American soil and the American tradition more directly perhaps than any of the other great American architects." Nevertheless he must be counted a part of the international revolt against the excesses of the Victorians and one of those who strove for a unity of the arts. Although Wright was born in the wilds of Wisconsin and Mackintosh in the industrial city of Glasgow, it is hard to miss the similarities between a Mackintosh interior and, say, Wright's dining room for the Robie House.

Both architects were rebels and individualists, but that doesn't explain their curiously similar solutions, which probably should be attributed to the spirit of the age. Wright recalled in *A Testament* of 1957 that when he started his architectural career in Chicago "the pre-Raphaelites had appeared in England but they seemed sentimentalist reformers. Beside the mark. Good William Morris and John Ruskin were much in evidence in Chicago intellectual circles at the time. The Mackintoshes of Scotland; restless European protestants also—Van de Velde of Belgium, Berlage of Holland, Adolph Loos and Otto Wagner of Vienna; all were genuine protestants, but then seen and heard only in Europe. Came Van de Velde with *Art Nouveau*, himself predecessor of the subsequent Bauhaus. Later, in 1910 when I went to Germany by instigation of Professor Kuno Francke, there I found only the rebellious 'Secession' in full swing. I met no architects." Wright was born in 1867 and Mackintosh in 1868. That Wright was associated with the Prairie school and Mackintosh has been classified as an Art Nouveau architect is not particularly important. Prairie school architects considered themselves responsible not only for the design of the house but for all the furniture and furnishings that went into it and so did Art Nouveau architects.

"The 'grammar' of the house," explained Wright in his *Autobiography*, "is its manifest ar-

The dining room with its high-backed chairs in Frank Lloyd Wright's own house in Oak Park, Illinois, of 1895 is his first known experiment in which everything "has a related articulation in relation to the whole and all belongs together because all together are speaking the same language." Dining table and chairs anticipate the dining room furniture in later Prairie houses.

Above: Oak side chair with upholstered seat designed for Wright's Oak Park house, c. 1904.

Opposite page: Wright's armchair of painted steel with an oak seat for the Larkin Administration Building in Buffalo, New York, of 1904 foreshadowed the tubular steel chairs of Mies van der Rohe, Marcel Breuer, etc., by some 20 years.

ticulation of all its parts—the 'speech' it uses. . . . When the chosen grammar is finally adopted (you go almost indefinitely with it into everything you do) walls, ceilings, furniture, etc., become inspired by it. Everything has a related articulation in relation to the whole and all belongs together because all together are speaking the same language." Mackintosh would have understood that.

In Wright's case, it all began in 1895 when he converted the kitchen of his own house in Oak Park, Illinois, into a dining room in which architecture, furniture, lighting, and ornamentation comprised an integrated whole. After that for Wright there was "*no* dichotomy between architecture and ornament, between structure and design, between the whole and its parts," in Henry-Russell Hitchcock's words. And that, he concludes, "differentiates Wright as much from Sullivan as from the later 'international' functionalists."

"I tried to make clients see that furniture and funishings not built in as integral features of the building should be designed as attributes of whatever furniture *was* built in and should be seen as a minor part of the building itself even if detached or kept aside to be employed on occasion," is the way Wright put it in his *Autobiography*. He goes on to say that he realizes "Human beings must group, sit or recline, confound them—and they must dine, but dining is much easier to manage and always was a great artistic opportunity. But arrangements for the informality of sitting in comfort singly or in groups still belonging in disarray to the scheme as a whole: that is a matter difficult to accomplish. But it . . . should be done, because only those attributes of human comfort and convenience, made to belong in this . . . integrated sense to the architecture of the home as a whole, should be there at all, in modern architecture. For that matter almost four-fifths of the contents of nearly every home could be given away with good effect to that home."

That last sentence is not very far from Morris's precept: "Believe me, if we want art to begin at home, as it must, we must clear our houses of troublesome superfluities that are forever in our way; conventional comforts that are no real comforts, and do but make work for servants and doctors: if you want a golden rule that will fit everybody, this is it: *Have nothing in your houses that you do not know to be useful or believe to be beautiful*." Nor is it far from Thoreau's "Why should not our furniture be as simple as the Arab's or the Indian's. . . . At present our houses are cluttered with it, and a good housewife would soon sweep out the greater part into the dust-hole." For his own cabin at Walden he had three chairs, "one for solitude, two for friendship, three for society." Rebels all—rebels

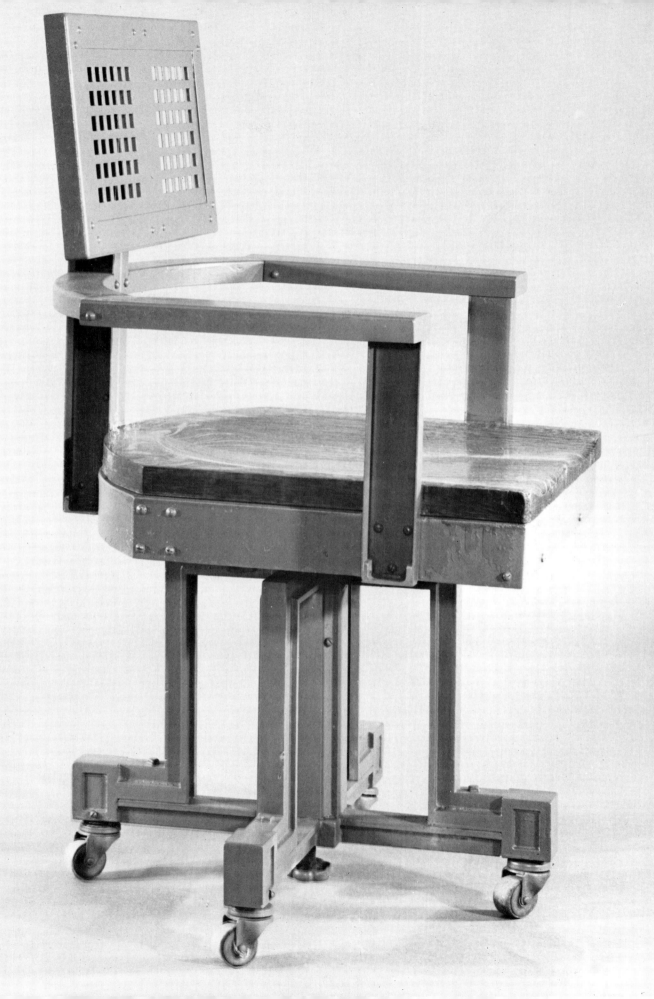

The circular and semicircular forms of this oak armchair for the Darwin D. Martin house in Buffalo, New York, of 1904 represent a departure from the strictly rectangular furniture of these years, but the splats extending from floor to crest are characteristic of the early furniture.

Above: All the furniture in the living room of the Darwin D. Martin house was designed by Wright and made by Matthews Brothers, Manufacturing Company of Milwaukee.

Right: The cantilevered shelves of this small oak table designed by Wright for the Darwin D. Martin house echo the cantilevered roofs of the house.

against the clutter and confusion that marked the interiors of their day. But Wright, unlike Morris, Thoreau, and the craft-oriented architects, recognized the machine as a means of achieving the simplicity he was after. "In the Machine," he said in his Hull House lecture, "lies the only future of art and craft." In the same lecture he forgave Morris for his hatred of it. " That he miscalculated the machine does not matter. He did sublime work for it when he pleaded so well for the process of elimination its abuse had made necessary; when he fought the innate vulgarity of theocratic impulse in art as opposed to democratic; and when he preached the gospel of simplicity . . . " Morris, Wright added, "pleaded well for simplicity as the basis of all true art. Let us understand the significance to art of that word—SIMPLICITY—for it is vital to the Art of the Machine."

Wright wrote and talked about simplicity all his life. When he started to practice in the 1890s, he later recalled, the house was "a bedeviled box with a fussy lid." He changed all that, first, with his Prairie houses and, then, his Usonian houses. They were not only simple, they were designed to be lived in. In his London lecture on "Organic Architecture" in 1939, he remarked that "it was Lao Tze, five hundred years before Jesus, who, so far as I know, first declared that the reality of the building consisted not in the four walls and the roof but inhered in the space within, the space to be lived in. . . . My own recognition of this concept has been instinctive; I did not know of Lao Tze when I began to build with it in mind," but discovered him much later in a little book in which Lao Tze "expressed precisely what had been in my mind and what I had myself been trying to

do with a building: 'The reality of the building does not consist of walls and roof but in the space within to be lived in.' There it was!"

It is difficult to miss the influence of traditional Japanese architecture in Wright's work no matter how much he denied it. He contended he was only influenced by Japanese prints of which he had a splendid collection, but his houses seem to say otherwise with their low hovering roofs and broad overhanging eaves, their open plans and built-in shelves, their appreciation of natural materials. Wright's Prairie houses also reveal something of the Japanese taste for informal, intuitively balanced composition. The Japanese, moreover, have always considered buildings as aspects of the natural scene as Wright did. That the Japanese are the only people in the world never to have developed furniture and Wright spent so much time designing it does not matter. Portable screens, shelves, and low tables—almost the only furniture to be found in a traditional Japanese house—have been interpreted by Wright for the West with built-in furniture wherever possible. In accordance with the Japanese custom of storing chests and tables when not in use behind the sliding doors of closets, Wright, as we have seen, wanted his clients to think of movable furniture as "a minor part of the building itself even if detached or kept aside to be employed on occasion." Siegfried Giedion put it well when he said that although Wright drew from the Far East, it was not "in the manner of the last century, as a substitute for creative impulse, but like Matisse with Negro or Persian art, from an inner sympathetic relationship."

It was, of course, almost essential to use Wright-designed furniture in his Prairie houses as well as in such later houses as Fallingwater,

Above: One of four armchairs made for the Francis W. Little's Peoria house of 1903 is of dark brown stained oak, which is typical of Wright's early Prairie house furniture.

Left: Library table made for the Francis W. Little's Wayzata, Minnesota, house of 1912–1914 no longer has such transitional elements as capitals and feet. Instead it exhibits the wide overhanging horizontals, open spaces, and blond unstained finish that marked Wright's later pieces.

Right: Oak side chair with upholstered seat and back designed by Wright for the Imperial Hotel in Tokyo of 1916–1922.

Below: Interior of Wright's Imperial Hotel in Tokyo of 1916–1922, showing his furniture.

Opposite page: One of the oak dining chairs with upholstered seat which Wright designed for the Hollyhock house in Los Angeles in 1902–1921. The hollyhock motif, a feature of the architecture, is used here in a highly conventionalized form as the back of the chair.

the Taliesins, and Usonians. If the available traditional furniture wasn't out of scale, it certainly looked out of place. Wright's furniture evolved as his houses evolved. "Every chair must eventually be designed for the building it is to be used in," he wrote in *The Natural House*. "Organic architecture calls for this chair which will not look like an apparatus but instead be seen as a gracious feature of its environment which can only be the building itself. . . . When the house-interior absorbs the chair as in perfect harmony, then we will have achieved not so minor a symptom of a culture of our own."

The early Prairie house furniture is highly architectural and seemingly rooted to the floor as the houses are rooted to the earth. For his later Usonian houses (usually designed for families with young children and geared to the increasing informality of living in the late '30s, '40s, and '50s) the furniture is more refined, lighter. There is less sense of occasion about it. The dining room in the 1907 Robie House, for instance, is set up for the almost sacrosanct act of family dining with its tall thronelike enclosing chairs. The Usonian house has no dining room, but a convenient cooking and dining space adjacent to, if not a part of, the living room. Light, low chairs—sometimes a bench—served for the diners. When Wright designed his first Usonian house for the Herbert Jacobses in 1936, he listed among the things that could be eliminated: "Furniture, pictures, and bric-a-brac" which he thought unnecessary "because the walls can be made to include them or *be* them." And among the essentials: "We must have as big a living room with as much vista and garden coming in as we can afford, with a fireplace in it, and open bookshelves, a dining table in the alcove, benches, and living room tables built in; a quiet rug on the floor."

Although Wright was designing 20th-century houses, his ideas about furniture were not unlike those of the Middle Ages when interiors were left as unencumbered as possible and tables, for instance, folded to the wall. His open planning also had its precedent in the Middle Ages when rooms were divided by mobile partitions hinged to the ceiling. Siegfried Giedion has pointed out that while such "lowerable screens" have been lost in Europe, they still exist in Connecticut where "stone houses of the first half of the seventeenth century had plank screens that were raised to the ceiling in summer and let down in winter to concentrate the warmth around the fireplace." The usual Gothic dining table or refectory table also seems to have been a portent of Wright's Usonian dining table. The Gothic table was usually set up for the meal and taken down when the meal was over, while fixed stone or wooden benches skirting the walls served as dining seats. Even the fireplace, so es-

Above: Looking toward the dining room from the living room in the Avery Coonley house in Riverside, Illinois, of 1908, one of Wright's great Prairie houses, just as he completed it.

Opposite page: Living room at Fallingwater, Wright's "house on a waterfall" at Bear Run, Pennsylvania, for Edgar Kaufmann in 1936–1937, showing cushioned stools and built-in upholstered wall bench. Tops of coffee and occasional tables echo the cantilevered forms of Fallingwater itself. The Wright-designed furniture was crafted for Fallingwater by the Gillen Woodworking Company of Milwaukee, successor to the Matthews Brothers firm which made furniture for some of Wright's early Prairie houses.

sential to the medieval house, was an integral part of every Wright house. In the Middle Ages, as Giedion says, they "knew well how the hearth might be woven into domestic life and the fireside given a meaning far beyond its bare usefulness." And so did Wright. He thought of the fireplace as the heart of the house. "It comforted me," he said of his Prairie houses, "to see the fire burning deep in the solid masonry of the house itself." His plans always started from a central chimney as the core of the house, just as they did in the early New England colonies. Wright, in fact, not only captured the spirit of a medieval room in his modern Usonian houses, but he came close to achieving Morris's ideal: "one great room where one talked to one's friends in one corner and ate in another and slept in another and worked in another." Wright designed houses for 20th-century families to live in, and like Morris, he felt the simplicity and openness of a medieval room was far more appropriate than the clutter and fuss of a Victorian parlor.

Wright used various cabinetmakers to execute

his furniture. Ever since the 1820s factories had been turning out furniture and they were a continuing factor in the decline of the traditional cabinetmaker who did everything by hand. By the 1890s when Wright began to design furniture for his houses, most of the large cabinetmaking firms in the Chicago area employed extensive machine equipment and were turning out many of the revival horrors that caused Wright and others to rebel. For his early furniture Wright apparently bypassed the large firms and turned to the small, relatively unknown shop of John W. Ayers. In *The Decorative Designs of Frank Lloyd Wright* David A. Hanks attributes the reason for this to the fact that Ayers respected Wright's unfamiliar ideas and was willing to execute his innovative designs while some of the larger firms were not. Ayers used machinery in his shop but finished pieces by hand. Later Wright used other cabinetmaking firms including the Matthews Bros. Furniture Company in Milwaukee. Matthews's successor, the Gillen Woodwork Corporation, executed the furniture for Fallingwater in 1937. Hanks has

also set the record straight on George Niedecken, who is usually credited with making most of Wright's early furniture. To begin with, Hanks states, Niedecken was not a cabinetmaker. He was an interior decorator and worked for Wright in that capacity—supervising and coordinating "all the details that went into the execution of Wright's interior," including the supervision of the making of the furniture.

The furniture in Usonian houses was fairly standard, according to Gordon Chadwick, the Taliesin apprentice who supervised construction of Wright's Usonian house for Loren Pope in Virginia (now the Pope-Leighey House, a National Trust property). "Mr. Wright," he explained, "would prepare a furniture plan which showed the dining table, modular chairs, bed frames and anything that was built in." Sometimes, he said, "the furniture plan included things which the client didn't require. Mr. Wright put a grand piano in every living room. That was not necessarily what the client wanted." While he modified the design of some of the pianos at Taliesin and refinished the wood, explained Chadwick, "he didn't mind the look of the traditional piano, no matter how unlike the rest of the furniture it was. He just liked pianos and thought of them as part of family life."

Usonian furniture was much simpler than the early Prairie house furniture, and as Hanks says, it sometimes gives the impression of folded paper. In fact it has been referred to as "origami" furniture. Wright designed it so that it could be built by millworkers or even the owners themselves instead of by expensive cabinetmakers. The building of furniture for two Wright houses was graphically described by Herbert Jacobs in answer to questions put to him by the present author in an attempt to discover how Wright's clients liked living with Wright-designed furniture and what discussions, if any, they had with Wright about furniture. Mr. and Mrs. Jacobs built and lived in two Wright-designed houses—the first Usonian house built in 1937 when Jacobs was a young journalist and their later "Solar Hemicycle" house built in the 1940s. The letter Jacobs wrote the author telling about the furniture for those two houses is worth quoting at length:

"As to Usonia No. 1 . . . Wright's floor plan specified the dimensions of the big living room table—4 by 8 ft.—and the dining table—26 inches by 8 ft.—but he did not design them or any other furniture for the house. On one of our early talks with Wright we said my wife's cousins, Harold and Clarence Wescott (Harold had spent a summer at Taliesin, and led us to Wright), would like to do the furniture. Wright approved, on condition that he review their plans. They had power tools, and had already done some 'modern' furniture for their parents. Wright's only suggestion, as I recall, was to 'keep things low.'

"We did send their preliminary sketches to Wright . . . but I believe all he did was to change slightly the vanes or panels attached to the table legs. Our only participation was to wonder whether the 26-inch dining table was wide enough. We took off a closet door, set up a service, and it seemed adequate—as indeed the actual table proved to be. The Wescott boys, who also did the upholstery, delivered everything several months before we could move into the house, which made things a bit congested in our rented flat.

"After we moved in, I made simple frames of one-inch stuff for our twin bedsprings, and a built-in frame for a spring in the back bedroom. I made a low child's bed out of the furnace crate (hemlock hard to saw, by the way) which freed the crib for the second child. The small bed could be taken apart with four screws, stored flat, and was reassembled for later child. I did make a floor lamp out of scrap lumber. . . .

"I also bolted arms and a back on a studio couch spring, trying to conform to the Wescott easy chair design, and it seemed to work, or at least Wright never objected. . . . The big living room table was pleasing to the eye, as was the other Wescott furniture, and served admirably for social occasions like buffet dinners, and equally well for more mundane things like assembly of a cookbook my wife wrote, and the many spreadings out of papers involved in my writing activities.

"For the solar hemicycle [the Jacob's second Wright-designed house] I do not recall any discussions with Wright about furniture. This house was different, in that we actively participated in the work, doing about half ourselves. With the exception of the kitchen cabinets and the five three-legged hexagon tables, made by the carpenter from Wright's design from the ends of mezzanine floor boards, I did all the built-in furniture, as well as partitions. Wright furnished a furniture sheet among the working drawings. Some things we built, some we didn't. First thing I built was a dining table, vaguely patterned after the one at Usonia No. 1, with detachable triangular leg frames, and three boards, or 34½ inches with fascia, wide. Alas, it was fairly attractive and serviceable, so we didn't build the more elaborate hexagonal one that Wright designed until 10 years later, when a son-in-law and I put it together in one day at a cost of about $15.

"We never did the dining chairs that Wright designed. The carpenter said they would involve so many cuts and machine resettings that each would cost over $100. We did not have that kind of money, and I am rather cool to Wright's chair designs anyway. We bought some Kentucky mountaineer chairs for $4 apiece, and they served well. I did build some hassocks of Wright's design, from the ends of partition boards, and one large one, five feet across, for near the fireplace. Did a 14-foot couch or seat at the end of the living room, with cushion of flour bags filled with cornhusks til we could afford a felt pad, and shelves at its ends. A son-in-law and I built a music cabinet fitted to the wall. He had been at Taliesin. Upstairs beds were simple pallets, and I did shelves and cupboards.

"After we finally built the proper dining table, I did the shelves and cupboards fitted to the curve of the wall, matching the table, and they were quite attractive. Also master bedroom shelves and counter in plans by Taliesin. The furniture layout showed about six triangular small tables suitable for buffet. We had one built, cost $30; didn't build any more. I still have it. The only other piece of furniture we retained is a floor lamp with curved standard which I made from the curved rib framing of the stairwell wall. Wright was so pleased with it that he said I should patent the design, but I never did.

Living room of Taliesin West, Wright's winter headquarters in Scottsdale, Arizona, of 1932, showing the large easy chairs, which reflect the angular shapes of the room, and built-in upholstered benches.

'Twas our only furniture discussion.

"The two easy chairs we made ourselves, copying from memory those for the Usonia No. 1 house. I did the frames, my wife did the upholstery. They worked very well—in fact I wrote a daily column and several books in one of them, typewriter on lap, and low hexagon table beside me. . . .

"You asked how I feel about architect-designed furniture. If it's cheap, comfortable, attractive and easy to build—great! I hope that's sufficiently equivocal." And all that written when he was in the process of getting his newest and entirely enchanting book to press—*Building with Frank Lloyd Wright* by Herbert Jacobs with Katherine Jacobs, published in 1978.

Beginning with the somewhat stolid furniture that suited the strong horizontality of the Prairie houses as well as the stability of family life at the turn of the century, Wright continually refined and rethought his furniture designs to suit the changing mores of family life until he achieved the great livability and practicality of the Usonian houses. Nevertheless, like Jacobs, he was never apparently completely satisfied with his chair designs. "My early approach to the chair was something between contempt and desperation," he says in *The Natural House*. And later he continues: "We now build well-upholstered benches and seats in our houses, trying to make them all part of the building. But still you must bring in and pull up the casual chair. There are many kinds of 'pull-up' chairs to perch upon—lightly. They're easier. They're light. But the big chair wherein you may fold up and go to sleep reading a newspaper . . . is still difficult. I have done the best I could with this 'living room chair' but, of course, you have to call for somebody to help you move it. All my life my legs have been banged up somewhere by the chairs I have designed. But we are accomplishing it now. Someday it will be well done." But, he added, "it will not have metal spiderlegs nor look the way most of the steel furniture these days looks to me."

That the furniture Wright designed for at least one Usonian—the Pope-Leighey House—has proved both livable and practical was eloquently conveyed to the author by Mrs. Marjorie F. Leighey who has lived with it for more than 30 years. She and her husband, Robert A. Leighey, purchased Loren Pope's little Usonian house in 1946. Mr. Leighey died in 1963, but Mrs. Leighey has continued to live there with the exception of a period between 1964 and July 1, 1969, when it was moved from its original site in Falls Church, Virginia, to the grounds of Woodlawn Plantation, Mount Vernon, Virginia, after being threatened with destruction by Interstate Highway 66. To save the house Mrs. Leighey gave it to the National Trust for His-

toric Preservation. The Trust moved it to its present site and she still lives in it. When asked how the Wright-designed furniture worked for her, functionally as well as esthetically, Mrs. Leighey told the author that the tables and chairs in the living-dining room "allow an almost unimaginable flexibility in the use of the space. It looks right, as though it was meant to be, whether arranged for a class, a large dinner, small lunch, or whatever. That it could lend itself to such a variety of positioning, without the room's losing attractiveness comes about, I think, because of the perfection of scale, furniture to ceiling height and wall spaces." As for the esthetics, she said: "To me, to my husband, to many, many others, there is great serenity along with the beauty here. I have given much thought to this, and can only conclude it arises from the perfect harmony and unity between furniture and house." She then quoted, "somewhat reluctantly," she said, "but to show others respond to this—it is not merely in my imagination—from a note a college professor sent after bringing his graduate students here: 'One of the most beautiful moments of my· life occurred . . . when my students and I sat at your feet, and—quite wondrously, a Peace came to us, in your beautiful house, your beautiful presence. May I give you back, in this moment a little of the love you gave us. . . .' " And Mrs. Leighey adds, "Now, that is F.L.W's work as well as mine, and how in the world can you ever get it in a book so that those who have not experienced it will understand?"

Frank Lloyd Wright would have liked that.

Above: Mahogany desk lamp built by a former guide at the Pope-Leighey house from a Wright design, c. 1905.

Opposite page: Dining area in the main room of the Usonian Pope-Leighey house of 1940–1941, now in Mount Vernon, Virginia. As Wright said of his Usonian houses, "a single spacious, harmonious unit of living room, dining room and kitchen. . . ."

GEORGE WASHINGTON MAHER 1864–1926

*. . . we must turn again to Nature,
and hearkening to her melodious voice,
learn as children learn the accent
of its rhythmic cadences.* LOUIS SULLIVAN

George Washington Maher was one of the early rebels in America's midwest who helped found the Prairie school. In fact he along with Wright and a few others might be called the Prairie pioneers who in the 1890s decided to attack the status quo and create a new American architecture of which furniture would be an important part. H. Allen Brooks has shown that it was in the midwest more than any other region of the country that "the *fin de siecle* represented the age of progressive spirits." He points to Hamlin Garland, Theodore Dreiser, Frank Norris, John Dewey, Jane Addams, among others, who, disillusioned with things as they were, decided to blaze new trails. In architecture, of course, it was a matter of getting away from the borrowings from other countries and other cultures that had brought about the rich eclecticism of the Victorians. Although Louis Sullivan's pleas for an architecture of democracy might be called the starting gun for the formation of the Prairie school, it was actually part of a worldwide revolt that was manifested in Art Nouveau, the Secessionist movement in Vienna, the Arts and Crafts movement, and so on. Maher, incidentally, seems to have been the first Prairie architect to be recognized in a European publication when, in 1899, *Dekorative Kunst* illustrated one of his houses.

Maher was born in 1864 in Mill Creek, West Virginia, where his father had been a recruiting officer during the Civil War. The family moved to New Albany in Indiana and then to Chicago where Maher at the age of 13 began his study of architecture as an apprentice in the firm of Joseph Lyman Silsbee where Wright and Elmslie were fellow draftsmen—a situation hardly less striking than the later coincidence that brought Mies van der Rohe, Le Corbusier, and Walter Gropius together in the Berlin studio of Peter Behrens. Silsbee, in fact, seems to have been as important a catalyst for the Prairie school as Behrens was for the Bauhaus.

In 1888 Maher left Silsbee's office to open his own practice in Chicago at the age of 23. The year before he had outlined his theories of an American architecture in a talk before the Chicago Architectural Sketch Club, in which he held that "Originality in American architecture rests . . . upon . . . studying the necessities of labor and life, and meeting them . . . there is as much chance of a national style forthcoming in this country as elsewhere in the world. . . . In most of our large cities a class of buildings can be seen which have no equal for interior arrangement . . . for nowhere are the wants of comfort and practicability so sought after as here. . . ." In the same talk he stated that a house should have massiveness and solidity in order to express substantiality. While most of his houses were massive and solid, his esthetic contribution to an American architecture seems to have been more in his theories than in his architecture. Maher was not, however, without followers and public acclaim.

For many of his residential commissions he designed furniture which carefully followed the pattern and decoration of what he called his "motif rhythm theory." The latter was a method he devised for achieving visual unity throughout his interiors. The "fundamental principle," he explained, was "to receive the dominant inspira-

Railing of the stairway in the Ernest J. Magerstadt house in Chicago of 1908 is related to the design of the side chairs in the dining room (shown on page 110).

tion from the patron, taking into strict account his needs, his temperament, and environment, influenced by local color and atmosphere in surrounding flora and nature. With these vital impressions at hand, the design naturally crystallizes and motifs appear which being consistently utilized will make each object, whether it be of construction, furniture or decoration, related." The motif, it seems, might be a lion as it was in the John Farson house in Oak Park (1897), a thistle as it was for the James A. Patten house in Evanston (1901), a hollyhock as it was for the Harry Rubens house in Glencoe (1902–1903), or a poppy as it was for the Ernest J. Magerstadt house in Chicago (1908). But Maher's theory was "inherently a decorative concept," as H. Allen Brooks has pointed out, "and only superficially applicable to architectural design." It was, however, applicable to furniture. And as a result the furniture Maher designed for his early houses was often more elaborate than most Prairie school furniture. Nevertheless it fell within the Prairie school philosophy which emphasized simple geometric shapes and honesty of expression. And in his later Magerstadt house the furniture became severely geometric and much simpler, probably as a result of Wright's influence.

Although for us Maher's houses may lack the esthetic appeal of some of the Prairie houses, they received international attention. The Patten house was illustrated in a 1903 issue of the influential British *Studio*, which proclaimed it "a gratifying example of art from the philosophical standpoint" and Maher's theory "at once novel and enduring." The American *Architectural Record*'s astute critic Arthur C. David, however, was not so flattering. In the April 1904 issue he referred to Maher as "assuredly the 'new architect' in his most garrulous and candid moment. He has not been afraid to design houses, which would impress any eye, not merely as extraordinary, but perhaps as grotesque. . . ." Inside the Patten house, he says, "one begins to realize the full proportions of Mr. Maher's enterprise," and he goes on to explain that the thistle motif "is varied ingeniously to cover large areas of wall, to surmount mantelpieces and side-boards, to figure curtains, and to supply decorative borders to wall surfaces tinted in solid colors." But while Davis found some of these designs "in themselves very beautiful, and one cannot help attributing to the architect, who is capable of handling such a motive with so much variety, so much originality and in a sense with so much propriety, very unusual powers of design," he

could not "say as much that is favorable of the hectic angel, into which the stem of the thistle flowers in specified places. To my sense," he tells his readers, "she is merely ornamental impertinence, which would become intolerable as steady company, and which is an example of the worst solecism which the architecture of ideas can commit." He speaks of the woodwork in the hall and dining room as "much more appropriate to a bar-room or a hotel than a private house," adding that "Mr. Maher, indeed, has throughout kept his structural members extremely massive, while his ornamental 'elements' have been made almost aerial in their lightness. Even the furniture is chunky and heavy—too much so for the taste of most people, but none the less very cleverly designed from the architect's point of view." Obviously it is all too much for Davis. "Just think," he exclaims, "of living in such a thorny environment! Think of being constantly entangled in such a system of 'rational aestheticism!'"

Maher was undoubtedly a dedicated architect who seriously tried to develop a new American architecture, but one suspects he needed a system in order to create a harmony which Wright, for instance, accomplished with the aid of his inherent taste and his infallible eye. "A true architect, like a true poet," as Maher himself said, "is born, not manufactured."

Above: Dining chair designed by Maher for the John Farson house in Oak Park, Illinois, of 1897 shows a European influence. The lion's head motif ornamenting the chair (see detail at right) was used throughout the house in keeping with Maher's motif-rhythm theory, his method of achieving visual unity.

Opposite page: Built-in buffet and chairs designed by Maher for the Ernest J. Magerstadt house. The severely geometric oak side chairs, probably influenced by Wright, are a departure from the elaborate style of his earlier furniture.

GEORGE GRANT ELMSLIE 1871-1952

*Without the Prairie school furniture
there could have been no Prairie house as we
know it, in terms of the interior space and
the completed design concept.* DONALD KALEC

"There in the Adler and Sullivan offices high in the Chicago Auditorium Tower I worked for nearly seven years—George Elmslie alongside—occasionally looking out through the romantic Richardsonian Romanesque arches over Lake Michigan, . . ." writes Frank Lloyd Wright in *A Testament*. Elmslie, in fact, had worked with Wright even before the Adler and Sullivan days. He was born in Scotland in 1871, emigrated to Chicago in the 1880s, and entered the office of Joseph Lyman Silsbee, first as an errand boy, then as apprentice in 1885, where both Wright and Maher were members of the staff. In 1890 he joined the staff of Adler and Sullivan.

Although much has been said and written about Sullivan's influence on Wright and Elmslie, Silsbee's was also important. In some ways Silsbee's ideas were closer to those of the Prairie school architects than Sullivan's. The latter had little interest in residential design while Silsbee helped introduce the Richardson Shingle Style house to the Midwest where it had an important influence on the Prairie architects. He also designed furniture for some of his own buildings.

Elmslie remained in Sullivan's office for almost 20 years to become a designer only second to Sullivan himself. He was, in Hugh Morrison's words, both Sullivan's "most faithful friend" and "one of his most talented disciples." In fact it seems likely that much of the later work in Sullivan's office was more Elmslie than Sullivan. In 1909 he left Sullivan to join George Feick and William Gray Purcell in partnership. After 1913 the firm became Purcell and Elmslie, and in 1917 Purcell took a position for two years in Philadelphia, then moved to Oregon. Purcell and

Elmslie, however, continued to collaborate on commissions until 1922 when the partnership was dissolved.

Because an extremely close design relationship existed between Purcell and Elmslie for some 15 years—although only seven of those years were spent directly together in partnership—it is often difficult, if not impossible, to definitely attribute the design of any particular job to either partner. This is also true of furniture, except in a few specific instances where there is clear evidence that Elmslie was the designer. Alan K. Lathrop, curator of the Northwest Architectural Archives at the University of Minnesota where the Purcell and Elmslie papers are housed, pointed out to the author that even before Elmslie joined the firm in 1910 he often aided Purcell with advice on some of his projects, and it is entirely possible he helped him with furniture designs before 1910 and after 1917. It is also quite possible, said Lathrop, that Elmslie designed more furniture than is evident on the surface during the years in between. That certainly would seem to be the case. Elmslie's extraordinary modesty has undoubtedly kept him from getting the credit he deserves as perhaps one of the most important Prairie school architects who designed furniture. It is highly probable that during his last years with Sullivan, Elmslie should be credited with most of the design, ornamentation, and furniture for such buildings as the Babson house in Riverside, Illinois (1907), the bank at Owatonna, Minnesota (1907–1908), and the Bradley house at Madison, Wisconsin (1909). It is almost certain that Elmslie was responsible for the design of much of the Bradley house furnishings including the ornamental glass win-

Left: Tall mahogany clock with brass inlay was designed in 1912 by Elmslie for the Henry B. Babson house in Riverside, Illinois. The house was originally designed in 1907 by Louis Sullivan when Elmslie worked for him. In 1912 Elmslie and his firm made additions to the house including eight pieces of furniture, of which this was one.

Below: Stencil design by Elmslie, c. 1915, may have been for a piece of furniture in the Beebe house in St. Paul, Minnesota.

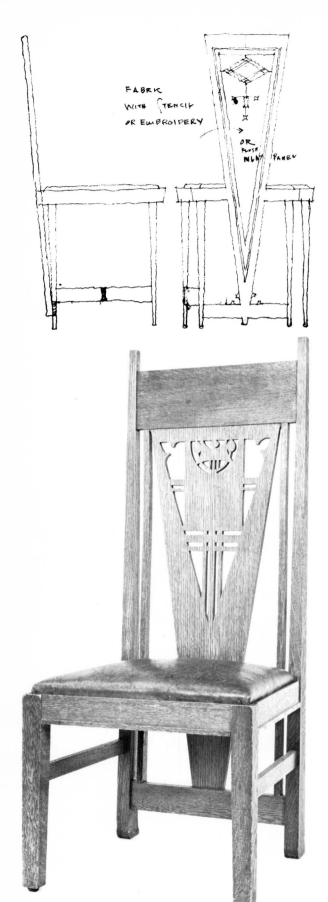

On the drawing:

FABRIC
WITH STENCIL
OR EMBROIDERY

OR
FLUSH
INLAY PANEL

dows, lamps, tables, and chairs; and it is known that a good share of the furniture and accessories in the Babson house came from his hand. Moreover, the original Babson house furniture was augmented in 1912 when Elmslie and his firm made additions to the house, which included eight pieces of furniture undoubtedly of Elmslie's design. In fact without Elmslie's furnishings, as David Gebhard put it, "the house appears bare and uninteresting." In view of the Prairie school custom of sometimes using Mission furniture in secondary rooms, it is interesting to note that a bed designed by Elmslie for the Babson house was mated with chairs and tables from Stickley's workshop.

The anonymity of the designers during the Purcell and Elmslie partnership was apparently intentional. Both men were involved with every phase of the total design of their buildings. They believed, as Gebhard has pointed out, "that the task of building was not that of a lone genius, but the coordinated effort of a number of men," and that is the way they worked. But even if Elmslie didn't design all the furniture that came out of the Purcell and Elmslie office, it is clear that he took a great deal of interest in its design. In the Purcell and Elmslie papers, for example, there is an office memo in Elmslie's handwriting dated April 6, 1913, about some chairs for the Merchants National Bank in Winona of 1912–1913 which says in part: "The Winona chairs are the toughest kind of a problem to get comfort and appearance with the present basis. I have been trying all kinds of variants from your sketches and really feel that a cushion panel back rest is the best of them all, only I would make it as wide as we possibly can. I feel that a narrow effect is sort of apologetic while if we make it wide it will appear more natural and not disengage the corners of the back so much. . . ." In another notation, he writes: "You *have* to do a little thinking on the chairs—they are *not* comfortable and must be made so. 4″–5″ will do it but how without narrowing the seat."

Like most of the Prairie school architects, however, Purcell and Elmslie's work was predominantly residential, the major part of it in Minneapolis and some in the smaller towns of Minnesota and Wisconsin. Also like most of the Prairie architects, Purcell and Elmslie involved themselves in the total design of their buildings from furniture and fabrics to landscape. Unlike most of the Prairie architects, however, they

Top: This Elmslie drawing marked "idea for chair" specifies for its back: "Fabric with stencil or embroidery or flush inlay panel."

Left: Oak side chair with leather upholstery, c. 1909, designed by Elmslie for the Charles A. Purcell house in River Forest, Illinois, is similar in style to a number of Elmslie-designed chairs with cutout geometric designs in their splat.

placed importance on ornament, which seems to show the influence of Sullivan. But, as Gebhard reminds us, "Elmslie had produced so much of the ornament which emanated from the Sullivan office, his post-1909 designs may be thought of as Sullivanesque only in the sense that he continued to adhere to Sullivan's belief in the inherent logic and significant place which ornament occupies within the total design of a building."

There is no doubt that Elmslie was a highly gifted ornamentalist and the individuality and appeal of much of the Purcell and Elmslie furniture is based on ornament. In fact ornament is one of the essential elements contributing to the overall harmony of their interiors. The richly ornamental cutout designs in the splats of some of the chairs carry motifs that often appear in the rugs, leaded glass, andirons, even table covers. Explained Elmslie: "These motifs are designed as an organic part of a structure, an efflorescence of the idea represented in the building itself. . . . The ornaments themselves represent the expansion of a single germinal idea and may be severe, restrained, simple or as elaborately evolved as desired for place and circumstance. After the motif is established the development of it is an orderly procession from start to finish, it is all intensely organic, proceeding from main motif to minor motifs, interrelating and to the last terminal, all of a piece. . . ."

Rhythm was a characteristic in design valued by many Prairie architects. Maher, as we have seen, had his "motif rhythm theory." Elmslie called rhythm "the underlying influence that induces the vital and spiritual essence of organic design to disclose itself. . . ." Some of Elmslie's motifs are reminiscent of the motifs Mackintosh used on cupboards and other pieces, and like some of Mackintosh's furniture, Elmslie's is more lyrical than most Prairie furniture.

We may not know exactly what Elmslie designed, but we have Purcell's assessment of his partner as he expressed it in a letter to Gebhard dated November 1955, in which he says Elmslie "was a man of quick imagination; his mind in architecture was highly articulate, succinct and competent. He was not a long distance talker, but he was by no means a silent person. He was a satisfactory companion in general conversation, very well read in literature. He kept his mind open to current thought and salted his good talk with Scottish humor and repartee." He also seems to have been an extraordinarily satisfying and cooperative partner who cared nothing about receiving credit for what were surely his designs.

The Prairie school, which was completely dead as a coherent school by the end of World War I, was short-lived as far as such movements go. Many have tried to explain its early demise. It has been blamed on the arrogance of architects who insisted on taking everything into their own hands from furniture to landscaping. But as Carl W. Condit says in *The Chicago School of Architecture*, "the sudden death and virtual oblivion of the midwestern architectural movement, which was so prolific up to 1915, continues to be one of the unexplained phenomena of American cultural history. The Chicago literary renaissance of the same period moved to New York and on to greater heights, but there was no place in the United States that was hospitable to original architecture." Only Frank Lloyd Wright managed to weather the years of discontent with a native American architecture.

Drawings by Elmslie for a chair for the Henry Babson house, marked in lower left: "chair for den living room nook."

FOUR CALIFORNIA ARCHITECTS

THE GREENE BROTHERS
BERNARD MAYBECK
R. M. SCHINDLER

The dreams and doings of Californians often astonish, infuriate, and sometimes enrich the rest of the country. The region seems to produce natural rebels who shy away from American traditions whether they be religious, architectural, political, or economical. The results, however, may well be more American than the old traditions which, after all, came from Europe. This had often been the case with California architecture whose uniqueness can partly be attributed to what David Gebhard and Harriette Von Breton have called the "conscious and unconscious give and take" between the vernacular of the builder and the designed forms of the architect. Certainly the work of Charles and Henry Greene took much of its inspiration from the shingle tradition of earlier California structures as did that of Bernard Maybeck, while the patio-oriented Spanish dwellings of Southern California strongly influenced the work of such architects as Irving Gill, Rudolph Schindler, and Richard Neutra.

Of course there are two Californias—the California of San Francisco and the California of Los Angeles—which sometimes seem poles apart particularly to each other. There is what Reyner Banham has called "the permissive free-swinging cultural style of Los Angeles," and while the San Franciscans may like to think of their cultural style as a little less volatile, it is nevertheless permissive. Altogether, however, from its northern border to Mexico, it seems to breed a truly indigenous domestic architecture as naturally as it breeds cults and sects.

But what about the furniture? The Californians discussed here, like the Prairie school architects, designed furniture to be compatible with interiors that were as remote from the claustrophobic Victorian parlor as they could be. Like the Prairie architects, too, they made their interiors at one with the architecture, and they made the architecture harmonize with its landscape. Also like the Prairie architects they spoke the language of the Arts and Crafts tradition, but that didn't mean mechanization should be banned. It meant honesty of construction, simplicity, and respect for materials. And also in line with the Prairie architects, the Californians insisted on maintaining human scale whether in their furniture, their houses, their banks, or their office buildings.

While these Californians believed in a "totally designed" environment that included furniture and fixtures as did the Prairie architects, the Art Nouveau architects, the architects of the Vienna Secessionists, and everyone else who designed furniture for their buildings, they were generally not so successful in attracting clients who went along with them. The Greene brothers, of course, were a notable exception as was Schindler who treated the furniture as a *fait accompli* by making it "impossible to tell where the house ends and the furniture begins." One can surmise, however, that Maybeck, Gill, and Neutra might have liked to complete many more interiors with furniture of their own design than they were given a chance to.

THE GREENE BROTHERS
CHARLES S. 1868–1957; HENRY M. 1870–1954

*If I were asked for some simple test
by which we might hope to know a work
of art when we saw one I should suggest
something like this: Every work of art
shows that it was made by a human being
for a human being.* W. R. LETHABY

To Charles and Henry Greene the furniture was as important as the architecture. In fact the quality of their most important houses is aptly described by William Jordy as "that of fine cabinetmaking given architectural scale and meaning."

The Greenes were building their California houses during the same years that Wright was building his Prairie houses and they have many affinities. If the Greenes designed vernacular houses which suited their California environment and Wright designed sophisticated houses which he not only suited to the prairie but to any environment he chose to work in, nevertheless they were impelled by the same things and most of those things go straight back to Morris: simplicity and honesty of material, houses that blend with their landscape, plans that are as asymmetrical and romantic as Morris's own Gothic manor house at Kelmscott.

Boston architect Ralph Adams Cram, who was a contemporary of Wright and the Greenes, wrote of the work of the latter in his *American Country Houses of Today* published in 1913: "One must see the real and revolutionary thing in its native haunts of Berkeley and Pasadena to appreciate it in all its varied charm and its striking beauty. Where it comes from heaven alone knows, but we are glad it arrived, for it gives a new zest to life, a new object for admiration. There are things in it Japanese; things that are Scandinavian; things that hint of Sikkim, Bhutan, and the fastness of Tibet, and yet it all hangs together, it is beautiful, it is contemporary, and for some reason or other it seems to fit California. Structurally it is a blessing; only too often the exigencies of our assumed precedents lead us into the wide and easy road of structural du-

plicity, but in this sort of thing there is only an honesty that is sometimes almost brazen. It is a wooden style built woodenly, and it has the force and the integrity of Japanese architecture. Added to this is the elusive element of charm that comes only from the personality of the creator, and charm in a degree hardly matched in other modern work."

Nor was Cram the only architect outside California to call the Greenes' houses beautiful. C. R. Ashbee, one of the leading architects of England's Arts and Crafts movement and founder of the Guild of Handicraft in 1888, visited Pasadena in 1909 and found the work of the Greenes "among the best there is in the country." Like Wright, he says of Charles Greene, "the spell of Japan is on him, he feels the beauty and makes magic out of the horizontal line, but there is in his work more tenderness, more subtlety, more self effacement than in Wright's work. It is more refined and has more repose. Perhaps it loses in strength, perhaps it's California that speaks rather than Illinois. Any way as work it is, so far as the interiors go, more sympathetic to me." Apparently Ashbee didn't meet Henry for he goes on to tell of visiting Charles's workshop "where they were making without exception the best and most characteristic furniture I have seen in this country. There were beautiful cabinets and chairs of walnut and lignum-vitae, exquisite dowelling and pegging, and in all a supreme feeling for material, quite

No house in the United States displays craftsmanship in wood superior to the best of the Greene brothers, of which the David B. Gamble house of 1908 in Pasadena, California, ranks high. This view of the dining room shows Greene-designed furniture and built-in cabinets all detailed as part of the overall design of the house.

Above: One of several chairs inlaid with fine woods and silver designed by Charles Greene for the Charles M. Pratt house in Ojai, California, in 1909.

Opposite page, top: Sideboard for Charles Greene's own house in Pasadena.

Opposite page, bottom: Partial view of the fireplace alcove with built-in seating in the Gamble house living room.

up to the best of our English craftsmanship, Spooner, the Barnslys, Lutyens, Lethaby. I have not felt so at home in any workshop on this side of the Atlantic—(but we have forgotten the Atlantic, here is the Pacific). Here things were really alive—and the 'Arts and Crafts' that all the others were screaming and hustling about, are here actually being produced by a young architect, this quiet, dreamy, nervous, tenacious little man, fighting single-handed until recently against tremendous odds." The day ended, Ashby tells us, having tea at Charles Greene's house. "We looked out on the mountains and discussed single tax, in the intervals of tea and fingering the surfaces of Greene's scholarly panelling."

The Greene brothers were born 15 months apart in a small town outside Cincinnati. The family eventually moved to St. Louis where the boys enrolled in Washington University's Manual Training High School. This course, unique in America at the time, required each student to study woodworking and metalwork with emphasis on understanding the inherent nature of wood and metal as well as the use of tools and machinery, along with a regular liberal arts curricula. In 1888 they entered the School of Architecture at the Massachusetts Institute of Technology, and after graduating Henry worked briefly in the office of Shepley, Rutan, and Coolidge, which had taken over Henry Hobson Richardson's practice at his death in 1886, and Charles worked in another Boston architectural firm. In 1893 Charles and Henry went to Pasadena ostensibly to visit their parents, but they were so captivated by the California scene that they stayed on to set up practice there. It is interesting to note that on their way to Pasadena they stopped to see the World's Columbian Exposition in Chicago, where they were impressed by the Japanese Pavilion, which also must have impressed Wright although he never admitted it.

Furniture was always close to the heart of both Greene brothers, but this was especially true of Charles. The first piece of furniture he is known to have designed was a simple square table with a geometric inlay on top which he presented to his English bride-to-be in 1901. That spring Charles and his wife spent their honeymoon in England when the Arts and Crafts movement was at its height. Soon after they returned home the first issue of Gustav Stickley's *The Craftsman* appeared with most of its pages devoted to William Morris and his philosophy. The Greenes were regular subscribers to *The Craftsman* and Randell Makinson believes Harvey Ellis's illustrations stimulated their own involvement with interior design and furnishings.

Left: Shoe bench designed by the Greenes for the entry hall of the Robert R. Blacker house in Pasadena of 1907.

Below, left: This Greene and Greene version of the Morris chair is made of teak. It was designed for the Robert R. Blacker house.

Bottom: Detail of the Greene-designed Morris chair shows the hardware for its adjustable back.

Below, right: Living room chair designed by the Greenes for the Robert R. Blacker house.

It took the Greene brothers about ten years to develop the individual style that impressed itself on California architecture for some time to come. Their stint at the Manual Training High School, their fascination with Japanese architecture, Charles's brush with England's Arts and Crafts movement during his honeymoon, and the indigenous architecture of California—all came together to produce the style which culminated in six or seven houses built from 1907 to 1909 that have been called "among the finest examples of the Arts and Crafts movement in America." The beautifully finished furniture and paneling that Ashbee found so sympathetic was by no means a minor part of the total effect of the Greenes' important houses. As Henry commented about one of them: "The whole construction was carefully thought out, and there was a reason for every detail. The idea was to eliminate everything unnecessary to make the whole as direct and simple as possible, but always with the beautiful in mind as the final goal." And Charles once compared a work of art with a piece of tapestry stating that "the same thread runs through the web, but goes to make up different figures. The idea is deeply theosophic, one life, many manifestations; hence, inevitably, echoes, resemblances—consonance." Thus, while an elegant piece of Greene furniture may be a masterpiece in itself, it is part of the larger masterpiece.

To admire the Greenes' furniture, moreover, is to realize that there was far more to it than design. It had to be crafted by someone who cared. Nor is it surprising that the Greenes had difficulty finding craftsmen who would or could produce the kind of work they demanded until they met Peter Hall and his brother John, self-taught craftsmen from Sweden. The Halls worked with the Greenes on their furniture for many years, and Charles was in the habit of spending several hours every day directing and working with the craftsmen.

The best preserved of the Greenes' houses is the one they designed for the David B. Gambles in 1908–1909. Little has been changed of the original structure, and almost all of the furniture, lighting fixtures, rugs, silverware, picture frames, linens, stained glass, and hardware that the Greenes designed for it remain in place. In 1966 the Gamble family presented the house, together with its interior furnishings, to the City of Pasadena and the University of Southern California, and it is now operated as a house museum. The Gamble house is indeed "a miracle," as Robert W. Winter says, for the Greenes lavished their talent on it "and even participated as artisans in various stages of the construction."

If in the final analysis the interiors of Wright's houses and Mackintosh's houses strike us as less conventional, more modern, it is perhaps because the Greenes were true craftsmen. They finished their furniture themselves. Wright and Mackintosh were craftsmen, but they were also artists who cared more for the overall effect than the comfort or finish of a particular chair. To Wright a chair was first of all an architectural problem. To the Greenes it was first of all a place for someone to sit, albeit a part of the overall architectural scheme. The Greenes' furniture, as Esther McCoy put it, "belonged to the floor, not to the wall." Wright and Mackintosh interiors have the boldness of art, while Greene interiors are probably more livable. "Soon," Wright wrote in his *Autobiography*, "I found it difficult, anyway, to make some of the furniture in the 'abstract.' That is, to design it as architecture and make it human' at the same time—fit for human use."

Noting the similarities between the dining rooms in the Gamble and Robie houses, William Jody rightly points out that the Greenes' room looks back to the handicraft past, Wright's to the future. If the chairs in the Gamble dining room are reminiscent of the earlier chair designs, those in the Robie dining room "possess an architectonic abstractness which completes the geometry of the room." Altogether the Greenes' interiors are self-effacing, as Ashbee said, while Wright's are sometimes more arrogant. It is quite likely, moreover, that Morris would have preferred the Greenes' California houses to Wright's Prairie houses. For he, too, looked back to the handicraft past.

The Greenes, like the Prairie architects, were forgotten after World War I. The ideals of Morris and the Greenes were no longer fashionable. Humanity, it would seem, lost out to machinery. Not until 1952 did the American Institute of Architects come to realize the true significance of the Greenes as "formulators of a new and native architecture."

BERNARD MAYBECK 1862-1957

Maybeck, for all his learning, was one of the great innocents, in every age always free. VINCENT SCULLY

Contrary to one's expectations of California's individualist architects, Bernard Maybeck, the most individualist of them all, studied at the École des Beaux-Arts in Paris, that stronghold of architectural tradition. But Maybeck fits the California mystique on other counts. He went in for health fads, and while several of the rebel architects we have been considering liked to design clothes for their wives, Maybeck may be the only one who designed his own clothes. Moreover he created an architecture that was decidedly idiosyncratic. There is a fairy-tale quality about some of Maybeck's work that recalls the work of that other great romantic individualist, Antoni Gaudi. Both were mystics and their buildings often represented a search for spiritual meanings.

Maybeck came by his interest in furniture naturally. His father was a woodcarver by trade who had emigrated from Germany in 1848, and his mother, like Wright's mother, decided her son should be an artist. Therefore when he didn't do well in school (which is not surprising for a nonconformist), he was apprenticed at the age of 17 to a woodcarver. This didn't last long because, as he himself explained, "I knew what I was doing but he didn't." He then went to work for his father at Pottier and Stymus in New York, a prestigious firm that made fine furniture and was responsible for furnishings for the Pullman Company's parlor cars. Here again Maybeck got bored and started to design a reversible Pullman seat on his own. He later sold his idea, which eventually gained widespread use in trains and streetcars. His obvious interest in designing decided his father to send him to Paris to study in the studio of Mr. Pottier's brother—a studio that happened to be across the street

from the École des Beaux-Arts. It was Maybeck's view of the comings and goings of student architects and particularly "a wonderful individual who was wearing a pot hat and kid gloves" that suggested to him his own next step, and he enrolled at the École. Although modern architects from Louis Sullivan on have rebelled against the methods of the École, Maybeck did not. As William H. Jordy put it, Maybeck accepted both worlds—"the elite world of the academician and the humble world of the craftsman, the realm of splendor and that of nature, a sentimental viewpoint toward building and one of common sense."

In 1886 after completing the course at the École, Maybeck returned home. He worked for a while with the New York Beaux-Arts firm of Carrère and Hastings (Hastings had been a roommate in Paris) superintending work on their Ponce de Leon Hotel in St. Augustine, Florida, among other things. It was doubtless Maybeck who was responsible for much of the hotel's fantasy for, as Wayne Andrews put it, "the firm was never again to design anything as rash as this hotel." H. Allen Brooks has added an interesting postscript to this. While searching the autobiography of the English furniture designer Walter Crane who spent nine months touring the United States in 1890–1891 for references to Chicago architecture, Brooks found that throughout the English designer's entire "coast-to-coast, and Maine-to-Florida tour," he only singled out one building for particular attention: the Ponce de Leon Hotel in St. Augustine.

Maybeck designed the deal table and chairs as well as the chandeliers in the refectory at Wyntoon of 1902–1903, the Hearst country house on the McCloud River in California, in association with Frederick H. Meyer.

The main room of the Bohemian Club's Grove Clubhouse of 1903 on California's Russian River shows the long table and three-legged chairs patterned after Flemish milking stools which Maybeck designed for it.

After his short stint with Carrère and Hastings, Maybeck wandered westward to San Francisco via Kansas City where he found his bride-to-be. In San Francisco he worked for a while as a furniture designer at the Charles M. Plum Company and then for the architectural firm of A. Page Brown. While with Brown, he did some work on the Crocker Building which included entwining his wife's initials in a design around the cornice. One is reminded of the Elizabethan Bess of Hardwick, another nonconformist builder, who surmounted the towers of Hardwick Hall with her own initials, except that Maybeck's grand architectural gesture was for love of another while Bess's was less altruistic. For a brief period before starting his own practice in San Francisco Maybeck worked in the office of Ernest Coxhead, the English architect who had brought to California some of the idealism of William Morris and who, like Maybeck, was enchanted with California's indigenous shingled houses. But nothing really influenced Maybeck. He was after beauty and it didn't matter how he achieved it.

In 1894 he accepted a teaching post in the drawing department at the University of California and was soon teaching a class in architecture at his own house, which marked the beginning of the University's College of Architecture. The Phoebe Apperson Hearst international competition for a master plan for the University's Berkeley campus was Maybeck's idea, and it was Maybeck who went to Europe in 1897 to distribute information about the competition. While in England he visited the architect Norman Shaw. He also went to Glasgow but apparently did not meet Mackintosh. In Austria he saw some of the work of the Vienna Seccession which had been founded that year, but he was not particularly impressed. He missed any reference to tradition.

In his own furniture designs as in his architecture Maybeck borrowed freely and with confidence. "No one," as Esther McCoy said of his Christian Science Church in Berkeley, "ever carried the burden of the past more weightlessly." She quotes Maybeck as saying, "When you think of things of the past they come alive again," and that was certainly true for him. "All ages were the present, and when he became a practicing architect he went to the past to be refreshed, as he dipped into the industrial world of the twentieth century, bringing together disparate elements in a timeless world of his own dramatic creation." The castle, Wyntoon, which he designed and built for Mrs. Hearst in 1902, was certainly one of those dramatic creations. In the first place, as Esther McCoy has suggested, it was hazardous for one who looked upon architecture itself as a major art to design space for Mrs. Hearst's art objects. By all accounts, however, Maybeck's castle (later destroyed by fire) must have overshadowed any art objects. The high stone-walled living room with its free-standing fireplace silhouetted against an arch filled with stained glass was not only pure Maybeckian Gothic but pure Maybeckian fantasy. Maybeck, as seems only plausible, also designed furniture for Wyntoon.

Just as Maybeck roamed freely between tradition and modern technology so did he roam freely between the ideas of the Arts and Crafts movement and those of an industrial age. Nevertheless he was a trained architect, and as Kenneth Cardwell points out in *Bernard Maybeck, Artisan, Architect, Artist*, while he appreciated much of the Arts and Crafts philosophy, he started his designs "on premises more sophisticated than those attributed to the Arts and Crafts movement. Exploitation of structural order, application of visual phenomena, and respect for new materials and industrial processes, as well as a firm belief in the expressive qualities of form were the bases for his work." In all likelihood it never occurred to Maybeck that one should be a follower of the Arts and Crafts movement *or* a follower of modern technology. For him both were valid. In Esther McCoy's words he believed as Morris did "that all worthy creations in architecture sprang from the fraternity between the artist and the workman, as in the Middle Ages, and that 'it is spoiled when the gentry gets hold of the idea.'" But he could see no reason why he shouldn't take advantage of technology and new materials. When he was commissioned to design the Christian Science Church in Berkeley, McCoy tells us, Maybeck wondered how he could "put

himself in the boots of a fellow in the twelfth century." He was certain of one thing, however, "the man of the Middle Ages would use 'the most modern materials he could lay his hands on,' and would combine them in such a way as to express the spirit of his faith."

One can also imagine that designing furniture for his buildings was not something Maybeck had any theories about as Wright and the other Prairie architects did. He designed furniture as he designed buildings, because he felt it should be that way. Furniture arose as naturally out of his plans as windows or stairways. His fireplaces, like Wright's, often had a built-in seat on one side—redwood in Maybeck's case—but they were not conceived as visual blocks any more than the fireplace was conceived as a focal point. The fireplace was there for its heat, the seat as a place to receive it. Proof of the serviceability and common sense of Maybeck furniture is that much of it is still being used. McCoy tells us that three generations of children grew up in one Maybeck house where a simple table of redwood boards he designed for the dining room is still in place. One of his earliest commissions came from San Francisco's Bohemian Club to which he belonged. The club had been holding summer encampments along the Russian River north of San Francisco and in 1903 decided to build a permanent structure. Maybeck was asked to design a clubroom that would serve as a meeting place, dining room, and bathing facility. For the clubroom he designed a large deal table surrounded by three-legged chairs derived from 17th-century Flemish milking stools, which all are still being used in the clubroom.

Maybeck's furniture then was rarely as fantastic as some of his architecture, but in that as in everything else he was a follower of no one. Maybeck could design both functional furniture and functional buildings, but he could also design the famous Palace of Fine Arts in San Francisco of which Philip Johnson once asked: "Who can use the Parthenon or Maybeck's Palace?"

R. M. SCHINDLER 1887-1953

*Only lately have we again discovered
the real height and breadth of a human
being. Ceilings shelter us instead of
crowning our position. Doors are to walk
through rather than to form an impressive
frame for one who carefully pauses on
the threshold. The chair supports
the back rather than to produce
an aura for our head.* R. M. SCHINDLER

It must have seemed perfectly natural for the Viennese-born Schindler to design furniture for his buildings. His father was a craftsman in wood and metal. The young Schindler studied in Vienna at a time when the arts were being swept by the spirit of revolt which had begun with William Morris and the Arts and Crafts movement and continued with Art Nouveau and the Viennese Secession. And designing furniture was a leitmotif of all these movements.

Schindler entered the Imperial Institute of Engineering in 1906 and before graduating enrolled in the Vienna Academy of Fine Arts where he trained under the great Otto Wagner who was a member of the Secessionist movement and designer of such innovative 20th-century architecture as the Austrian Postal Savings Bank of 1904–1906 with its curved glass roof and utterly simple bentwood and metal furniture. He knew the Viennese architect, writer, and teacher Adolf Loos who also considered it de rigueur to design furniture for his buildings. It was a time, in fact, when Vienna was literally swarming with geniuses, architectural and otherwise. Kafka, Schiele, Kokoschka, Klimt, Freud, Rilke, Gustav Mahler, Ludwig Wittgenstein, Albam Berg are but a few of the others. Most of the Viennese artistic world, moreover, gathered in the dazzling black and white Fledermaus Cabaret which opened in 1908 with its playfully simple black and white tables and chairs, all designed by architect-designer Josef Hoffmann who taught at the Arts and Crafts School and helped found the Wiener Werkstätte in 1903. It is also quite possible that Schindler saw the work of Charles Rennie Mackintosh when it was so enthusiastically received in Vienna in 1900.

But notwithstanding the geniuses all around him, Schindler was fascinated by Frank Lloyd Wright whose work he became familiar with through the Wasmuth portfolio published in Germany in 1910. Adolf Loos, who had spent some time in the United States in the 1890s and knew about Schindler's interest in Wright, persuaded him to accept a position with Ottenheimer, Stern and Reichel in Chicago. Of course when he arrived in Chicago in 1914 there were geniuses there too, although hardly on the scale of pre-World War I Vienna. But Wright was there and it was his genius that brought the Viennese Schindler to America's midwest.

While with Ottenheimer, Stern and Reichel, Schindler designed several buildings including the Buena Shore Club in Chicago which contained some of the built-in furniture that he later developed and refined in his residential work in Southern California. In 1917 Schindler realized his original ambition and started working for Wright at Taliesin. In 1920 he went to California to supervise construction of Wright's Hollyhock house for Aline Barnsdall in Hollywood. It was Schindler, in fact, who designed most of the original furniture for the Barnsdall house with the exception of the dining table and chairs which were Wright's design.

Schindler set up his own practice in Los Angeles in 1921. His first furniture, as might be expected, was not unlike Wright's, but it was lower and more comfortable. In the Lovell

Low armchair designed by Schindler for the living room of the Dr. Philip Lovell beach house in Newport Beach, California, in 1925–1926 sits beside a Schindler-designed floor lamp, which is a vertical column of alternating wood and exposed light bulbs.

beach house—designed by Schindler in 1922 but unappreciated until much later as "one of the really crucial examples of the new architecture of the 20s," in Henry Russell-Hitchcock's words—there is a built-in sofa with adjacent book shelves as innovative as the house. While still a student in Vienna, Schindler had written a manifesto on modern architecture in which he proclaimed: "The old problems have been solved and the styles are dead. . . . The architect has finally discovered the medium of his art: SPACE." And it was that medium, space, that informed all his work—furniture as well as architecture. Schindler later recalled that when he first saw the portfolio of Wright's work in Vienna, he realized "Here was 'space architecture'. . . . Here was the first architect. And the timeless importance of Wright lies especially in these first houses." In view of Schindler's interest in space it is perhaps worth noting that he, like many European architects who designed furniture, studied painting and was influenced by the work of the cubists as well as by Cezanne's concept of space.

Space was Schindler's reason for designing the "Schindler Unit Furniture" that he used in his minimum houses of the 1930s. These units were designed to conserve maximum floor space and could be combined in a variety of ways. In a series of articles on "The Contemporary House" which Schindler wrote for *The Architect and Engineer*, he explained in the December 1935 issue that "the modern architect who has become the space architect, sees the house as an organism in which every detail, including the furniture, is related to the whole and to the idea which is its source." In the following issue of January 1936, he goes on to explain that the "Space Architect sees the house (or the whole town) an articulation of the one cosmic space. The house becomes an organizer in which all rooms are related to each other representing variations of one basic theme. The house becomes a weave of a few basic materials used to define his space forms. The furniture which is stationary (beds, etc.) become part of the weave until it is impossible to tell where the house ends and the furniture begins. The few pieces which are necessarily movable (chairs, etc.) become so in an accentuating degree. Moving, they are unfit to define the space conception and must therefore be eliminated architecturally for the sake of clarity. They are either folded up and stored away or made transparent to become inconspicuous. This is the real meaning of the metal chair. Its essence is its transparency—the lack of which immediately delegates to the realm of idle phantasies all the 'fashionable' designs in which bulging upholstery masses are suspended on snaky metal braces.

"The folding chair is the more radical solution of the space architect's problem—it avoids blur-

Built-in sofa and adjacent bookshelves in the Lovell beach house recall Schindler's words: "it is impossible to tell where the house ends and the furniture begins."

ring of the space scheme by leaving the realm of furniture altogether; it becomes part of the occupant like his shoes and clothes and will develop his final shape out of this new constellation. . . ." Thus Schindler had the same difficulty with movable furniture that Wright did, but his words, at least, make the problem seem easily solvable. Not only must the furniture define space, as Schindler saw it, but it must conform to the more relaxed posture of the time: "Our houses should give us ease and freedom of action—a request which 'period furnishing' is unable to satisfy."

The Schindler Units developed in 1931 were composed of a few simple units which, in Schindler's words, "allow rearrangement, addition, and substraction with ease." He wanted to achieve forms that would not become furniture shapes when placed against a wall. "The stationary furniture especially," he explained, "stops leaning against the wall and tries to merge with the floor." His units are thus low and wide. "Placed one above the other they establish several horizontal planes throughout the room, giving the furniture the character of floor terraces." Because no unit has a front or back, nor is it symmetrical it "permits the establishment of form relationships with its neighbors. The result is consequently not the formless pile of self-centered elements which the usual type of unit furniture produces, but a form organization with definite character and variable individuality." Schindler goes on to explain that large sofa pillows are also part of his scheme and can be turned into armchairs "by simply adding an adjustable back and arms. Several such seats and backs joined together form the couch, which may be of any length, or a corner seat." This, of course, is an idea very much in fashion today, but one wonders how many are aware that it began with Schindler more than 40 years ago.

Schindler's minimum houses included, in addition to his unit furniture, well-planned storage cabinets, built-in dressing tables and cabinets in the bathrooms as well as other built-in pieces; and the cabinetwork was always superb. He invented undercut grooves to replace drawer pulls in 1926 because he thought shiny hardware "places an object out of reach of a close personal relationship." Before developing his unit furniture he designed a variety of stools, tables, and sideboards on the job from leftover scraps of wood which, in the words of Esther McCoy, had "great charm and spontaneity and were so satisfactory they are still in use in many early houses." By 1940 Schindler was using plywood extensively inside and out. He used it for built-in cabinets as well as movable furniture. He preferred fir plywood, according to David Gebhard, not only because it was cheap but "because it looked common and inexpensive." Schindler designed more and more of his furni-

ture so that it could be built easily by the carpenter on the job rather than by a cabinetmaker, just as Wright designed the furniture for his Usonian houses.

Although Schindler left Vienna before the formation of Gropius's Bauhaus, it is obvious that many of his ideas grew out of the same soil. He, however, considered the work of the Bauhaus an expression of the "minds of a people who had lived through the first World War, clad in uniforms, housed in dugouts, forced into utmost efficiency and meager sustenance—it had no thought for joy, charm, and warmth." One can only assume that in Schindler's case, it was the magic of southern California that made the difference. Reyner Banham has called Schindler "the master of the International Style in Los Angeles," and that was even before New York's Museum of Modern Art had made Americans aware of such a thing through its famous 1932 exhibition, "The International Style: Architecture since 1922." But Schindler would not have been flattered. He didn't think much of the International style especially when it came to furniture. "Most of the buildings which Corbusier and his followers offer as 'machines to live in,' equipped with various 'machines to sit and sleep on,'" he wrote in *Dune Forum* of February 1934, "have not even reached the state of development of our present machines. They are crude contraptions to serve a purpose. The man who brings such machines into his living room is on the same level of primitive development as the farmer who keeps cows and pigs in his house. Mere instruments of production can never serve as a frame for life. Especially the creaks and jags of our crude machine age must necessarily force us to protect our human qualities in homes contrasting most intensely with the factory."

He was only a little more understanding but no less condemnatory when the following year he wrote in *The Architect and Engineer* of December 1935: "The architect is a new hand at furniture designing, which accounts for many of his recent mistakes. During the period of his initiation, striving strenuously for unity, he tried to make the furniture an integral part of his architectural scheme without sufficient regard for use. The resulting lines and materials fitted admirably into the setting; but the furniture remained angular and unwieldy. The realization of this defeat threw him into the camp of the mechanist. . . ." Furniture, in its mature form, Schindler contended, "is the result of many complex forces to which the architect must submit and which he must keep in proper relations." Later he says that although "furniture may have civilisatory use, in its ripe form it has undoubted cultural meaning. All thoroughbred western furniture will show dynamic conven-

tionalisations of biological parent forms. And this is the real reason why we had to abandon the earlier stiff architectural designs of Frank Lloyd Wright and others—their unpractical unwieldiness being only a superficial excuse for the switch towards the 'Functionalist.'"

However, as Schindler points out in another place, the basic idea of his unit furniture is "thoroughly modern and could not have been conceived in a period without machine production." His unit scheme, he adds, "illustrates at the same time that most of the sloganists advocating machine production do not yet understand its essential feature. The machine which is used to fabricate whole objects: houses, desks, etc., takes its production scheme from the craftsman. The latter, however, maintains a certain aliveness in his product by his inability for exact repetition. The machine, for which exact repetition is the very essence, when misused in such a way will cause a deadly standardization of our lives." And, Schindler concludes, "Only by confining the machine to making parts (units) which, through the very fact of their precision, may be joined freely, can we subdue its mechanical ferocity to individual expression. The machine, contrary to common opinion, can develop such individualisation to a degree of which the handicrafter could never have dreamed." The Schindler Units are made up of machine-made parts which can be assembled and rearranged into furniture "which will respond to the particular conditions of any room, according to the individual character of the occupant."

Schindler, it can be seen, was only second to Wright in the amount of thought he gave to furniture. And, like Wright, he never stopped designing it. Furniture, for Schindler, was perhaps an even more important part of his architecture than it was for Wright. The furnishings, he said, "merge with the house, leaving the room free to express its form."

Southern California seems a natural setting for Schindler's ideas—his furniture as well as his open, patio-oriented houses. It is, in fact, strange that so many of the architects who created an indigenous American architecture on California soil were trained overseas—Maybeck in Paris, Schindler and Neutra in the creative and fashionable avant-garde atmosphere of pre-World War I Vienna. The Greenes, of course, were an exception and so was Irving Gill. As Reyner Banham notes when speaking of the contingent of German-speaking architects in southern California—Kem Weber, Schindler, Neutra—"So there they were, face to face with Southern California, afloat in its atmosphere of permissive extravagance, but with little cultural support except their original debts to Vienna and the *Wagnerschule*," and he wonders if it was not "this sense of an old indebtedness that prompted someone to serialize Otto Wagner's *Moderne Architektur* in the *Southwestern Builder and Contractor* from July 1938 onwards." The *Wagnerschule*, however, was only the starting point for the Los Angeles school fostered by that German-speaking contingent.

No matter where these California architects came from, where they were educated, or what influenced their designs, the results are not only individual but as much a product of America as the Pueblos of New Mexico and Arizona. It can only be the influence of the land. It was certainly in Europe that Schindler's ideas were incubated, but it was in the special atmosphere of Southern California that they came into their own. The architect, as Schindler himself said, "is both the child and creator of a culture. His source is the life character of a group, nationally, racially, or locally defined, a source emitting a subtle unconscious influence to which he is forced to submit."

Top: Interior of the summer house designed by Schindler for C.H. Wolfe on Catalina Island in 1928, showing built-in living room furniture and the raised bedroom behind it, seems to follow Adolf Loos's idea that interior space should be thought of as a series of vertically related horizontal platforms.

Bottom: Schindler's unit furniture in the living room of the W.E. Oliver house in Los Angeles of 1933 shows what he meant when he said furniture should merge with the house leaving the room free to express its form.

THREE ART NOVEAU ARCHITECT-DESIGNERS

Art Nouveau, that "short but very significant fashion in decoration" around the turn of the century, as Nikolaus Pevsner defines it, was dedicated to bringing all the arts together. Artists, designers, and architects were committed to the oneness of design, and like Morris before them, many concerned themselves with the total decoration of a room or an entire house. Whistler, Tiffany, Gaudi, Mackintosh, and Guimard are but a few. Fine artists carved furnishings and designed stained-glass windows; architects designed furniture, fabrics, wallpaper, and cutlery. Art Nouveau, as Walter Crane had said of Morris's Arts and Crafts movement, was "turning our artists into craftsmen and our craftsmen into artists."

The term "Art Nouveau" derives from S. Bing's *Maison de l'Art Nouveau*, which opened in Paris in 1895 and for which painters and architects were commissioned to design furniture and decorate rooms. Bing's shop was a showcase for the new furniture, interiors, painting, ceramics, fabrics, metalwork, and anything else that fit the Art Nouveau idea of unifying all elements of life. Bing commissioned the Belgian architect Henri van de Velde to design four complete rooms for his shop. He commissioned Vuillard and Bonnard to make designs for stained glass executed by Tiffany. Vincent Van Gogh was a customer and Marcel Proust informs us that Robert de Saint-Loup had decorated his home with furniture from Bing's. His first *Salon de l'Art Nouveau* included posters by Mackintosh and Beardsley, glass by Tiffany, sculpture by Rodin, and jewelry by Lalique.

Bing later explained that at the time of its creation, *L'Art Nouveau* "did not aspire in any way to the honor of becoming a generic term. It was simply the name of an establishment opened as a meeting ground for all ardent young spirits anxious to manifest the modernness of their tendencies, and open to all lovers of art who desired to see the working of the hitherto unrevealed forces of our day. . . ." He goes on to explain that it was "only in relation to art as applied to decoration, to furniture, to ornamentation in all its forms, that the need of a new departure was felt. This department of art, in reality the most essential to man, being closely connected with his daily existence, had been at a standstill for nearly a hundred years."

While Art Nouveau artists and architect-designers shunned all relation to the past, they did not exist in a void. The Gothic revival, the work of the Pre-Raphaelites, Impressionism, and Richard Wagner who tried to synthesize music and drama were in their immediate background, and of course they were direct heirs of William Morris whose name was synonymous with reform in the applied arts. Nature was their main source of inspiration as it had been for Morris. Even the femme fatale with her languid curves and flowing hair who undulates through Art Nouveau like a leitmotif seems to have had her source in Morris's wife Janey who inspired so many paintings by Rossetti as well as Morris. She even fascinated Henry James who described

HECTOR GUIMARD
ANTONI GAUDI
CHARLES RENNIE MACKINTOSH

her in 1869 as "an apparition of fearful and wonderful intensity." Robert Furneaux Jordan has suggested that a femme fatale was so important to the Victorians that she demanded a setting and one that "clearly could never be anything so specific as Gothic." In architecture, he points out, that setting "became progressively less real, less stylistic, more abstract—the painter's attenuated lilies transmuted into ornament tended to become long stalks with little buds, until attenuation and swooning curves were all that was left. Those swooning curves, however, . . . could be painted panels, they could be stained glass, they could be wallpaper. They could be steel—for steel is dactile and can be curved, drawn out and shaped." And they could be wood—for hadn't Michael Thonet discovered how to bend wood to make his famous chairs as early as the 1840s?

Perhaps more than anything else the Art Nouveau architect-designers were disgusted, as Henri van de Velde put it, by "the insane follies which the furniture makers of past centuries had piled up in bedrooms and drawing rooms. . . . Processions of fauns, menacing apocalyptic beasts, benevolently hilarious Cupids (bawdy in some cases and complacently anxious to please in others), and swollen-cheeked satyrs in charge of winds."

Thus architects as farflung as Victor Horta and Henri van de Velde in Belgium, Hector Guimard in France, Charles Rennie Mackin-tosh in Scotland, H. P. Berlage in Holland, Antoni Gaudi in Spain, and Eliel Saarinen in Finland decided to design their own furniture as Morris and his followers had decided to do. There is nothing arbitrary about the Art Nouveau furniture these architects designed. It is so much a part of its setting that one can rarely do justice to an individual piece outside of its intended context. Art Nouveau furniture, in fact, is an organic part of the interior as no other architect-designed furniture is—not even Frank Lloyd Wright's.

Probably the three most significant Art Nouveau architect-designers were France's Hector Guimard, Spain's Antoni Gaudi, and Scotland's Charles Rennie Mackintosh, all of whom were important for their furniture designs, their originality, and because they marked an important step in the transition from historicism to the Bauhaus and the modern movement. Moreover the interiors of these three architect-designers are totally dissimilar in their overall effect, indicating a wider originality in Art Nouveau than is usually realized. Certainly the sophisticated furniture and interiors of Mackintosh and the fantastic furniture and interiors of Gaudi are two extremes of a theme that had more homogeneity in France, Belgium, and Germany. All three, however, designed furniture and interiors that more than do justice to Morris's lifelong campaign to raise the artistic level of the lesser arts.

HECTOR GUIMARD 1867–1942

For a rather short period—thirty or forty years—Art Nouveau dominated all forms of creative expression, from the poster art of Toulouse-Lautrec to the furniture of Guimard. PETER BLAKE

It was Hector Guimard who gave Paris its famous Art Nouveau street furniture with his entrances for the Métro stations. His houses also helped make Art Nouveau part of the Paris scene, but it is the interiors with their sometimes playful and sometimes sinister furnishings that demonstrate to an amazing degree that synthesis of the arts which Morris advocated. Guimard was so convinced that as an architect it was his duty to preside over the design and execution of every detail of his buildings that he apprenticed himself to every type of structural and decorative craft. This was evident in a Guimard house where furniture, wallpaper, staircases, fireplaces, doorknobs, lighting fixtures, cutlery, and the building's facade were unmistakably the products of a single mind. Guimard, like Morris, even carried this integration into the design of his wife's clothes. He signed his work "Hector Guimard, Architecte d'Art," perhaps a little self-consciously albeit accurately.

Guimard was born in Paris and studied at the École Nationale des Arts Décoratifs for three years before entering the École des Beaux-Arts in 1885. Although he didn't stay to receive a diploma from the Beaux-Arts, it was there that he became impressed with the theories of Viollet-le-Duc who believed that the architect must analyze the masterpieces of the past and then learn to make his own synthesis serving the conditions and using the materials dictated by his own age. In other words he must derive from the past not in order to revive it but in order to develop an entirely new style. Guimard began his practice in 1888 with this firmly in mind. But it was probably his meeting with the Belgian Art Nouveau architect Victor Horta in 1895 that helped him find his way to his own new style.

Horta was also an admirer of Viollet-le-Duc's theories and had already completed his famous Tassel house in Brussels when Guimard met him in Belgium.

Along with his desire to create a total work of art in a new style for a new age, it was Guimard's stated ambition to modernize the French decorative arts and—while Rococo furniture and decoration was an important influence—he came close to doing just that. It is not easy to assess Guimard as an interior designer since so many of his interiors have disappeared, but there is no doubt he should be ranked high as a furniture designer. Sherban Cantacuzino has even called him "probably the equal of the best Rococo designers of the 18th century" in addition to lauding him as a pioneer of industrial design for both his superbly executed furniture and his Métro entrances.

The Castel Béranger of 1894–1898 in Paris was not only the first building for which Guimard designed furniture, but his first to express the Art Nouveau style. In his early furniture such as that for the Castel Béranger and the Coilliot house in Lille, the carving is bold and there is a strong suggestion of natural forms. Guimard like Gaudi didn't imitate nature merely for its decorative effect. He saw its value as a structural force. "When I design a piece of furniture or sculpt it," Guimard told Victor Champier in *Revue des Arts Décoratifs* of 1899, "I reflect upon the spectacle the universe provides. Beauty appears to us in a perpetual variety. No

Skylighted gallery in the Mezzara house in Paris of 1910–1911 shows the remarkable unity Guimard achieved in his later work between the architectural elements and furnishings of an interior space.

parallelism or symmetry; forms are engendered from movements which are never alike. . . . For construction, do not the branches of the trees, the stems, by turn rigid and undulating, furnish us with models? You will tell me that if I apply the example of the stem's movements, and the disparities within these movements, to furniture, to everyday objects . . . I will end up with the effect of cut-outs. Inaccurate! You only have this impression because you are accustomed to furniture conceived as antique monuments. These dominant lines which describe space, sometimes supple and sinuous arabesques, sometimes flourishes as vivid as the firing of a thunderbolt, these lines have a value of feeling and expression more eloquent than the vertical, horizontal and regular lines continually used until now in architecture. . . . Let us be inspired by these general laws. Let us bend before . . . the examples of the great architect of the universe."

The desk which he designed for his own studio at the Castel Béranger and the buffet and fireplace he designed for the Coilliot house are but two examples of his early furniture for which "the branches of the trees, the stems, by turn rigid and undulating" did indeed furnish Guimard with exemplary models for construction. "Here is an art that both abbreviates and amplifies the immediate facets of Nature; it spiritualizes them," as the critic Gustave Soulier wrote about Castel Béranger in close collaboration with Guimard.

In his later furniture the decoration becomes both more delicate and more elaborate or, in Guimard's own words, "as though the entire piece is enveloped in a mysterious veil." Attention has shifted "from raw, undecorated linearity to highly plastic volumes of space enriched by 'civilizing' ornament,' as Lanier Graham puts it in the catalog of the Museum of Modern Art's 1970 exhibition, *Hector Guimard*. "Hard dark mahogany is replaced by soft, blond pearwood. Symmetry eventually replaces asymmetry."

In 1909 after many years of bachelorhood Guimard married the American painter Adeline Oppenheim and built his own house in Paris— his last design, in fact, that was a totally integrated environment inside and out. The Guimard house is not only a masterpiece of Art Nouveau but a fine example of the "Style Guimard," as he liked his later work to be called. Its furniture and all its other decorative objects, as was usual with Guimard, were designed for their specific architectural context. The dining room with its lavalike walls and the sinuous lines of the furniture may seem to us more reminiscent of a backdrop for a cartoon by Charles Addams than a Morris interior or anything done by Wright, but who can say it doesn't follow the latter's dictum: "Furnishings should be consistent in de-

Above: This desk of olive wood with ash panels designed by Guimard for his own use, c. 1899, is, in Robert Schmutzler's words, "among the most incredible but convincing pieces of Art Nouveau furniture."

Left: Fruitwood side chair designed by Guimard, c. 1908 (see also opposite page).

Opposite page: Dining room in Guimard's own Paris house of 1909–1910 is in the purest Style Guimard.

sign and construction, and used with style as an extension in the sense of the building which they 'furnish.' "

Whether one singles out Guimard's "designs for buildings, furniture, wallpaper, or doorknobs; whether one discusses his treatment of space, mass, light, volume, color, texture, or line; whether one considers him as an architect, planner, craftsman, draftsman, graphic designer, industrial designer, jeweler, or sculptor; more often than not, these aspects are only partial components of a single comprehensive aesthetic," as Lanier Graham says. "The totality of his concern for the quality of life and the humanity of his planning with a new style for a new age, are only part of Guimard's relevance for our own time."

Later generations may have thought of Art Nouveau as strangely overdone with an emphasis on novelty and not much else. But from our technology-minded, materialistic point of view, there is no doubt that the high standard of craftsmanship, the spontaneity, the idealism of Art Nouveau in general and Guimard in particular do indeed have a relevance for our time. Far from thinking of Art Nouveau as lacking in seriousness, our own contemporary critic Vincent Scully compares the interiors of Victor Horta, for instance, with "a Bergsonian world which embodies the endless continuities that move through all things, including man, and in which all separateness drowns."

And listen to Guimard's own opinion of Art Nouveau as he stated it in *Architectural Record* of June 1902: "It is upon us architects that falls more particularly the duty of determining, by

Above: Side table from the Nozal house bedroom, c. 1904–1907, in Paris (see also opposite page, top).

Left: Hector Guimard's own office, c. 1897–1899, showing the architect seated at his drafting table.

Opposite page, top: This unmistakably Art Nouveau bed flanked by a side table (see also above) and night stool was designed by Guimard for the Nozal house.

Opposite page, bottom: Buffet and fireplace designed by Guimard for the dining room, c. 1901, of the Coilliot house in Lille is a remarkable Art Nouveau symphony.

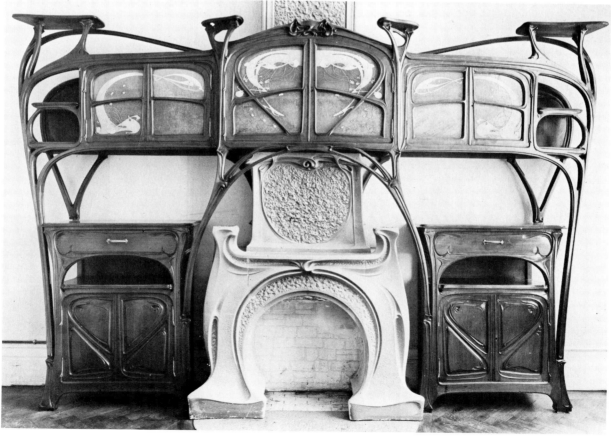

Bronze umbrella stand, c. 1902, and two carved walnut chairs designed by Guimard possibly for his own use.

our art, not only the artistic, but also the civilizing and scientific evolution of our time. Nature is a big book from which we draw inspiration, and it is in that book that we must look for principles, which, when found, have to be defined and applied by the human mind according to human needs. From this study I obtain these principles which should have a predominating influence in all architectural productions, viz.: 1. Logic. . . . 2. Harmony, which means putting the constructions into full accord, not only with the requirements to be met and the funds available, but also with the surroundings. 3. Sentiment, which, partaking at the same time of logic and harmony, is the complement of both, and leads by emotion, to the highest expression of art.

"These are the principles which I have desired to exemplify in all my edifices. . . . I cannot say that all these productions illustrate the three principles which I have just laid down. For the most part they infringe them, for that undefinable thing called *taste*, which makes us like a chair, a clock, a vase or a jewel; taste, which is the embodiment of *esprit*, charm, emotion, life, whether in cloth or metal, an article for use or an ornament, is a quality which is lacking in the greater number of those who believe themselves to be modern creators. . . ."

It is hardly surprising that in 1925 when Guimard was nearing 60, he expressed his reservation about the lasting values of machine-inspired art. "Today's fashion of the Naked corresponds to a whole state of mind: we no longer believe in mystery." Nevertheless it was Guimard along with other Art Nouveau and Arts and Crafts architect-designers who prepared the ground for the nudity of the Bauhaus and the International style by freeing those later architects from eclecticism. In fact didn't Walter Gropius, Mies van der Rohe, Le Corbusier all train in the office of Peter Behrens who had started out as a painter and craftsman of Art Nouveau persuasion, although he later rejected it? And there are many other close connections between Art Nouveau and the Bauhaus.

Like the Rococo of the 18th century, Art Nouveau was spontaneous, exuberant, and imaginative. It inspired an emotional response. Ours is an age of realism, of machines, and we may believe even less in mystery now than in 1925 when Guimard noted that it had lost its appeal. It is not by chance that his superbly executed furniture, which probably represents some of the last significant examples of craftsmanship, evokes a kind of mystery that no machine could achieve.

Angled cupboard from the Nozal house is, like much of Guimard's furniture, original in shape.

ANTONI GAUDI 1852-1926

. . . have you noticed, in walking about this city, that among the buildings with which it is peopled, certain are mute: others speak and others, finally—they are the most rare—sing? PAUL VALÉRY in *Eupalinos, or the Architect*

The forms of the Catalan architect-designer Antoni Gaudi are especially infused with the action of nature and, as Vincent Scully says, are therefore "somehow real." He was probably the most mystical as well as the most eccentric of the Art Nouveau architect-designers. "Who," asks Pevsner, "would be ready to live in rooms of such curvy shapes, under roofs like the backs of dinosaurs, behind walls bending and bulging so precariously?" And he answers himself: "Who but an out-and-out aesthete or a compatriot of Gaudi and Picasso." It also might be asked who could design furniture for such extraordinary rooms, and of course the answer is no one but Gaudi, although Picasso might have tried.

It was not Gaudi's intention to reconstruct natural forms nor to stylize them anew, as George R. Collins has pointed out, "but to produce a type of poetic metamorphoses of them, working according to natural laws, which he considered to be the primary rules of the art of architecture." His furniture as well as the elevations and floor plans of his buildings were conceived with that idea.

Gaudi was born near the Mediterranean city of Reus in Catalonia, the fifth child of a coppersmith. He went to school in Reus but preferred to spend his time on the shore contemplating the rhythmic movement of the sea. "All great feats are accomplished by the sea," he once told a journalist. "The sea has been and must be involved in the most stupendous enterprises of humanity." It was undoubtedly from the sea that Gaudi acquired his lifelong love of the undulating forms of nature as well as some of his mysticism. He entered the School of Architecture in Barcelona in 1869 but did not graduate until 1878, having spent much of his time on outside architectural work in order to finance his education.

Even more than most Art Nouveau architect-designers Gaudi conceived each work as a totality and moved freely from ceramics and stained glass to furniture and ironwork. His furniture as well as everything else is an integral part of the precisely conceived whole while at the same time each item is an entity, complete in itself. In fact the unifying connection between structure and furnishings is what makes it possible to trace the evolution of Gaudi as an architect through his furniture. As his architecture evolves in the direction of functionalism so does his furniture. Although his first pieces of furniture like his architecture were medieval, he went on to develop his own highly personal designs, culminating in the furniture for the Casa Batlló which even today, as José-Luis Sert has noted, is "astonishingly modern in appearance."

Furniture was an aspect of architecture which Gaudi never disdained. He designed his first piece immediately after completing architectural school in 1878 for a Gothic chapel and continued to design furniture throughout his career. Among his early interior furnishings are a set of carved wooden armoires for liturgical vestments and other pieces he designed for the church of the Sagrada Familia in Barcelona—a work he undertook in 1883 that would occupy his entire life off and on. The year Gaudi graduated he met the industrialist Eusebio Güell who was to become one of his important patrons and for whom he designed a variety of buildings along with the furnishings. The Palau Güell, a town house Gaudi designed for Güell in Barcelona in 1885–1889, not only

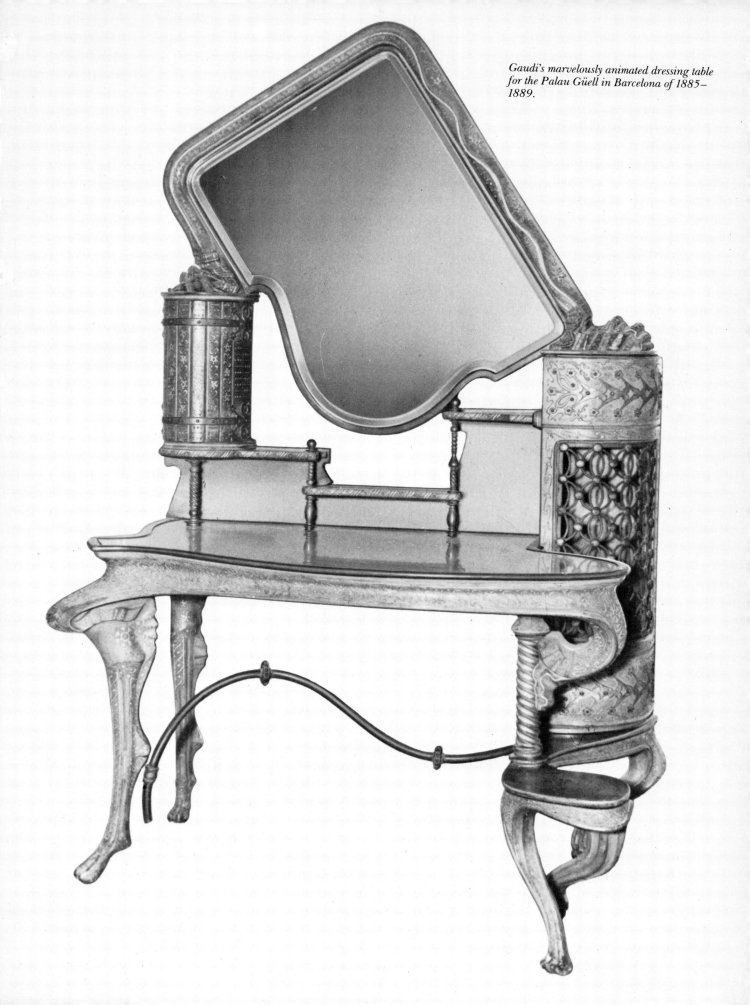

Gaudí's marvelously animated dressing table for the Palau Güell in Barcelona of 1885–1889.

Above, left: This deceptively simple carved oak side chair for the Casa Batlló of 1904–1906 has been called Gaudí's "final display of expressionist functionalism." Its concave seat and the angle of its back make this chair amazingly comfortable.

Above, right: This armchair is one of the pieces Gaudí designed for the offices in the Casa Calvet in Barcelona, c. 1901–1902, which marked his turning away from any reference to tradition into his own world.

Right: Gaudí's benches for the crypt of Santa Coloma de Cervelló, begun in 1898 (shown on pages 148–149), with their rough wooden seats on spidery legs are intensely individual, like everything he did.

has lavish interiors but some of what was surely Gaudi's more exotic furniture including a chaise longue on twined metal legs which Henry-Russell Hitchcock thinks "offers startling premonitions of that of the mid-twentieth century." There is also a remarkably animated dressing table which, in Robert Venturi's words, "represents an orgy of contrasting dualities of form; extreme inflection and continuity are combined with violent adjacencies and discontinuities, complex and simple curves, rectangles and diagonals, contrasting materials, symmetry and asymmetry, in order to accommodate a multiplicity of functions in one whole." Only the imagination of Gaudi could have conceived such a piece.

Also for Eusebio Güell, Gaudi later designed the chapel of Santa Coloma de Cervelló of 1898–1915 on an industrial estate outside Barcelona. Although only the crypt of the chapel was ever completed, its innovative structural logic has been astonishing architects and laypeople ever since. Its effect, as Hitchcock observed, is more prehistoric than medieval—"perhaps one should say outside time." And the benches Gaudi designed for it are no less outside time. With their rough wooden seats on spidery iron legs they give the impression of animated prehistoric insects. The Santa Coloma benches also represent, as Pevsner has pointed out, "one of the few cases of design trying to do what painting was doing at the same moment, that is, scrapping all the agreed conventions of art."

At about the same period that Gaudi designed the Santa Coloma benches he designed furniture for the Casa Calvet in Barcelona of 1898–1904, which is surprisingly non-Gaudian in that it is almost conventional. Much of the furniture for the upper floors is also more or less conventional, but some sketches Gaudi made of the chairs for the ground floor offices have a special interest. George Collins has pointed out that about the time Gaudi designed these chairs he "arrived at the concept of an architectural structure that echoed the efficiency of nature and an architectural style that substituted natural order for the traditional historic orders. . . ." And Collins sees the sketches Gaudi made for the Casa Calvet office chairs as examples of his struggles with the problems arising from this conception. "By observations (i.e., sketching) and by testing," explains Collins, "he had reduced the idea 'chair' to its primary structure (both for sitting and leaning back upon), arriving at an almost insectile, skeletal frame that supports the plaques on which one sits and leans; the plaques seem to have been formed from the impress of a human body, so that they will hold the latter as a chalice would. 'Originality,' Gaudi said, 'means to return to the origin.' To understand the dimensions of this transformation in his concept of 'chair' one has only to compare the rigid, mechanistic assemblage of historically-derived and animal-decorated parts that characterized

Gaudi's sketches of chairs for the Casa Calvet offices show his attempt to reduce the idea of a chair to its essentials.

his early efforts in furniture with his later 'natural' creations. . . ."

And thus with the Casa Calvet office furniture, Gaudi moves away from identifiable tradition into a world of his own. By the time he got to the Casa Batlló in 1905–1907—the facade of which Collins has aptly equated with the "bubbly surface of a Mediterranean wave spreading over a rocky beach"—the furniture is both entirely functional and wholly involved in the pattern of curves that controls the interiors. From beginning to end Gaudi's furniture plays a perfect accompaniment to his spirited architecture, and both are imbued with his unique prophetic vision but always subject to his stated credo: "The beauty and the logic of structure transcends all styles." Whatever Gaudi designed—a light fixture, a chair, a staircase, a house, a church, an iron gate—was pure Gaudi, but, as Collins has observed, it is the ironwork outside and the furniture inside that lends his buildings a sense of animation even when they are deserted.

Gaudi worked closely with the craftsmen at a building site, thus establishing an intimate master-apprentice relationship. He was essentially the medieval craftsman, in Pevsner's words, "whose final decision could only be taken as he watched over the execution. . . . In him one idea of William Morris had come true. What he built was 'by the people' and no doubt 'a joy for the maker' i.e. the actual mason as well."

There are few words of Gaudi's extant to tell us much about either the man or his work, but this can hardly matter since his biography is to be found in his architecture and the furniture that is so much a part of it. All his visions and his artistic beliefs are there. Gaudi's coworkers later remembered being more affected by his religious faith and his sincere belief in architecture as a way of life than by his theories. And the faith and belief they speak of is most apparent in his famous unfinished church of the Sagrada Familia in Barcelona which occupied so much of his life. Louis Sullivan called it "spirit symbolized in stone!" And indeed all Gaudi's mystic expressionism is in that fantastic church, which is dedicated, among other things, to the expiation of the sins of the materialistic age. Here, too, Gaudi reveals his affinity with Morris. He envisaged a colony of artisans clustered about his church as in the Middle Ages "from which will rise the noises of work, like the buzzing of bees, toward the sunlit church, a mystical hive," as he once described it to a visitor. Certainly Vincent Scully is not wrong in calling Art Nouveau "especially profound when its influence touches Antonio Gaudi, to whom continuous structure had indeed always been sympathetic."

The insectlike benches (shown on the bottom of page 146) are perfectly at home in the fantastic crypt of Santa Coloma de Cervelló, for which they were designed.

CHARLES RENNIE MACKINTOSH 1868–1928

Around 1900, a magnificent gesture—we shed the tatters of an old culture. LE CORBUSIER

The Scotsman Charles Rennie Mackintosh was not only the British link with Art Nouveau as it was developed on the Continent in the 1890s, he was one of the strongest links between Art Nouveau and the Bauhaus. Pevsner, moreover, calls him "the European counterpart of Frank Lloyd Wright and one of the few true forerunners of the most ingenious juggler with space"—Le Corbusier. Thus Mackintosh, perhaps more than other Art Nouveau architect-designers, was an important part of the continuing evolution of design, although Gaudi's imaginative structural innovations have been recognized by José-Luis Sert among others as being far in advance of their time.

After Mackintosh began practicing architecture in 1889 as an assistant in the Glasgow architectural firm of Honeyman and Keppie, he attended evening classes at the Glasgow School of Art where he and three fellow students formed a group called "The Four" who, in true Art Nouveau fashion, experimented with several arts including furniture design, book illustration, painting, leaden glass, and posters. As the 25-year-old Mackintosh put it in a lecture he delivered in 1893: "Architecture is the world of art and as it is everything visible and invisible that makes the world, so it is all the arts and crafts and industries that make architecture . . . architecture is the synthesis of the fine arts, the commune of the crafts." Although the statement is a plagiarism from a book by W. R. Lethaby, *Architecture, Mysticism and Myth*, published the previous year, it is a good indication of Mackintosh's thinking as well as that of all the Art Nouveau architect-designers.

In 1891 he went to Italy with the prize money from a student competition and it was on his re-

turn to Scotland at the end of the year that his career began. In 1894 he was commissioned by a Glasgow firm of cabinetmakers and started designing several pieces that were simple, severely rectangular "only relieved by the occasional long, taut, sweeping curve that so characterized his graphic work," as Robert Macleod describes them in his 1968 biography of Mackintosh. For his furniture he used dark brown or green stains, avoided varnish, and the result was not far from the simpler products of the English Arts and Crafts movement. The main difference, in Macleod's words, "lay in Mackintosh's tendency to make the structural members slender, often extremely so, with a resulting delicacy and refinement that contrasts with the English homely robustness." The British precedent for this linear quality was the highly popular furniture style initiated by Whistler's English architect friend E. W. Godwin. And of course the drawings of Aubrey Beardsley were another influence. From the beginning, then, Mackintosh's furniture is simple and austere and closer to the work of the modern movement than to Continental Art Nouveau.

In 1900 Mackintosh married Margaret Macdonald, another member of The Four as were her sister Frances and the latter's husband Herbert McNair. Also in 1900 the Glasgow group was invited to exhibit at the 8th Secessionist exhibition in Vienna where the Mackin-

A Mackintosh fireplace surrounded by some of his furniture includes an oak table and barrel-shaped chairs designed for domino playing. The table is one of a series made first for the Argyle Street Tearooms in 1897 and later repeated in the Ingram Street Tearooms about 1911 where it was joined by the chairs.

toshes were received with great acclaim. While the *Neue Freie Presse* wrote somewhat derisively of the "foreign 'moderns' " who "Opulently . . . indulge in pretended simplicity . . . prehistoric magic images, hiding-boxes of the sorcerer, furniture for fetishes . . ." a more sympathetic review of their work was written by the critic Ludwig Hevesi: "One of the interiors . . . lies quite beyond good and evil. . . . In the total there is a simplicity which appears to enjoy itself with virtuosity. From an iron stable lantern or from two lumps of lead it fashions a charming lamp which even gets bought. . . . The artists hardly spend their family life in such rooms but perhaps they have a special ghosts' room in the house, hobgoblin's closet or something like that, as other people have a guest room, and this is the way it looks. . . ."

The most appreciative and most descriptive account of Mackintosh's work, however, is to be found in Friedrich Ahlers-Hestermann's book *Stilwende*: "Here we found the strangest mixture of puritanically severe forms and lyrical sublimation of the practical. These rooms were like dreams; everywhere there are small panels, grey silk, the slenderest vertical shafts of wood, small rectangular sideboards with upper edges that jut out, so smooth that their different parts merge into one, so straightforward that they look as innocent and serious as young girls about to receive Holy Communion—and altogether unreal. There was also a decorative piece like a jewel, destined for some place or other, and it seemed inconceivable that its lines should be anywhere broken, lines of a shy elegance . . . like a tenuous and distant echo of van de Velde. The fascination that these proportions exerted, and the aristocratically spontaneous certainty with which a piece of enamel or stained glass or wrought iron was placed, enchanted all artists. . . . Here were mysticism and asceticism, although far removed from the Christian sense of the former word, with a strong scent of heliotrope, and a feel of well-cared-for hands, and of delicate sensuality. As if in contrast to the exuberance of what had gone before there was scarcely anything in these rooms except two upright chairs, with backs as tall as a man, which stood on a white carpet, looking at each other over a slender table, silently like ghosts."

But ghostlike or not there is no hesitation in a Mackintosh chair. It is as direct as an abstraction by Franz Kline. And, as Ahlers-Hestermann implies, Mackintosh's furniture is always a poetic part of the interior it furnishes. Perhaps Pevsner best explains the essence of a Mackintosh interior when he says that to understand the architect "it is essential to grasp the fusion in his art of puritanism and sensuality. The enchanting curves of Art Nouveau have the same importance as the austere verticals of the incipient Modern Movement, and the blacks and whites

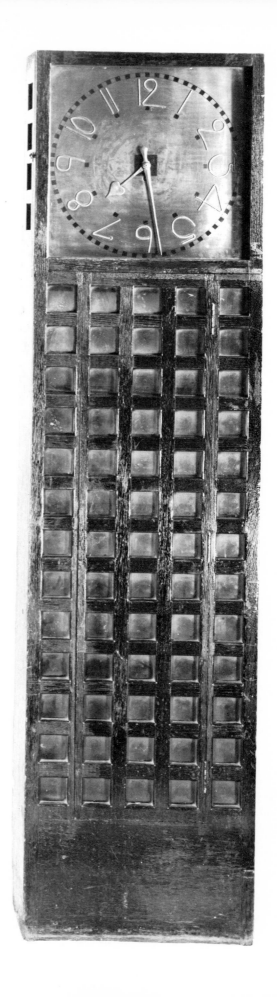

Opposite page: Tall clock of 1904 designed by Mackintosh for the Willow Tearooms is of oak with a dark stain finish.

Right: Mackintosh designed this small table, c. 1906, for the music room of Miss Cranston's own house, House'hill, at Nitshill, Glasgow. Of oak with a dark stain finish, it was originally painted white.

Below: Dining table and chairs designed by Mackintosh for B. Lowke in 1918.

are as essential as the soft pinks and violets. Everything is extremely seductive, but far from pure." Thus Mackintosh's puritanical high-backed chairs are as much a part of the harmony of his rooms as the sensual color schemes or the wall panels in which, as Pevsner notes, he discovered the necessity and the possibilities of abstract art "several years before Picasso and Kandinsky had begun their efforts to liberate art from nature."

As a result of the highly successful Scottish exhibition in Vienna, Mackintosh and his Viennese colleague Josef Hoffmann seem to have become admiring friends and near collaborators. Dr. Eduard F. Sekler tells us that a Mackintosh cabinet shown at the Secession was purchased by Dr. Hugo Henneberg for whom Hoffmann was designing a house. The Mackintosh cabinet was placed in the house right beside a writing desk that Hoffmann had especially designed for the purpose. And in 1902 both Hoffmann and Mackintosh designed rooms for Fritz Wärndorfer's house in Vienna. Another indication of the close ties that existed between Mackintosh and his Viennese colleagues is a letter the Scottish architect wrote to Wärndorfer in 1903 about the projected Wiener Werkstäate, which was founded that year by Hoffmann, Koloman Moser, and Wärndorfer. In his letter Mackintosh suggests that if they want to achieve an artistic success with the Werkstäate, "every object which you pass from your hand must carry an outspoken mark of individuality, beauty and most exact execution. From the outset your aim must be that every object which you produce is made for a certain purpose and place. Later . . . you can emerge boldly into the full light of the world, attack the factory-trade on its own ground, and the greatest work that can be achieved in the century, you can achieve: namely the production of objects of use in magnificent form and at such a price that they lie within the buying range of the poorest. . . . But . . . first the 'artistic' (pardon the word) scoffers must be overcome; and those who are influenced by these scoffers must be taught . . . that the modern movement is not a silly hobby-horse of a few who wish to achieve fame comfortably through eccentricity, but that the modern movement is something living, something good, the only possible art. . . . Yes—the plan which Hoffmann and Moser have designed is great and

Opposite page: Main bedroom in Hill House at Helensburgh of 1902–1903, one of Mackintosh's significant architectural achievements, shows how he built furniture into the room as an integral part of the whole. A medley of strict verticals and horizontals is contrasted with such unexpected curves as those in the linear decoration of the wardrobes.

Right: The chair from which this tall ladderback chair of ebonized wood was reproduced still occupies its original position in the Hill House bedroom (see opposite page).

splendidly thought through. . . . If I were in Vienna, I would assist with a great shovel! . . ."

I n the meantime Mackintosh was gaining a reputation in his native Scotland with, among other things, a series of tearooms he designed in Glasgow for Miss Catherine Cranston—a lady who had not only a flair for the dramatic but an urge to lure the citizens of that industrial city away from hard liquor to her hygienic and high-styled tearooms. They combined the facilities of gentlemen's lunch clubs with the gentilities of ladies' afternoon tea. Mackintosh executed work along with other designers in some of the earlier Cranston tearooms, but the Ingram Street Tearooms of 1901 was all Mackintosh—china, silverware, chairs, tables, vases, tablecloths, carpets, murals, and so on. And for the Willow Tearooms of 1902–1904, he designed the building itself as well as the interiors and all their furnishings. The elegant and sophisticated atmosphere that characterized all four Cranston tearooms, however, was obviously Mackintosh's doing. A wall decoration in one of the earlier tearooms features the femme fatale, so typical of Art Nouveau, but here she takes on a Celtic air and might easily be imagined as the occupant of one of Mackintosh's high-backed chairs.

As an example of the Scottish architect's sometimes "quixote delight in pursuing functional considerations to inventive ends," Macleod points to the chairs he designed for the earlier Argyle Street Tearooms of 1897 where the "buttock-shaped recesses in the wooden stool surfaces would certainly require a posterior commitment of unreasonable accuracy." Although one usually associates Mackintosh with those distinctive, high-backed, thronelike chairs, he also designed low, almost cubical ones. Both types were used in the tearooms as well as in many other Mackintosh interiors. Macleod's description of the two chair types is worth quoting. The low chairs, he says, were "in fact based on the cube, that simplest and most static of proportional forms, but the constituent parts were assembled as lapping planes, maintaining their separate identity. The very tall chairs, which tended to be more conventional in their assembly, were nonetheless so attenuated as to make them entirely linear objects, and to deny any determinate relationship between, say, seat and back." This is easily established, Macleod points out, "by comparing two similar chairs in which the height of the backs differs by several inches; a variation which in conventional chairs would have a critical visual effect becomes quite irrelevant. Similarly in his fondness for thin, over-

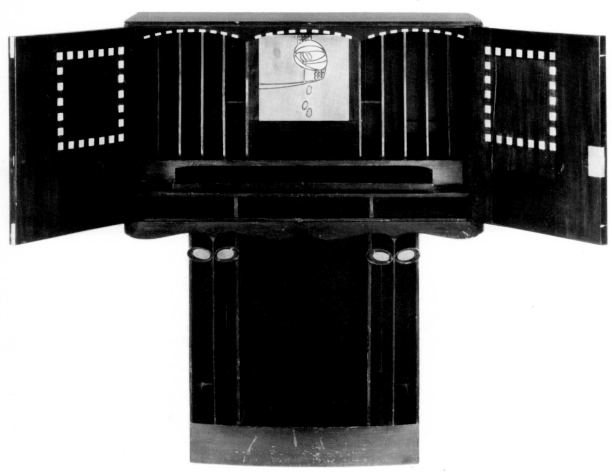

Above: This Mackintosh chair with its sloping arms and slats that grow progressively wider as they reach the floor has the sureness of all his furniture as well as his architecture.

Left: High-backed oak chair with a dark stain finish was one of those designed for the central tables in the Argyle Street Tearooms, c. 1897. The same design was used by the Mackintoshes as their own dining chairs.

Opposite page: Desk designed by Mackintosh for himself in 1904 brought $177,456 at auction in 1979. Of dark stained wood, the twin doors covering the upper writing cabinet are enlivened with crosshatches of honey-toned wood. Stylized mauve glass flowers accent the semiopen base. With its twin doors open, Mackintosh's desk reveals a glittering panel of leaded green, white, and mirror glass set in zinc and mother-of-pearl squares inset in the doors and under the arched framing.

lapping planes as tops for tables, chests of drawers, and indeed buildings, the emphasis is entirely on surface and plane rather than on any precise proportional relationship with the other parts of the assembly."

Mackintosh used furniture, much as Wright did, to define space. His chairs, particularly the characteristic high-backed ones, often act as screens effectively shutting one off from everything behind as the chairs do in Wright's Prairie house dining rooms. But while Wright would have been glad to do without movable furniture altogether, Mackintosh's movable pieces are as much a part of the room as the walls. To remove them is to deface the picture. Mackintosh's furniture, moreover, retains its interest out of its context as Wright's rarely does. Altogether the Scottish architect's interiors create an extraordinary sensation of organic wholeness, but because of his "real grasp and control of the actual functioning of the room," as Macleod explains it, they are not oppressively immobile. "People, curiously enough, are not out of place within them, although it must be acknowledged that certain kinds of furniture would be." Neither Wright nor anyone else brought internal space more boldly to life than Mackintosh did.

That his designs and his words were not far apart can be deduced from his own statement: "The only truly modern individual art in proportion in form and in colour is produced by an emotion, produced by a frank and intelligent understanding of the absolute and true requirements of a building or object—a scientific knowledge of the possibilities and beauties of material, a fearless application of emotion and knowledge, a cultured intelligence, and a mind artistic yet not too indolent to attempt the task of clothing in grace and beauty the new forms and conditions that modern developments of life—social, commercial, and religious, insist upon."

Mackintosh, like all Art Nouveau artists and architects, was preoccupied with beauty. He believed, moreover, that all creative effort must not only be stimulated by nature but grow out of function. Beyond that we have the splendid effectiveness of his furniture in the setting for which he intended it. Although, as has been said, the character of Mackintosh's furniture derived from Gothic chairs and cabinets (as Morris's also did), it underwent fascinating transformations in his inspired hands. Everything he did, in fact, had an entirely personal stamp. Sometimes his furniture is painted white, sometimes it is stained dark green or black, and sometimes it is decorated with a stenciled flower design or other ornamentation, but it is always pure Mackintosh.

Art Nouveau in the hands of Mackintosh and a few others was not so much a strange interlude in the continuing evolution of architecture and design as it was one of the last chapters of a story that probably began when Noah designed the ark. After Art Nouveau, the machine took over in earnest and became the determining factor in design in spite of a few valiant attempts to counteract it. In America Art Nouveau never achieved anything like its European popularity except in the work of Tiffany and possibly the architecture of Louis Sullivan. One explanation of this is that to America with its comparative youth, the machine was never the traumatic experience it was to older countries with their long history of handcrafts.

Mackintosh's active career lasted less than 20 years. He received his first major commission for the Glasgow School of Art in 1896, followed by a number of important private commissions including two significant houses—Windy Hill in Kilmacolm of 1899–1901 and Hill House in Helensburgh of 1902–1903—and he designed furniture and furnishings for all of them. His career virtually ended in 1913 when he resigned from the architectural firm that had become Honeyman, Keppie and Mackintosh in 1904. He went to England where his work had never been appreciated and eventually to the south of France. But no matter how brief his career nor how few his commissions, his influence was amazingly extensive on the Continent as well as in America. Mackintosh was admired by Le Corbusier, Gropius, and other members of the modern movement. Mies van der Rohe called him "a purifier in the field of architecture," and he was that in the field of furniture design too. His austere white interiors, unified and uncluttered, with fitted cupboards and tall rectilinear furniture, have all the spirit of the best modern design of the 1930s, and his masterpiece, the Glasgow School of Art, has often been considered closer to the work of the modern movement than that of Art Nouveau. Mackintosh died in 1928 a poor and forgotten man, but in 1979 the desk he designed for himself in 1904 sold in London for $177,456—a record high for a piece of 20th-century furniture. But is that not the often-told tale of genius?

This early photograph of the library in Mackintosh's Glasgow School of Art of 1897–1899 shows the original center table and Mackintosh's version of a windsor chair. The carvings which decorate and perforate the five vertical stretchers at each end of the table correspond to the decoration on the gallery pendants.

THE MODERN MOVEMENT

What a difference between an Adam or Chippendale chair and Rietveld's Zigzag chair or Breuer's Wassily chair. The 18th century—as well as most of the 19th—believed in concealing structure, the 20th in emphasizing it.

The machine was fully accepted by the post-World War I architects and designers. "The Bauhaus believes the machine to be our modern medium of design and seeks to come to terms with it," Walter Gropius wrote in 1923. But the difference between the 18th and 20th centuries is not only the difference between the hand and the machine, but a difference between life styles. Life in the 18th century and much of the 19th was horse-drawn—leisurely, decorous, and gracious. An aristocratic culture prevailed. It could afford and had time for the luxury of ornament in its furniture as well as its literature and art. Tradition was master. By comparison, life in the 20th century became hurried, tense, machine-propelled. It developed furniture that was as appropriate for an office as a house; it stripped literature and art of ornament. A democratic culture with all its waywardness held sway. "Progress" was the key. It is the difference between a Watteau and a Mondrian, between a restoration comedy and *Finnegan's Wake*.

Furniture needed to be recreated to harmonize with the new architecture and new life style, and it needed to conform with contemporary machine methods. Moreover the new designers were aware of what Morris understood intuitively: the machine was a real danger to the design of furniture. While the machine made possible cheap and accurate reproductions of old handcraft patterns, it turned out dead copies of those patterns whose beauty depended on the life-giving talent of the hand. The designer of furniture, then, was faced with a new problem. Not only did he have to work with a manufacturer who employed machines, he had a whole new array of materials to work with including steel, aluminum, plastics, and plywood. Although technology was not new, these new 20th-century designers were among the first to realize that the machine had its own characteristics and could produce esthetically pleasing objects if the designer understood its potentialities as well as its limitations.

The main difference between Morris's ideas and those of the modern architects was that Morris repudiated the machine and tried to restore the medieval status of the craftsman. The Bauhaus, however, considered the machine an extension of the hand, a thing to be used and tamed by the individual. Thus, in the view of the Bauhaus, the craftsman might be brought back into the industrialized 20th century. Artists and architects alike embraced the imagery of industry and technology. Perhaps Marcel Breuer explained it best when he wrote in 1934: "The origin of the Modern Movement was not technological, for technology had been developed long before it was thought of. What the New Architecture did was to civilise technology. Its real genius was a growing consciousness of the spirit of our age." It also should be mentioned that the modern movement did not spring full-blown out of the Bauhaus. It was probably Mackintosh who first used the phrase when he explained to Fritz Wärndorfer in 1903: ". . . the modern movement is not a silly hobby-horse of a few who wish to achieve fame comfortably through eccentricity . . . the modern movement is something living, something good, the only possible art. . . ." The term "modern," in fact, had acquired currency as far back as 1896 when Otto Wagner published his *Moderne Architectur*, and the Art Nouveau glassmaker and furniture designer Emile Gallé was talking about "modern furniture" in 1900.

For our purposes, however, the modern movement began immediately after World War I when an intellectual quickening in the arts was exemplified by De Stijl in Holland, Cubism in France, and Constructivism in Russia and when architects took it upon themselves not only to design the furniture for their buildings but to set standards for the future. Furniture, they decreed, must participate in the new architectural spirit. There were of course architects in earlier periods such as Robert Adam who made names for themselves as chair designers, but, as Peter Collins points out in *Changing Ideals in Modern Architecture 1750–1950*, it wasn't until this century that "the ultimate test of architectural genius became whether or not one could design a new kind of chair." And it might be worth noting that architects have been responsible for the only really significant innovations in furniture design and furniture technology in this century.

The five architects discussed in this chapter were chiefly influenced by the ideas of the Bauhaus and De Stijl. The Bauhaus was founded at Weimar in 1919 by Walter Gropius. "The ultimate aim of the visual arts," stated Gropius in the Bauhaus manifesto, "is the complete building!" The purpose of the school, he said, was "to educate architects, painters, and sculptors of all levels . . . to become competent craftsmen or independent creative artists and to form a working community of leading and future artist-craftsmen. These men of kindred spirit," he added, "will know how to design buildings harmoniously in their entirety— structure, finishing, ornamentation, and furnishing." For more than a decade the Bauhaus was a focal point of creative energy in Europe. It was at the Bauhaus in 1925 that Breuer produced the first tubular-steel chair.

De Stijl was a movement in Holland made up of a group of artists formed by Theo van Doesburg at Leyden in 1917 who sought to attain a plastic language which would be valid in both architecture and painting. The Dutch group, particularly Van Doesburg and Rietveld, reduced furniture design to its essentials, remolding the chair along uncompromisingly geometric lines.

Like Schindler, these architects had a new conception of space which gave furniture a new meaning. But whereas Schindler made his Unit Furniture an actual part of the floor, these architects wanted furniture that was self-sufficient and would allow space to flow freely through it, and they wanted it to take up as little room as possible. Thus the use of plywood and steel tubing. Wright also wanted furniture that would take up as little room as possible and would allow space to flow through it, but the difference is obvious to anyone who compares a room in a Wright Prairie house with a room by Mies or Breuer.

Although they shared many ideas with the architects of an Arts and Crafts or Art Nouveau persuasion, the architects of the modern movement, unlike their predecessors, designed furniture that could be mass produced. It was no longer a question of designing particular pieces for particular interior spaces. Although Wright sometimes used the same chair in different houses, those chairs were not mass produced in the same sense and not used by other architects. Of course some of the chairs of the modern movement such as Mies's Barcelona and Tugendhat chairs were originally designed for a particular place, but no matter how diverse the pieces produced by these architects they were compatible with one another. The diversity, in fact, is extraordinary.

As might be expected when painters and architects become allied as they did at the Bauhaus and among the De Stijl group, they shared the same vision. Sir John Summerson has suggested that it was actually the abstract and Cubist painters who opened up a world of form which was subsequently explored by the architects. But Theodore Brown in *The Work of G. Rietveld* makes a good case for a reverse influence. While Rietveld's Red and Blue chair of 1918 bears an obvious visual relationship to a Mondrian painting, Brown points out that the Dutch architect "had combined lines, primary colors and unbroken planes in a manner anticipatory of Mondrian's mature works." Perhaps, Brown says, "the two phenomena were simply parallel." In any case, there is no doubt that there was a give and take between architecture and painting that hadn't even existed among the Art Nouveau designers who moved freely from fine art to furniture and almost everything in between. The architects built in a painterly way and the artists painted in an architectural way—especially the Cubist and De Stijl artists. Everyone designed furniture including Mondrian, and Le Corbusier was a painter before he was an architect. By the time Aalto began designing his plywood chairs in the 1930s, the rectilinear geometry of a Mondrian began to be replaced by the serpentine curves of an Arp.

Almost all the architects of the modern movement were socially conscious. They wanted to design chairs as well as houses, factories, and entire cities that would make the world a better place. It may have been naive, but it partook of an optimism and enthusiasm that are missing today. It produced, moreover, some handsome chairs and handsome buildings.

GERRIT RIETVELD 1888–1964

Our furniture, be it chairs, tables, or cupboards, represents the abstract-concrete objects of our future interiors. THEO VAN DOESBURG

The Dutch were the first to project the new ideas of the modern movement into furniture design, and Gerrit Rietveld was probably the most successful of them. He once said, "To sit is a verb too," and he truly explored some of the more unusual ways that verb can be conjugated.

Rietveld was born in Utrecht. He left school in 1899 when he was eleven to work in his father's cabinetmaking shop. He couldn't have been much older than that when he designed a table and chairs to be used in the gatehouse of a castle near Utrecht, which, in the words of his biographer Theodore Brown, were "admirably adapted to the medieval character of the room." But while that furniture was still more or less traditional, around 1917 Rietveld began to design pieces that were fully attuned to the new architecture, perhaps more so than the furniture of any other modern architect. His famous Red and Blue chair of 1918, for example, may have been less successful in a traditional sense than some of Wright's early chairs, but it served as a remarkable archetype of the new architectural theories, particularly those of the De Stijl movement.

Most furniture historians seem to be a little embarrassed by the early furniture designed by the pioneers of the modern movement, which is not surprising since it ignores traditional considerations such as comfort and beauty while going merrily on its own eccentric way. Obviously considerations other than comfort determined its design in Rietveld's case no less than in Wright's. And Rietveld, it is worth noting, had thoroughly familiarized himself with Wright's furniture when he copied some of it for the owners of a Wright-influenced house designed by the Dutch architect Robert van't Hoff. The latter was so impressed by the copies that he introduced Rietveld to members of the De Stijl movement. In 1919 Rietveld joined De Stijl and thus became familiar with and known to Holland's avant-garde artists and architects. The De Stijl group believed the age demanded a new beauty in painting, sculpture, and architecture and set about achieving it. Of course in the revolutionary years following World War I such an aim was not limited to the Netherlands nor was it limited to architects and artists. It need only be remembered that in 1918 when Rietveld's Red and Blue chair appeared, James Joyce was trying to get *Ulysses* published. Mondrian looked at painting as if it had never existed before, and Rietveld approached a chair as if no such thing had ever been constructed. "Moving around or within a rectangular building or object," Mondrian said, "it can be seen as two-dimensional, for our era abandons the static vision of the past." Mondrian believed, as Peter Collins explains it, that his abstract paintings "expressed a three-dimensional reality whereby the whole of nature was to be conceived as essentially a series of planes, and that even architectural compositions must be thought of as a similar series of planes, rather than as volumes and masses bounded by traditional facades." Thus the aim of the De Stijl group which clustered around Mondrian was "to destroy the isolation of objects in space and to treat form and space as something universally integrated. . . ." And so the De Stijl architects, as Wright had done before them, created more open plans, and Rietveld, as Wright had tried to do before him, created furniture that allowed space to penetrate it and pass through it, thus destroying its isolation in space.

Gerrit Rietveld's famous Red and Blue chair of 1918 was called by Siegfried Giedion a manifesto which guided the direction of an entire development.

The rectangle, as Mondrian saw it, was a form "where lines cross or touch tangentially, *but do not cease to continue. . . .*" And that can serve equally well as a description of Rietveld's Red and Blue chair, his 1919 buffet, or his Schroder house, as it does for a Mondrian painting. Thus it isn't surprising that the Red and Blue chair is often called the most compact visual statement of the principles of De Stijl nor that it formed the basis of Rietveld's own architecture. Siegfried Giedion refers to both the chair and buffet as "manifestoes" which "guide the direction of an entire development," adding that "No assembly line, no routineer, can supply the fantasy they embody. As furniture is broken down to make a fresh start possible, its elements resolve into a system of struts and planes. Its form is as neutral as possible." Rietveld himself said that with his Red and Blue chair "an attempt has been made to have every part simple and in its most elementary form in accordance with function and material, the form, thus, which is most capable of being harmonized with the whole. The construction is attuned to the parts to insure that no part dominates or is subordinate to the others. In this way the whole stands freely and clearly in space, and the form stands out from the material."

Color, too, was an important element of the Red and Blue chair. The back is painted red, the seat blue, the frame is black with the ends of each rail painted yellow. When placed against a dark wall and floor as it was in the Schroder house, the black frame becomes submerged in its background while the bright colors increase the discontinuous quality. "The clearer and purer the architecture, the less color is needed," Rietveld later admitted, but, he added, "frequently space is improved by color through the absorption of some planes and reflection of others."

Although Rietveld studied architecture, he was first of all a furniture maker and designer. The chair came first, the house later. The year before he died he told an interviewer that when he made the Red and Blue chair, "I did not realize that it would have such an enormous significance for me and also for others, nor did I imagine that its effect would be so overwhelming even in architecture. When the opportunity arose for me to build a house based on the same principles, I naturally did not let it pass by." He was, of course, referring to the Schroder house of 1924–1925 which, according to Reyner Banham, is one of "two works of world consequence" for which Rietveld was responsible. The other, of course, is the Red and Blue chair.

Mrs. Schroder, who commissioned Rietveld to design a house for her in Utrecht, was much more than just a client. She actually collaborated with Rietveld on the design of the

Above: The so-called Military chair, because it was designed by Rietveld in 1923 for a military club, is of ebonized oak with seat and back lacquered white.

Opposite page: The Zigzag chair designed by Rietveld in 1934 was made of elmwood with an untreated surface. Other versions lacquered red or green edged in white were used by him in several country houses he designed between 1938 and 1942.

Rietveld designed this crate furniture in 1934 using precut boxwood parts to be assembled by the user.

house, particularly the interior. She was, in fact, apparently responsible for the extreme openness and flexibility of the upper floor plan. In 1929 Henry-Russell Hitchcock called the Schroder house "one of the most original achievements of the New Pioneers" and particularly noted the ingenious moving partitions which "made it possible to utilize the upper story as one room or four, and the furniture, of which Rietveld had previously been particularly a maker, completed the extraordinary effect of a piece of abstract sculpture enlarged to architectural size." In addition to the Red and Blue chair the Schroder house was furnished with many Rietveld pieces designed especially for it, including lamps and storage cabinets.

Rietveld designed other buildings but comparatively few of them were constructed. He was, however, continually experimenting with new chairs. In 1923 he exhibited a chair at the Bauhaus in Weimar and with the painter Huszar designed a model room for an exhibition in Berlin for which the so-called Berlin chair was designed. Theodore Brown has pointed out that in the Berlin chair Rietveld literally "sketched" a model of the space construction of the Schroder house built the following year. In the 1920s he experimented with tubular steel furniture, and in 1927, a few years before Aalto began to work with bent plywood, he designed a bent fiberboard chair in order to exploit the properties of curved surfaces. In 1934 he designed what might well have been the first knock-down furniture consisting of precut parts made of wood generally used for crates and easily assembled by the layperson into bookcases, chairs, and tables at little cost. Also in 1934, still trying to find a form that would interrupt even less space in the volume of a room, Rietveld came up with his famous Zigzag chair. Made simply of four planes of wood, it blends into space in a most self-effacing way and has the added advantage of stacking for easy storage. Even if Peter Blake has called the Zigzag chair "some sort of climactic crisis" of the "Modern Movement's love-hate relationship with the human anatomy," it follows De Stijl principles, and as Daniele Baroni points out in *The Furniture of Gerrit Thomas Rietveld*, the Dutch architect's "introduction of the oblique line brought into the vast panorama of chair design a completely new morphology which no one before him had ever imagined." Made of

elmwood, the original version was left in its natural state, but versions lacquered red or green and edged in white were used by Rietveld in some country houses he designed between 1938 and 1942. In 1942 he designed a stamped aluminum chair. And a few months before his death he designed a new chair for a jewelry shop he remodeled in The Hague called the "Steltman" chair after the client for whom it was designed. It was made of natural oak and constructed of parallelepipeds which form a series of L shapes. The idea of the Steltman chair, as Daniele Baroni puts it, "was a perfect exemplification of neoplasticism and shows how Rietveld was the most representative architect of the De Stijl group in an absolute sense."

Some of Rietveld's chairs may seem entirely dissimilar, but one idea informs them all, and that is best explained by the designer himself: "The fact that I am constantly concerned with this extraordinary idea of the awakening the consciousness, may account for my work to be inevitably oriented toward spatial problems. Scaling an undefined space to human proportions may be achieved by a line drawn on a road, a floor, a wall, a covering surface, a combination of vertical and horizontal planes, curved or flat, transparent or massive. It is never a partitioning or closing off, but always a defining element of what is here and there, above and below, between and around."

We may not think Rietveld's chairs either beautiful or functional, but, as Theodore Brown has said, they "are not only refreshing excursions into the realm of materials and techniques but are suggestions of new ways of seeing and of sitting." They were so unlike any traditional idea of a chair in the 1920s that it is not surprising that they were rarely appreciated by the ordinary person. It took other New Pioneers at the Bauhaus and elsewhere to grasp what Rietveld was trying to do and appreciate the results. "Every true creation," as Rietveld put it, "(whether it appears in the form of invention, building, painting, dance or music) alters the insight, the demands and needs of former times. Therefore, a creation must conquer the era rather than to simply fulfill its demands and necessities."

Certainly in the realm of furniture Rietveld will always be considered a great innovator and purifier as Mondrian was in painting.

MARCEL BREUER Born 1902

The tubular steel chair is as truly a part of the heroic period of the new architecture as are the transparent shells of glass that replace bearing-walls. SIEGFRIED GIEDION

Marcel Breuer, who flew in an airplane before he rode in an automobile, must be given credit for being the first architect to come up with furniture that was both a valid machine product and esthetically appealing. He got his inspiration for his tubular steel chairs, stools, and tables from looking at the handlebars of his bicycle. "Mass production and standardization," Breuer told Paul Heyer (*Architects on Architecture*), "had already made me interested in polished metal, in shiny and impeccable lines in space, as new components of our interiors. I considered such polished and curved lines not only symbolic of our modern technology, but actually to be technology." Although Breuer was not yet an architect when he designed his first chair, he recognized that the approach to designing a chair was not dissimilar to that of designing a building. "The stresses on a chair," he once said, "are heavier than those on the factory floor."

Breuer was born in Pécs in southern Hungary, the son of a doctor. When he was 18 he left Pécs to enter the Vienna Art Academy, but, according to his own statement, he walked into the academy and out again. "I saw it was not for me." After that abortive attempt to study painting and sculpture, Breuer left for Weimar to enter Gropius's recently formed Bauhaus. He, like many another youth, had been attracted by the leaflet Gropius had sent out claiming that the Bauhaus would "one day want to conceive and create the new building of the future . . . that will rise to heaven from the hands of millions of craftsmen as a crystal symbol of a new faith."

Breuer was at the Bauhaus from 1920 until 1928, first as a student and then as a master and head of the carpentry and furniture depart-

ment. While there he devoted some time to painting, but, as is well known, it was his furniture experiments that eventually resulted in a new look for the chair, certainly one of the oldest pieces of household equipment. (Of course Rietveld's Red and Blue chair had appeared in 1918, but, innovative as its form was, its material was the traditional wood.) Henry-Russell Hitchcock, in his introduction to a 1938 Breuer exhibition at Harvard's Graduate School of Design, found Breuer's furniture of an "elementary nature," but "elementary in a deep sense, built up from an analysis of details of function and expressed in basic geometrical forms without reference to existing or earlier traditions."

In 1923 the Bauhaus presented a small exhibition house designed by the painter George Muche and furnished with Breuer's furniture, many pieces of which he had built by hand in the carpentry shop. Wolf von Eckardt tells us that this early wood furniture was produced at a time when it was said that Breuer "slept in the bathtub of some den which he shared with two women." But whatever may have been the outcome of the bathtub episode, this early furniture and the handlebars of his bicycle soon led to the invention of the first tubular steel chair in 1925—a steel chair not intended for the kitchen or the barbershop but for the living room. This, of course, was the famous model he later called the "Wassily" chair named after the painter Wassily Kandinsky for whose house on the Bauhaus campus it was designed. In the Wassily chair, as Hitchcock said, Breuer clarified the germ of an idea contained in his early wood chairs—"the separation of functions in any design-object, and the expression of that separation by visual

The Wassily—first bent tubular-steel chair designed by Breuer at the Bauhaus in 1925. "I considered such polished and curved lines not only symbolic of our modern technology, but actually technology itself."

and structural means." For Breuer, the framework which is the weight-supporting unit in any design became a distinct entity expressed in structural terms. The nonstructural parts with which the human comes in contact were of a less abstract, softer character. Thus the back and seat of Breuer's first tubular-steel chair were conceived as quite separate from the supporting parts, as they had been in Rietveld's Red and Blue chair. In Breuer's chair, however, steel tubes replace the wooden rails of the supporting structure, and fabric replaces the planks of the seat and arms. In Breuer's chair the elasticity of the steel tubing worked with the taut canvas to spring the seat, the back, and armrests. Unlike the traditional deck chair, Breuer explained in *Berliner Tageblatt* of October 19, 1929, the "taut cloth forming the back rests and seats" of his chair "are of a material so far used for tropical belts and boot-laces—the traditional materials

thus take on a new meaning, with unknown and so far overlooked potentialities. . . ." And thus bicycles, belts, and bootlaces are brought together to make the first bent-steel chair to inhabit the living room—"a delightful Constructivist object," as Hitchcock calls it, "overly complicated, perhaps, but extraordinarily refined." Wright, of course, had designed metal furniture in 1904 for the Larkin Company administration building in Buffalo but certainly not for his houses. Metal for the home was a daring departure in the face of Arts and Crafts traditions which were still flourishing in the 1920s.

"A frequent criticism of steel furniture," Breuer wrote in 1927, "is that it is cold, clinical, reminiscent of an operating theatre. But these are concepts which flourish from one day to the next. They are the product of habit, soon destroyed by another habit." And of course he was right. "Basically," he pointed out, "a well-

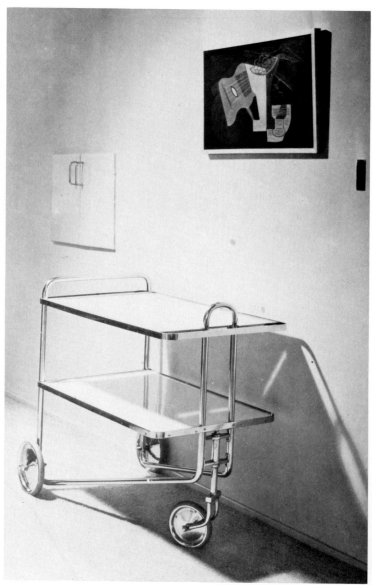

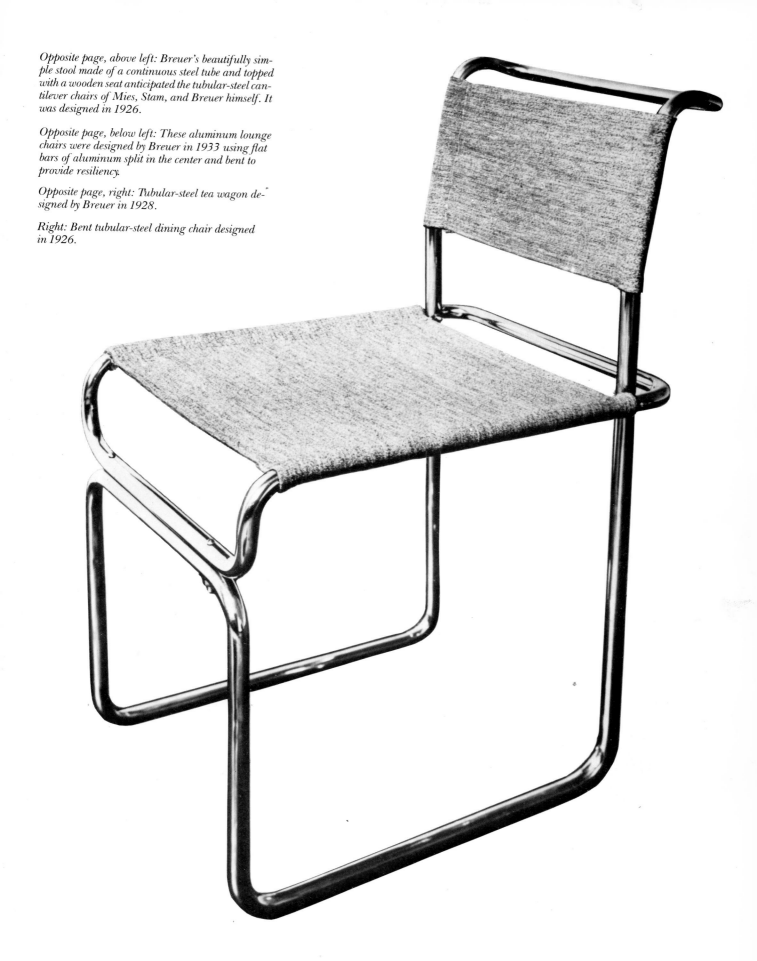

Opposite page, above left: Breuer's beautifully simple stool made of a continuous steel tube and topped with a wooden seat anticipated the tubular-steel cantilever chairs of Mies, Stam, and Breuer himself. It was designed in 1926.

Opposite page, below left: These aluminum lounge chairs were designed by Breuer in 1933 using flat bars of aluminum split in the center and bent to provide resiliency.

Opposite page, right: Tubular-steel tea wagon designed by Breuer in 1928.

Right: Bent tubular-steel dining chair designed in 1926.

Right: Breuer's tubular-steel cantilever armchair with caning framed in bentwood. This chair was designed shortly after Breuer left the Bauhaus, c. 1928.

Below: Lounge chair of tubular steel with natural woven reed and beech wood armrests designed by Breuer, c. 1930.

Opposite page: Dining area in the second Breuer-designed Geller house at Lawrence, Long Island, in 1967–1969, with the architect's ever-popular tubular-steel cantilever chairs.

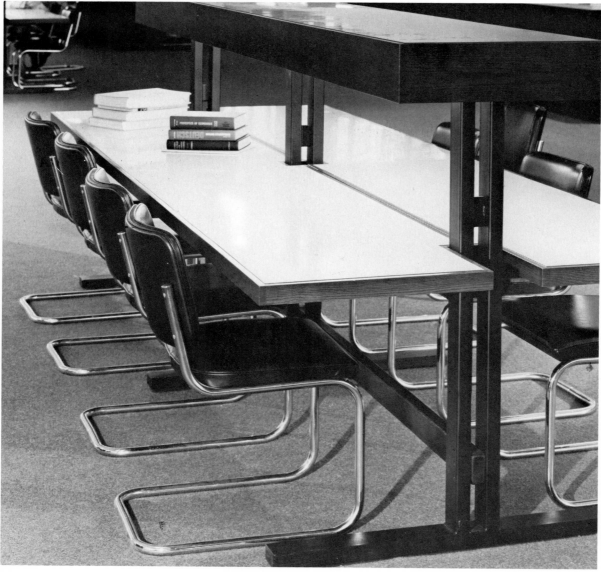

constructed steel chair will be better able to cope with static loads than an equally well constructed wooden chair, which means that for the same static loads, a steel chair can be substantially lighter. A chair made of high-grade steel tubing (a highly elastic material) with tightly stretched fabric in the appropriate places, makes a light, completely self-sprung seat which is as comfortable as an upholstered chair, but is many times lighter, handier and more hygienic, and therefore many times more practical in use." He goes on to explain that the "severe rationalisation of components—the use of the same components in this type of furniture, the possibility of reducing them to two-dimensional parts (over fifty club armchairs can be packed into a space of one cubic metre, with obvious advantages for transport), and a full regard for industrial and manufacturing considerations all contributed to the social yardstick of a price which could be paid by the broadest possible mass of the population. And I might say that without meeting the yardstick, I could not have found the project particularly satisfactory."

After the Bauhaus moved to Dessau and Gropius's new buildings were completed in 1926, Breuer furnished them, as well as the masters' houses, with his tubular steel furniture. By this time there were many more designs including the remarkably simple stool made of continuous steel tubing and topped with a wooden seat. Breuer continued to develop his chairs along Constructivist lines—the structural frame becoming increasingly lighter, the seats and backs becoming softer. And all along, as Hitchcock says, "his chairs developed visually from an angularity reminiscent of Cubist painting to smooth, flowing curves. All along the trend was toward more organic forms."

Although Breuer has always been identified with the invention of the steel cantilever chair and his experiments were certainly headed in that direction, he was not the first to introduce it. That honor was apparently shared by the Dutch architect Mart Stam and Mies van der Rohe, both of whose steel cantilever chairs were shown at the 1927 Weissenhof Housing Exposition in Stuttgart which Mies directed. While Breuer's pioneering tubular-steel furniture did appear at the Weissenhof Exposition in Gropius's prefabricated units, his version of the cantilever chair was not produced until a year later. Stam, it seems, had seen Breuer's tubular-steel furniture in the Bauhaus buildings in 1926 and produced his own S-shaped steel cantilever chair soon afterwards. In the meantime, Mies had been working on a steel cantilever chair, and the timetable of events as he relayed it to Nikolaus Pevsner in 1935 is undoubtedly reliable. Breuer's chairs, Mies told Pevsner, were the first to employ tubular steel, but they were still rigid.

Above: Stacking chairs with heavy, laminated frames and light, bent plywood seats and backs, c. 1936.

Opposite page, top: Breuer's cutout plywood furniture in the dining room of the Koerfer house of 1936–1937 in Moscia, Tessin, Switzerland.

Opposite page, bottom: Breuer-designed reading table with integral lighting fixtures and tubular-steel cantilever chairs in the library of St. John's Abbey and University, Collegeville, Minnesota, of 1953–1968.

He described Stam's somewhat crude cantilever chair of 1926, which was made of gas pipes as well as an improved version done in 1927 for the Weissenhof Exposition. But Stam's chair, Mies explained, was not resilient, as the curved sections of the tubular frame had been reinforced by the insertion of solid bars. Therefore, Mies concluded, "I was the first to have exploited consistently the spring quality of steel tubes. I made the experiments in early summer of 1927 and applied for a patent on August 24, 1927." Breuer's cantilever chair was produced in 1928. It was plainly an idea that was in the air, but it is ironic that Breuer who had done the preliminary work and whose cantilever steel chair is the model that has been copied all over the world could not patent his chair. Siegfried Giedion believed the cantilever chair was rooted in a specific demand of the time. The objective was to find a chair "that would seem to hover above the ground like cantilever concrete slabs or houses on stilts, houses surrounded by air. One was drawn to things that seemed to defeat gravitation. This emotional need," he concluded, "is as innate to our own time as the buttress to the Gothic and the undulating wall to the Baroque."

In 1928 Breuer left the Bauhaus and moved to Berlin to try his hand at architecture on his own, but it couldn't have been a worse time. The economic crisis precluded almost all building, and while Breuer fulfilled a couple of architectural commissions, he spent most of his time continuing his furniture experiments. In 1933 he entered an international competition for aluminum furniture held in Paris and won two first prizes. Breuer went to England in 1935 after Hitler made it impossible for anyone to practice modern architecture in Germany, espe-

cially anyone who had been connected with that "hotbed of cultural Bolshevism," as the Nazis called the Bauhaus. Shortly after he arrived he met Jack Pritchard, head of the Isokon firm, who agreed to produce some of the bent plywood furniture Breuer had developed partly from his winning aluminum designs. Although one usually associates Breuer with tubular-steel furniture, he consistently experimented with wood and was particularly attracted to plywood, a material whose possibilities increase with testing. Of his Isokon designs, the elegant form-fitting plywood reclining chair was the most famous, but he also designed a series of simple stacking tables and two types of dining chairs which are also stackable. The chairs have heavy laminated frames and light bent plywood seats and backs.

In 1937 Breuer arrived in the United States where he had been invited by Gropius to join him in partnership and teaching at Harvard's School of Architecture. The partnership lasted until 1941, and in 1946 Breuer left Harvard and moved to New York. He designed no more chairs but there was no need to. "I tried always, in my furniture, to find the last solution," he once said. "My philosophy, to find the simplest way." Furniture, however, never seems to have been far from his mind. Concrete benches and granite tables were often as much a part of his architecture as they were of Le Corbusier's.

When Morris couldn't find the furniture he wanted, he designed it, just as Thoreau made the few pieces for his cabin at Walden and Wright completed his Prairie houses with his own furniture designs. And so too Breuer continued that tradition, creating furniture for the living rooms of the modern technological age.

Above: "Canaan" desk designed by Breuer for his own house in New Canaan, Connecticut, in 1951.

Opposite page: Breuer's own house in Lincoln, Massachusetts, of 1939 designed in partnership with Walter Gropius. This view of the living room shows "Isokon" chairs beside the fireplace and a Calder mobile overhead.

LUDWIG MIES VAN DER ROHE 1886-1969

A chair is a very difficult object. A skyscraper is almost easier. That is why Chippendale is famous. MIES VAN DER ROHE

Mies could not have been far behind Wright in the quantity of furniture designs he made. In the Mies Archive at New York's Museum of Modern Art there are 774 furniture drawings, and he himself spoke of the "graveyards of chairs" when referring to the rejects of his experiments for the renowned Barcelona chair. This is not surprising since Mies's elegantly austere interiors are almost unthinkable without Mies furniture. Mies, however, was never as insistent about having his own furniture in his interiors as Wright was. He often said he designed interiors so that the occupants could live in them as they pleased. The architecture of "nothingness," he thought, allowed those who used the building the opportunity for complete self-expression. "Architecture," Mies said, "is the will of an epoch translated into space—living, changing, new," and indeed the elegant, understated buildings and furniture he created are the will of his epoch—an epoch in which science and reason held supreme. And even if he thought a building should be designed so that it could be adapted to new situations or new ways of life, his tremendous care with the design of his own buildings and their furniture suggests that he would have preferred that they stay the way he did them. As Philip Johnson once pointed out: "Mies gives as much thought to placing chairs in a room as other architects do to placing buildings around a square."

Mies was the last director of the Bauhaus, and is usually recognized as one of the three pioneers of modern architecture along with Wright and Le Corbusier. And it is no coincidence that all three designed furniture. Besides the fact that traditional furniture was completely inappropriate for the new architecture,

the growing influence of industrial design made architects feel challenged to design furniture for their buildings. While the Art Nouveau and Arts and Crafts architects believed the house and all its furnishings should be the creation of the architect, the Bauhaus made it official. As Gropius later wrote in his essay, "Is There a Science of Design?" published in 1947, "the process of designing a great building or a simple chair differs only in degree, not in principle." This may or may not be true, but there can be little doubt that designing furniture was on the minds of most architects worthy of the name in the decade after the First World War, and Mies was probably the most influential of them.

Mies was born in Aachen, Germany, the son of a stone mason. In 1905 when he was still in his teens he was apprenticed to Bruno Paul, the leading furniture designer of the period, who was strongly influenced by Art Nouveau. Mies next worked in the office of Peter Behrens, architect and apostle of the Arts and Crafts movement, where Corbusier and Gropius were already working. Behrens, too, was dedicated to the integration of all design and became one of the first industrial designers in the modern sense. When Mies went to work for him, he was the industrial design consultant for a large German electric company for which he designed their factories, their lighting, their typefaces, and probably their furniture. But while Mies followed his teachers in recognizing the importance of furniture as an element of architecture, his own furniture designs surpassed all their work in its longevity. In fact one of his designs—a reclining frame chair inspired by the deck chairs on ocean liners—was produced for

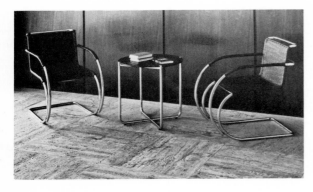

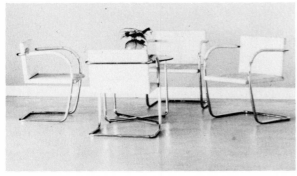

Top: Mies's tubular-steel cantilever chairs and coffee table on the upper level of the Tugendhat house.

Above: Brno chairs with tubular-steel frames and coffee table on the main floor of the Tugendhat house.

From left to right: Original tubular-steel stool with lacquered frame and cane seat designed by Mies in 1927; current model of Mies original tubular-steel cantilever chair designed in 1927; tubular-steel M chair, a version of the Brno chair; current model of the Brno armchair of 1930 designed for the Tugendhat house in Brno, Czechoslovakia. This chair was Mies's attempt to improve on his original tubular-steel cantilever chair of 1927.

the first time by Knoll International in 1977, some 45 years after Mies designed it. And the Barcelona chair, which he designed for the German Pavilion at the 1929 International Exposition in Barcelona, has been used ever since by countless architects and designers all over the world. Henry-Russell Hitchcock has called Mies's Barcelona Pavilion "one of the few buildings by which the twentieth century might wish to be measured against the great ages of the past," and that applies to the elegant furniture that was such an integral part of it. Oddly enough the so-called Barcelona chairs, which have rightly been termed the most beautiful of modern chairs, were designed as a sort of latter-day royal throne. The main function of the German Pavilion in Barcelona, points out Ludwig Glaeser, curator of the Mies van der Rohe Archive at the Museum of Modern Art, was to serve as a setting for an inaugural ceremony in which the Spanish king, Alfonso XIII, was to sign his name into a golden book. Thus the two Barcelona chairs Mies designed for the pavilion were obviously intended for the king and his queen Victoria Eugénie. The only other seats in the pavilion were ottomans placed at a respectful distance from the Barcelona "thrones." The ottoman, in fact, turned out to be one of Mies's most versatile pieces of furniture. Aligned in rows in the Barcelona Pavilion

the ottoman anticipated its later elongation into a bench, according to Glaeser, for Mies's 1962 apartment building at 2400 Lakeview Avenue in Chicago. He also converted the Barcelona ottoman into a coffee table for his own apartment in Chicago by replacing the seat with a travertine top. And of course the Barcelona chairs might almost be called the American equivalent of a royal throne so prevalent have they become as the de rigueur furniture of important spaces in offices and public buildings.

But to go back to 1927, Mies, as First Vice-President of the *Deutscher Werkbund* (founded by architects and industrialists to improve the quality of industrial design in Germany), became the director of the Werkbund's Weissenhof Housing Exposition in Stuttgart, which, in Peter Blake's words, "represented a kind of summary of the total achievement of modern European architecture and furniture up to that moment." Not only were several rooms in the Mies-designed apartment house furnished with his tubular-steel cantilever chairs, his tubular stool, and coffee table with a circular glass top, but Breuer's pioneering tubular-steel chairs and tables, as we have seen, furnished Gropius's prefabricated units, and the Dutch architect Mart Stam furnished his model house with his own tubular-steel cantilever

chairs which he designed in 1926. The first tubular-steel chair, of course, was Breuer's Wassily chair developed at the Bauhaus in 1925. Mies's first tubular-steel chair had its unveiling at the 1927 Weissenhof Exposition.

In 1930 Mies designed a series of new chairs for his Tugendhat house in Brno, Czechoslovakia, which he placed in that elegant setting along with several Barcelona chairs. The Tugendhat house has been called "the first glass house" just as the Barcelona Pavilion has been called the first monument to the International style. Writing of the Tugendhat house in *The Master Builders*, Peter Blake says: "As in every one of his designs, from skyscrapers to dining chairs, Mies reduced each object to its essential elements, and then refined each detail to a point of almost breathtaking beauty and eloquence. There was nothing in this house which did not reflect this process of distillation to the point of utter perfection—not a window mullion, not a heating pipe, not a lighting fixture, not an ash tray." And certainly not a chair or table. The Tugendhat chair, which is based on the cantilever principle of the tubular-steel chairs, is a more complex design than the Barcelona and has never gained the popularity of the latter. Knoll, however, began manufacturing it in 1977 after it had been out of production for more than 40 years so it may yet gain the acclaim of its sister chair,

the Barcelona. The Brno chair, also designed for the Tugendhat house, represented an effort to improve on the original tubular-steel cantilever side chair and make a more comfortable dining chair. This, too, was put into production by Knoll in 1977. The classic square glass-topped coffee table supported by a cross of four bar angles also made its debut at the Tugendhat house. In view of Mies's preoccupation with steel tubing, it comes as a surprise to learn that the furniture he designed for the upper rooms of the Tugendhat house was made entirely of wood. Later, however, as his drawings show, he experimented with ideas for bentwood chairs probably inspired by Aalto.

In 1930 Mies succeeded Gropius at the Bauhaus and remained its director until Nazi intervention forced it to close in 1933. In 1938 he left Germany and settled in Chicago, and that same year he was made Director of Architecture at Armour Institute (later known as the Illinois Institute of Technology) where he remained until he retired 20 years later. Although Mies was continually developing and improving his furniture, he didn't design any new pieces after the 1930s, with the exception of some fascinating studies he made in the early 1940s of plastic chairs. He regarded the existing pieces, Arthur Drexler tells us, as definitive statements which he felt would serve all purposes in his future work. The conchoidal chair studies he made in the 1940s were unlike anything he had done before. Astonishingly sculptural in form, there are literally hundreds of sketches showing numerous variations of the chair. There are one-piece chairs with and without arms, two-piece chairs with and without arms, all with the seat surface modeled after an ordinary tractor seat, but none

of them was ever put into production. Mies, in fact, made many sketches for all his chairs, probably many more than we know. In a 1956 recording, "Conversations Regarding the Future of Architecture," he said: "I often throw things out I like very much. They are dear to my heart, but when I have a better conviction, a clearer idea . . . then I follow the clearer idea. . . . I don't want to be interesting, I want to be good."

Mies's fine sense of proportion, impeccable craftsmanship, and sure knowledge of what to leave out have made his furniture, particularly the Barcelona chair, the most esthetically pleasing of all the furniture produced by the architects of the modern movement. Perhaps it was what has been called his "incredible modesty" that made his hand so sure. But whatever it was, to quote Peter Blake, "no sculpture by Brancusi outdazzles a chair or a table by Mies van der Rohe."

Mies, of course, had his critics. Lewis Mumford, for example, says in *The Highway and the City* that Mies's "hollow glass shells . . . existed alone in the Platonic world of his imagination and had no relation to site, climate, insulation, function, or internal activity; indeed they completely turned their backs upon these realities just as the rigidly arranged chairs of his living rooms openly disregarded the necessary intimacies and informalities of conversation." Nevertheless one can look at those crystalline glass shells with their rigidly arranged chairs and wish the world was like that. A Mies house is precise, lyrical, and leaves room for fantasy. It is like poetry whereas most houses are like prose. A Mies house suggests something more rather than merely expressing what is.

Opposite page, top: Interior of the Barcelona pavilion showing Barcelona ottomans and table placed against marble walls in the reception area.

Opposite page, bottom: The three chairs shown here are the so-called Tugendhat chairs of 1930 in the sitting area of the Tugendhat house for which Mies designed them.

Right: Mies's sketches of the early 1940s for the conchoidal chair, which was never produced, and the classic tractor seat.

LE CORBUSIER 1887-1965

A great epoch has begun.
There exists a new spirit.
There exists a mass of work
conceived in this new spirit,
it is to be met with particularly
in industrial production. . . .

LE CORBUSIER, *Towards a New Architecture*

If Le Corbusier had never designed a single piece of furniture for his own buildings, he still should be acclaimed for having rediscovered Thonet's bentwood chair. Originally designed by Michael Thonet in the first half of the 19th century, it was Le Corbusier who made it almost an indispensable component of the modern interior. Corbu, however, *did* design furniture for his buildings.

Like Wright and Mies, he tried to give form to a poetic vision. He came out of the same milieu as Mies and believed that "the sphere of architecture embraces every detail of household furnishing, the street as well as the house, and a wider world still beyond both." But unlike Wright, Corbu didn't look at furniture as a necessary evil. He thought of it as no less a decorative and essential element of his architecture than his corkscrew staircases. He believed built-in storage walls or dividers (*casiers standard*) would take care of everything that needed to be put into drawers or cupboards while leaving the space free for chairs and tables which he saw as sculpture. Mies probably did too, but, unlike Corbu, he rarely explained his thoughts.

Charles-Edouard Jeanneret (he assumed the name of Le Corbusier in 1923) was born at La Chaux-de-Fonds just across the French border in Switzerland. His father was a craftsman in enamel; his mother was a musician. He entered a local art school when he was 13. At 17 he designed and built his first house at La Chaux-de-Fonds and subsequently set out to educate himself as an architect. That education consisted largely of a four-year walking tour through Europe and the Middle East during which he observed both great and humble architecture at close range and recorded his observations in drawings. He spent six weeks on the Acropolis observing and drawing and found the Parthenon "a pure creation of the mind." In 1908 he went to work in the atelier of Auguste Perret in Paris where he stayed 15 months. He then entered the studio of Peter Behrens where he met Mies and Gropius. He also worked briefly with Josef Hoffmann in Vienna. It hardly needs to be said that all three of the architects with whom Corbu apprenticed designed furniture.

In 1911 his former teacher L'Eplattenier at the Art School in La Chaux-de-Fonds asked him to return to form a new section which would cover every aspect of design from doorknobs and flatware to furniture and architecture. It was, as Corbu once pointed out, a program similar to the later Bauhaus. The furniture Corbu was designing during this period was surprisingly revivalist, and, as Charles Jencks has pointed out, he was specifying "Louis XIII" and "Directoire" furniture in his buildings. In 1917 he settled in Paris where he made his first paintings and in 1918 had his first exhibition with Amédée Ozenfant. In 1920 he founded an avant-garde magazine with Ozenfant, *L'Esprit Nouveau*, that covered not only architecture but all the arts and sciences. In 1921 he opened his own atelier with his cousin Pierre Jeanneret and from then on devoted part of his time to painting and part to architecture.

At the 1925 International Exposition of Decorative Arts in Paris, Corbu furnished his Pavillon de L'Esprit Nouveau with built-in storage cabinets and tables of his own design along with paintings by Picasso, Gris, Léger, Ozenfant, and himself. His cabinets had tubular-steel legs and his table tops were placed on welded tubu-

The fauteuil grand confort *designed by Le Corbusier with Charlotte Perriand in 1928 has cushions placed within a tubular-steel cage.*

Corbu's sexy armchair with pivoting backrest designed with Charlotte Perriand in 1928 is an elegant version of the traditional British officer's chair. The arms are two continuous leather straps; the seat and back are black canvas.

lar frames, but he didn't attempt to design a tubular-steel chair until a few years later. Breuer produced his first tubular-steel furniture at the Bauhaus that same year. Le Corbusier also used Thonet's circular bentwood chair for the first but by no means last time in his pavilion. In the *Almanach d'Architecture Moderne* of 1925, he explained: "We have introduced the humble Thonet chair of steamed wood, certainly the most common as well as the least costly of chairs. And we believe that this chair, whose millions of representatives are used on the Continent and in the two Americas, possesses a nobility of its own."

It is easy to understand why Thonet's chairs caught Corbu's eye. They are not only functional but fit Corbu's idea of chairs as sculpture in space, especially the model used in his pavilion. That particular armchair, as Italian architect and architectural historian Renato De Fusco has suggested, may well have been Corbu's adaptation to his own design of one of the most typical of Thonet chairs. The proportions of the Corbu chair, De Fusco convincingly argues, have been modified—"the seat has become a complete circle, the back lowered below the shoulders so as to lend greater support to the waist, while a double curve connects loosely the arms and this low back." And the resulting chair, he points out, is "far removed from the taste of the nineteenth century and very close to the characteristics of purist painting and sculpture" and of course Corbu's own ideas.

Although Le Corbusier's Esprit Nouveau Pavillon had a tremendous influence on young architects from all over, it was relegated to an out-of-the-way spot at the exposition, which may have been the result of his proclamation: "We do not believe in interior decoration." Wright would have applauded, but it is not surprising that the promoters of the Exposition of Decorative Arts did not. Writing about the "New Spirit in Architecture" shortly before the exposition, Corbu says ". . . we are confronted by a new phenomenon: mechanisation. The methods of building a house on a human scale are so topsy-turvy, so greatly enriched and so different from what we are accustomed to that everything handed down to us from the past is no longer any use, and we are cautiously seeking a new aesthetic. We are on the brink of a new approach which we shall try to give expression to."

Such was Corbu's philosophy in the early 1920s. And by the time he died in 1965 he along with a few others had to a great extent done just that. Houses were not the same. Metal furniture was as welcome in a living room as it was in an office. Thonet bentwood chairs were not only de rigueur for modern dining areas but for fine restaurants around the world. Corkscrew staircases were almost a cliché, and New York City, at least, would be unthinkable without its millions of roof gardens half way to the sky.

The first important group of chairs, tables, and cabinets Corbu designed was done in 1928 with the young French architect Charlotte Perriand who started working at Le Corbusier's atelier in 1927. This furniture made its initial appearance in a house at Ville d'Avray which was remodeled by Corbu and Pierre Jeanneret and included the well-known reclining chair (*chaise longue basculant*), the armchair with pivoting backrest (*fauteuil à dossier basculant*), and the easy chair (*Grand Confort*). Corbu tells us how two of these chairs came about in his article, "The Furniture Adventure," published in 1929 when they were exhibited together with some handsome storage-wall units in a model apartment designed by Corbu for the Salon d'Automne. Of the armchair with a pivoting backrest (a reworking of the British Officer's chair), he says he remembered a 14-horsepower sports model Voisin "with a spring cushion arranged on the floor; and I travelled 500 km at a stretch on it without feeling tired; I bear it in mind when I furnish my drawing room. Here we have the machine at rest. We built it with bicycle frame tubes and we covered it with a magnificent pony skin; it is so light that it can be pushed with the foot, it can be moved by a child."

Of the reclining chair, he says, "I thought of the cowboy from the Wild West, smoking his pipe, his feet in the air higher than his head, against the chimney piece: complete rest. Our reclining chair can be put into any position; my weight alone is enough to keep it in the position chosen: no mechanics. This is the real machine for rest, etc."

The *Grand Confort* was intended to replace the traditional easy chair with its five bulging leather upholstered cushions hugged within its framework of shiny chromium tubes. Of all Corbu's "machines for sitting in" perhaps this one seems least machinelike, and it *is* comfortable, which is more than can be said for most of the chairs designed by the architects of the modern movement. In shape, the *Grand Confort* is not unlike Josef Hoffmann's cube chair for the Palais Stoclet in Brussels of 1905, but in concept it is quite different.

Another piece shown at the Salon d'Automne was the *Siège tournant*, a padded stool with four steel tube legs and a steel tube that loops around the back and threads through a tubular leather backrest, thus illustrating, in Renato De Fusco's words, "another feature of Le Corbusier's design, where the obviousness of the solution recalls an *objet-trouvé*."

Not only are all these chairs being produced today, but, as Peter Blake puts it, they "have spawned entire schools of furniture design"

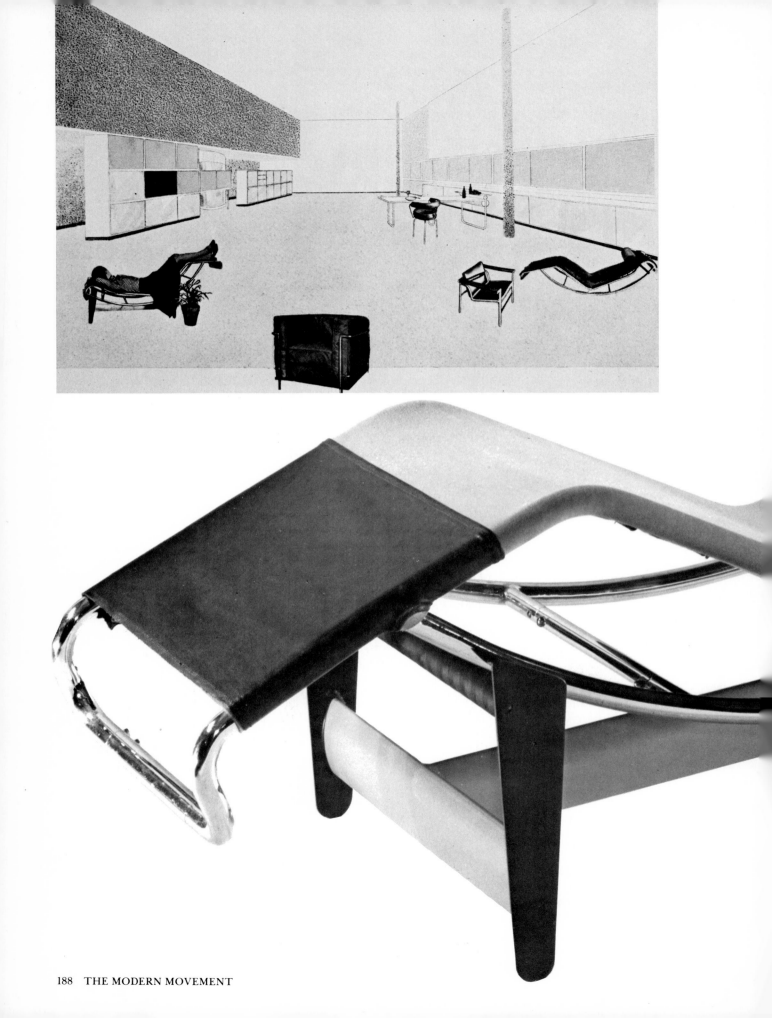

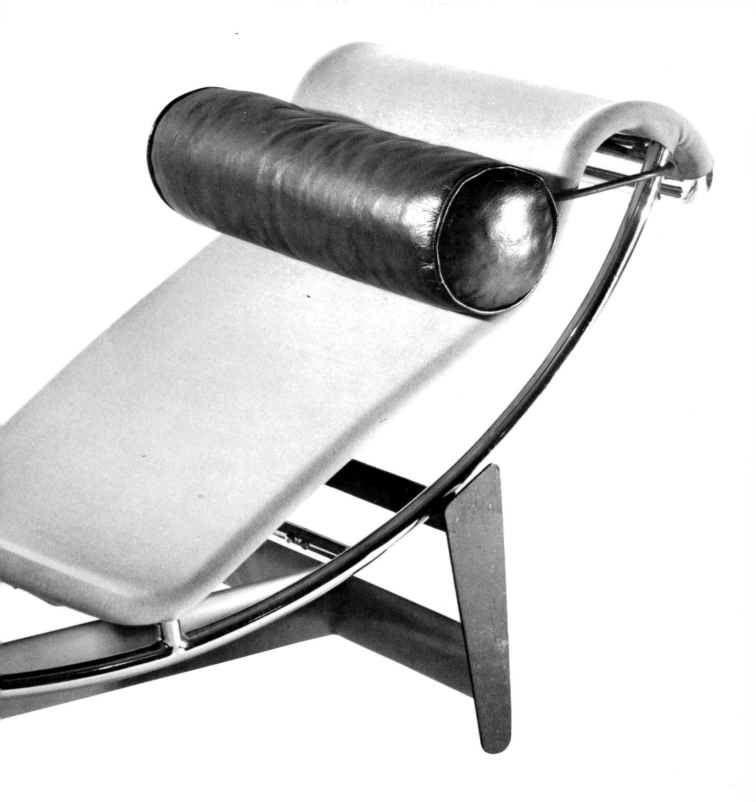

*Above: "This is the real machine for rest,"
Corbu said of the* chaise longue bas-
culante *he designed with Charlotte Perriand in 1928.*

*Opposite page: Collage of Corbu's Pavillon
de L'Esprit Nouveau, Paris, of 1925.*

since their original appearance. In Blake's words, Breuer's chairs were "entirely rational, technically impeccable, and, incidentally, very handsome," while Corbu's chairs were "neither particularly rational, nor especially easy to manufacture." He compares the latter with "expensive tarts: elegant, funny, sexy, and not particularly sensible." But, he adds, "Nobody has improved upon them to date."

It might be worth remembering that Corbu designed his sexy and elegant furniture, which is a status symbol today, during the halcyon 1920s when everything else that was new from cloche hats to brass- and wood-fitted motor cars seems hardly less outdated than hoop skirts and horse-drawn buggies. Or, as E. N. Rogers put it: "A chair by Le Corbusier is as valid as a Savonarola, or the Barcelona chair of Mies van der Rohe, or the furniture of Thonet, in short, as those few objects among so many which have existed whose age may be measured in centuries or decades, yet belong to all time."

Probably Le Corbusier and Wright were the architects of the 20th century who roamed the farthest and with the most freedom. Both were artists beyond the confines of architecture—Wright was a musician, Corbu a painter and sculptor—and both wrote extensively about their work and their ideas. It is not surprising that both designed furniture. Corbu, however, seems to have understood better than Wright that people will insist on bringing their own taste, furniture, and other human trivia into a house. Neither is it surprising that although one seldom finds paintings in a Wright interior, his spaces were invariably planned for a piano. Corbu, however, often made paintings, sculpture, and tapestries important elements of his dynamic spaces.

Except for an occasional table or storage unit for a particular house, Corbu designed almost no furniture after the small group of tables, chairs, and cabinets of 1925 and 1928, but, as Blake says, in those few pieces "he produced a sufficient number of ideas, both of detail and of over-all form, to inspire a dozen or more furniture designers for many years to come." In any case he had an artist's eye that recognized pure forms in existing furniture as it did in everything else. One only need look at photographs of his own apartment and studio to realize that he knew how to find the right pieces—graceful sculptures in space—whether they be simple wire or bentwood chairs. And it is perhaps typical of Corbu that if he wanted some particular seating in a particular place, he "sculpted" it. At the Villa Savoye there is the concrete slab that makes a table on the sun terrace and the large sculptured basin and cast chaise longue in the bathroom. On the roof garden of the Unité d'Habitation in Marseille there is the row of

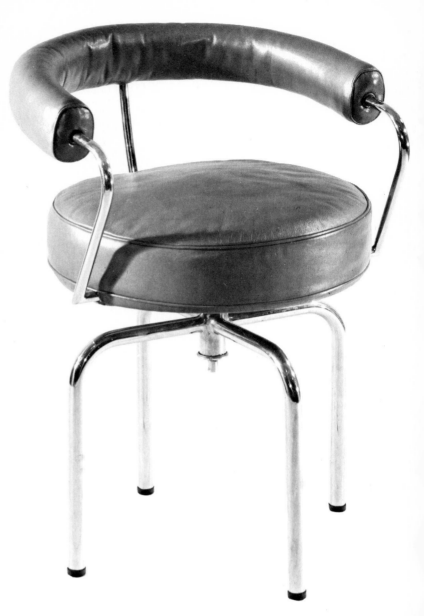

The siege tournant, *designed by Corbu and Charlotte Perriand in 1929, is of tubular steel and leather.*

curved concrete benches where mothers sit to watch their children, and there is a window seat in each apartment—an L-shaped form which is actually, as Charles Jencks has said, "not so specifically a seat as it is also a table, a structural stabilizer, an outdoor storage container, a place for children to hide under, and a part of the modular order which merges with several other visual contexts." At the steel and glass Maison de l'Homme exhibition pavilion in Zurich, there is the pressed-steel curved seating from which one can view the park. On one side of the nave in the Chapel at Ronchamp are the rough sculptural benches.

Corbu never considered furniture unimportant and gave it considerable thought to which both his drawings and his writings attest. In *Towards a New Architecture* of 1923 he includes a "Manual of the Dwelling" in which he tells "the modern man" to "Demand bare walls in your bedroom, your living room and your dining room. Built-in fittings to take the place of much of the furniture which is expensive to buy, takes up much room and needs looking after. . . . Buy only practical furniture and never buy decorative 'pieces'. If you want to see bad taste, go into the houses of the rich. . . ."

In 1929 he wrote, "Renewal of the plan of the modern house cannot be undertaken effectively without examining the question of furniture. This is the Gordian knot. It must be cut, otherwise any pursuit of the modern idea is vain." In another place he says ". . . I have noticed that, according to the hours of the day, the nature of our preoccupations, the posture we adopt in a drawing-room (and which we change three to four times during the evening), there are several ways of being seated. You sit 'actively' for working. I sit down to chat; a certain armchair gives me a decent and polite position. I sit down 'actively' to deliver a speech, to propose a thesis, to outline my point of view: how suitable this high stool is for my posture! I sit blissfully and I am relaxed: this Turkish stool of the *cavedjis* of Constantinople, 35 cm high and 30 cm in diameter, is a marvel; I could sit on it for hours without tiring, just sitting on my backside! And if there are 15 of us in the small drawing-room of our little

house, and we want to sit and do nothing, the lady of the house takes from a cupboard the 15 stools stacked one inside the other." And in still another place: "Furniture consists of tools, and servants, too. Furniture serves our needs. Our needs are everyday ones, regular, always the same. Our furniture fulfills constant, daily regular functions. All men have the same needs at the same times, everyday, all their lives. The tools which would fulfill these functions are easy to define, and progress, which brings us new techniques (tubular steel, pliable metal sheeting, autogenous welding) provides us with means of production which are infinitely more perfect. . . ."

But while Corbu thought of a chair as a tool, he could not have designed a chair without style. For that matter he could not have designed a tool without style. Everything he did possessed style. All his work was one—architecture, painting, sculpting, chairmaking, writing. It is perhaps even less possible to examine his furniture separate from the rest of his work than it is with Wright. Furniture to Corbu was a part of architecture just as all the arts were, including his own paintings, sculpture, and tapestries. Nevertheless there was a "Hierarchy," as he called it: "first, the Sistine; in other words, works of art in which passion has really inscribed itself. Afterwards machines to sit on, machines for classification purposes, lighting machines. . . . To speak truly, decorative art is utensils, beautiful utensils."

The arts, Corbu made clear, must be seen together. And while the architects of the Arts and Crafts and Art Nouveau movements may have believed this, no one had been quite so successful in bringing them together in a livable, esthetic whole. "But where does sculpture begin, where does painting begin, where does architecture begin?" he once asked. For his furniture he may have been inspired by a cowboy with his feet in the air or the seat of an automobile, but it went through the transforming filter of Corbu's undeniable artistry. Perhaps he more than any other architect of the modern movement understood how to replace the ornament of earlier architecture with forms that were ornament in themselves.

ALVAR AALTO 1898–1976

How did the capital of the Ionic column come into being? It originated from the bending of the wood and the curving of its fibres under a load. ALVAR AALTO

Finland abounds in birch forests so it is not surprising that the Finnish architect Alvar Aalto substituted birchwood for steel tubing in his chairs. Finns had long heeded the resilient quality of birch in the manufacture of skis, but Aalto was the first to give it expression in furniture and it seems extraordinarily right that he should have done so. Aalto was surely a creature of his northern land where the woodland god Tapio presides over a wide domain—more than two-thirds of Finland is forested. A deep sensibility of those abundant forests as well as of the myriad lakes that weave a watery web across southern Finland permeates everything Aalto did from his bent birchwood chairs to his characteristic slender wood columns and his undulating wood ceilings. But if Aalto's roots were deep in Finnish soil, he was by no means provincial. He mastered the expression of his time and, in Siegfried Giedion's words, "fused it with the things of his native surroundings." Frederick Gutheim put it another way. In Aalto, he wrote, "we see the regional expression that does not deny the universality of art." And Reyner Banham attributed part of Aalto's genius to his ability "to strike a resonance with folk traditions without ever copying them or being sentimental, without ever ceasing to be his own immensely sophisticated and hard-headed self."

But while Finland was important in his work, his regionalism was always tempered by his genius and his humanity. Giedion was not alone in commenting on Aalto's real interest in the desires and experiences of all kinds of people. And, as Aalto himself put it: "True architecture—the real thing—is only to be found where man stands in the center." It naturally follows that the design of an Aalto building

or chair was first of all prompted by its users. If it was a house, a factory, a library, a sanatorium its design grew out of the human actions that would take place in it. If it was the plywood seat of a chair or a door handle, it was molded to the human form. His chairs are not like Wright's or Rietveld's—interesting as designs but uncomfortable as chairs. Aalto's chairs are certainly interesting as designs, but at least part of that interest derives from the fact that they are a direct response to ways of sitting and to the material. He never forgot, as John E. Burchard noted in *Architectural Record* of January 1959, that "his stairs and his terraces and his rooms and his walls are made for men of ordinary size," and that applies to his furniture as well.

This extraordinary Finn was born in Kuortan in the central part of his northern country, the son of a surveyor. He built a house for his parents while he was attending the Technical University in Helsinki from which he received a diploma in architecture in 1921. In 1923 he opened his office at Jyväskylä, moving to Turku in 1927 and to Helsinki in 1933. In 1925 he married Aino Marsio who had been a fellow architecture student at the Technical University and who was to become a close associate in all his work until her death in 1949. In 1952 he married architect and designer Elissa Makiniemi with whom he also worked in partnership.

Aalto started designing furniture in the 1920s during the period that Breuer was developing his tubular-steel furniture at the Bauhaus. But if Breuer was a pioneer in developing a modern tubular-steel esthetic, Aalto was certainly a pioneer in creating a modern bentwood esthetic. Aalto recognized tubular-

Birch stools designed by Aalto in 1954 have a fan-shaped joint that attaches to the leg in an organic way on the horizontal level by gluing.

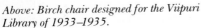

Above: Birch chair designed for the Viipuri Library of 1933–1935.

Above, right: Bent plywood armchair with upholstered seat and back, one of many versions designed by Aalto in the 40s, 50s, and 60s.

Opposite page: The Paimio chair designed by Aalto in 1930–1933 has a plywood seat suspended within a closed ribbonlike frame of laminated wood.

steel chairs as being technically rational because they were light in weight and could be mass produced easily: "To achieve a springy seat merely with a few bent tubes and some tightly stretched bits of leather is in itself a clever technical solution." But he didn't find them rational from a human point of view: "We . . . probably agree that objects which can with justification be called 'rational' often suffer from considerable lack of human qualities."

Although Aalto had designed some traditional furniture, his first modern piece seems to have been a birch stacking chair with straight legs, plywood seat and back, which he designed in 1927 for the assembly hall of his Civil Guard House in Jyväskylä. In his recent book, *Alvar Aalto and the International Style*, David Pearson does much to clarify when and how Aalto's furniture came into being and to explain his experiments with wood. It seems that in 1929 when he was preparing for the "700 Year Exposition" in Turku, of which he was one of the two principal designers, he met Otto Korhonen, a local manufacturer of furniture. Korhonen asked Aalto to design his exhibit at the fair and soon became a close associate in the development of all his subsequent furniture. It was in the Korhonen exhibit that Aalto's first molded plywood chair was

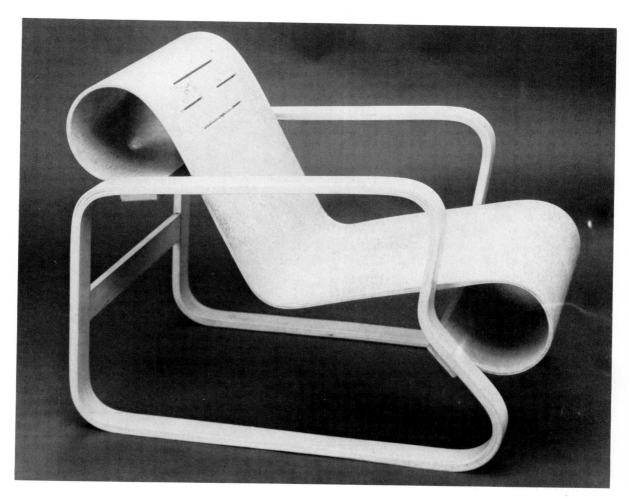

shown. This chair, however, was mounted on a tubular-steel frame apparently because bentwood structural experiments made at the time were not considered successful. But this initial failure to provide his molded plywood seat with a satisfactory wooden leg, explains Pearson, was ultimately overcome in the model called the "Paimio" chair by "making the laminated leg a closed form of veneered layers bound together with glue and curved in forms much like those Thonet had used earlier." The flowing lines of the Paimio chair, with its undulated plywood seat suspended within this ribbonlike frame, are all of a piece with Aalto's curving walls and undulating ceilings. It has been suggested that he got his incentive from the curved contours of the Finnish lakes, but wherever the inspiration came from, the Paimio chair is certainly one of the most elegant of modern chairs. It was not produced for the tuberculosis sanatorium at Paimio of 1928–1933 as is generally supposed, but took its name because it was developed during the period Aalto was working on the design of the sanatorium. Nevertheless the latter did represent the first instance of Aalto's total involvement in the design of a building. All the furniture, lighting fixtures, and other interior components of the Paimio

sanatorium came out of his head, heart, and imagination, as was to happen in much of his future work. J. M. Richards, former editor of *Architectural Review*, who visited Paimio shortly after its completion, spoke of Aalto's furniture as "lending the interiors a gaiety of style not always to be found in buildings of this purpose."

After the Paimio chair, Aalto and Korhonen continued to experiment with methods of forming a bent structural support of laminated wood without utilizing a closed form. And eventually, Pearson tells us, they solved the problem with neither a closed form nor steam bending but by "backsawing the portion to be bent into leaves of wood which in their small cross sections could be formed around a radius. This invention, patented by Aalto, made it possible to bend and glue, in a permanent right angle, wooden strips of sufficient thickness to be used as a structural support for a chair." The technique was finally put into production around 1933 for the famous stool that initially appeared in the Viipuri Library. While bentwood chairs had existed in the 19th century, no one had been able to produce an all-plywood chair until the mid-1930s when Aalto and Korhonen developed the spring leaf support and integrated it with the molded seat. Although it has been said that there was "no precedent technology for this chair—which depends on a compression spring of birch veneers welded together—in the manufacture of furniture or wood products," Pearson points to the birch baskets and other wooden forms which one still sees for sale in the markets of Helsinki. Unlike popular wicker techniques, this Scandinavian craft form is a well-developed tradition which depends on the use of thin but unsoaked strips of hardwood cut from newly fallen trees to yield a molded, rounded corner. And, says Pearson, obviously this method was partly a precedent for Aalto's technique. Nevertheless, he adds, its adaptation to furniture design must stand as Aalto's major contribution in that area. "The spring made of seven layers of birch, is thickened at the points of greatest stress and reduced at the base and toward the rear of the seat. Like the Paimio chair, the molded seat was joined to the supporting legs only along the two extremities to give a more resilient nature to the body." The spring leaf chair was produced in a variety of shapes including several upholstered versions, a chaise lounge, and a popular webbed sling model.

After the 1930s Aalto's designs depended more on the backsawn leg bend and were conceived along straighter and more traditional lines. The bent form, as Pearson explains it, "was ingeniously intersected with an identical shape at right angles to produce a fused leg, utilized both for a four-leg stool and a frame for the well-known glass-top coffee table. Still later he joined five of these bents to form a table or stool leg that had a splayed shape over its 90-degree profile, giving it the strength of a gusset. This leg component was jointed to a plywood base to produce a stool or table."

The 1930s marked the beginning of Aalto's association with Artek, the company founded by Aino and Alvar Aalto with Maire and Harry Gullichsen mainly to manufacture and distribute Aalto's birch plywood furniture but also as a place to exhibit paintings, sculpture, and generally promote the manufacture and distribution of well-designed homefurnishings and housewares. Artek is still the exclusive distributor of Aalto's furniture. The Gullichsens (he was an industrialist and she a painter) were longtime friends and patrons of Aalto's.

Mass production and standardization, in Aalto's eyes, were good to a point, but beyond that they became despotic. Perhaps with the help of Finland's small economy, he was able to find manufacturers who were geared to making only 150 chairs or 400 copies of a lighting fixture, but such limited runs would be out of the question in most industrial countries. In that way Aalto bypassed the necessity of choosing between the expense of a uniquely crafted item or

Opposite page, top: Several versions of the birch chair originally used in the Viipuri Library of 1933–1935.

Opposite page, bottom: Birch stacking stools of 1930–1933 first used in the Viipuri Library and a favorite ever since.

Below: Aalto's famous teacart of 1933 is an adaptation of the closed circle structural shape of the Paimio chair frame, as is this serving cart of 1936–1937.

Above: Elegant simplicity marks this glass-topped coffee table and four-legged stool. Both have laminated birchwood legs that branch out into a right angle at the horizontal plane to form the frame for the table top on the right and the webbed seat on the left, c. 1947.

Opposite page, top: Section of the living room in Aalto's own house in Helsinki of 1934 seems to reflect his own words that every house ought to be the expression of the family's "distinctively private ideas of life."

Opposite page, bottom: Lecture room of the Viipuri Library showing Aalto's upholstered chairs with an open bent structural support of laminated birchwood in 1935.

mass production in the usual sense with all its unattractive implications. It wasn't necessary to use the chairs designed for a sanatorium, for instance, in a library, office, or house. A chair could be designed for its particular place and function although it might be used again in another setting if it happened to fit the individual characteristics and needs of that building, and thus Aalto could have complete control of his buildings inside and out. When he designed the furniture for his library at Viipuri of 1930–1935, he gave special attention to pieces that would not only be right for a public library but equally versatile as mass-produced items in comparatively small quantities. The little round stool, so popular today, with its three wooden legs that bend into the circular seat, was first designed for the Viipuri Library but has been used in innumerable places since by Aalto and many others. Any one of Aalto's chairs was not only the result of "a painstaking study of posture, the properties of laminated wood and esthetic considerations, but also of the study of efficient (and consequently economical) mechanical methods of mass-production," as John McAndrew, former curator of New York's Museum of Modern Art, noted back in 1938. And that remained true throughout his life. "Technology and economy must always be combined with a life-enriching charm," as Aalto himself put it in 1953.

It has been convincingly argued that it was Aalto's experiments with curved laminated wood for his furniture that informed much of his subsequent architecture, and certainly his highly effective use of birch and other wood in both his architecture and furniture are complementary. Even more than most architects of the modern movement Aalto believed buildings should be conceived as total artistic expressions. That is what animated his furniture designs as well as his designs of hardware, lighting, and other parts of his integral architecture. It is also why Giedion believed that Aalto's genius could not be apprehended in a single piece of furniture, a living room, or a house, but "must be seen together with his large-scale planning and the structure of the country." So whether the furniture informed the architecture or vice versa really doesn't matter. They are part of one another. "The vertical, bearing portion of furniture forms," he once wrote, "is truly the small sister of the architectural column."

Aalto, along with Le Corbusier, was a painter and sculptor as well as an architect. In 1967 his friend and favorite critic Göran Schildt asked him if he considered his paintings and sculpture independent of his architecture, and Aalto replied that they were "a part of my method of working, which is why I unwillingly see them as separated from my architecture, as if they could express something beyond it. Many

architects have devoted themselves to painting as a separate activity. For me the situation is different. One could say that I don't regard my sculptures and paintings as something that belongs to these professions. It is difficult to prove from case to case but they are for me branches of the same tree whose trunk is architecture."

And that takes us right back to William Morris's remark about architecture: "Noble as that art is by itself, and although it is specially the art of civilisation, it neither has existed nor ever can exist alive and progressive by itself, but must cherish and be cherished by all the crafts whereby men make things which they intend shall be beautiful and shall last somewhat beyond the passing day. It is the union of the arts, mutually helpful and harmoniously subordinated one to another which I have learned to think of as architecture." Aalto, in fact, had much in common with Morris and the adherents of Arts and Crafts traditions and certainly not the least of them was his belief in the oneness of the arts. Not only was Eliel Saarinen a hero to the young Aalto, but it is interesting to note that the first furniture designed by Alvar and Aino to be seen by the public was adapted from traditional cottage-style pieces including a hoop-back Windsor chair, a gate-leg table, and glass-front cupboard, which, according to Pearson, are almost faithful copies of Morris and Co. designs. Two of the important houses Aalto designed—the Villa Mairea of 1938–1939 near the small Finnish village of Noormarkku for Maire and Harry Gullichsen and La Maison Carré of 1956–1959 at Bagoches-sur-Guyonne in France for the Paris art dealer Louis Carré—are thoroughly integrated expressions of his art as well as of his appreciation of the desires and activities of people. He not only designed furniture, lamps, fabrics, hardware, and other equipment for both houses, but he designed their surrounding landscapes as well. In fact these two houses are splendid examples of Göran Schildt's statement that in all Aalto did "from the organic design of curved wooden furniture and lamps to the attunement of every

structure with the landscape, there is evidence of the deep harmony the Finnish architect felt between man and nature." The site for La Maison Carré is a hill surrounded by an oak grove and the garden surrounding the house was created from Aalto's detailed plan. The Villa Mairea is also sited on a hill surrounded by a pine forest. Wood, of course, is used prominently in both houses, and both blend art with the life of the house. The Gullichsens gave Aalto a free hand to experiment as much as he wanted to, and the resulting Villa Mairea has been called one of the masterpieces of domestic architecture of the modern movement along with Mies's Tugendhat house, Le Corbusier's Villa Savoye, and Wright's Fallingwater.

That Aalto should have designed furniture is perhaps even more to be expected than that other architects did. He never wrote much about his architecture, but what he did write was invariably concerned with humanity, and in all of architecture furniture is what comes closest to humanity. And always, as Gutheim put it, "Aalto's appreciation of nature begins with man and in the end returns to man." Seldom have a man and his work been so much at one, and seldom has furniture been so attuned to its environment.

As for Aalto the man, we can do no better than quote what J. M. Richards wrote about his first meeting with him in 1933: "when his birch-wood furniture was seen for the first time outside Finland, at an exhibition in London, and I remember that it struck me then how closely the style of design revealed in it accorded with Aalto's own personality. The furniture had a freshness and unexpectedness which was derived from his adventurous exploration of new techniques. It had wit, which it owed to an unusually direct connection between ends and means. It was original, not as a result of trying to be so, but because of the serious thought that had been given to basic principles. Aalto's personality, too, showed freshness, wit and originality, and the reasons were the same."

Top: Living room of the Maison Louis Carré in Bazoches, France, designed by Aalto in 1956–1958.

Bottom: Fireplace area in the living room of the Villa Mairea designed for the Gullichsens in Noormarkku in 1938–1939 is eminently livable as are all Aalto's residential interiors.

TWO POST-WORLD WAR II ARCHITECTS

Eero Saarinen and Charles Eames are the post-World War II architects who best exemplify the continuing ideas of the modern movement. Designing chairs came just as naturally to them as designing buildings. In Eames' case perhaps even more so. Saarinen was brought up with the idea that architects design furniture as a matter of course. His famous father, architect Eliel Saarinen, was a fine early modernist who followed the Arts and Crafts tradition of his native Finland and considered furniture a natural part of the architect's job. Eliel was working in Finland before the First World War when Mackintosh was working in Scotland; Voysey in England; Otto Wagner, Adolf Loos, and Josef Hoffmann in Vienna; when Wright was building his Prairie houses in America's midwest and the Greene brothers were designing their California masterpieces—all architects who personally made furniture a part of its surrounding spaces.

In 1922 Eliel was awarded second prize for his Chicago Tribune Tower design, and in 1924 he accepted an invitation to become visiting professor of architecture at the University of Michigan. There he met newspaper publisher George G. Booth whose interest in the Arts and Crafts movement led him to commission the Finnish-born architect to design the Cranbrook School for Boys on his estate in Bloomfield Hills, a suburb of Detroit. Not only did the school emphasize craftsmanship and foster the collabora-

tion of artists, but it was so successful that in 1926 Booth commissioned Eliel to design and later direct the Cranbrook Academy of Art. In 1929 the Kingswood School for Girls was added—a project in which the entire Saarinen family participated. Eliel's wife Loja executed rugs and tapestries, his daughter Pipsan decorated the auditorium, and his son Eero designed the furniture.

Ever since he designed his own house in Finland, Eliel had followed his conviction that, particularly in residential work, the architect should design the entire building including the furnishings. So it is not surprising that when he designed a house for himself and his family on the Cranbrook campus, he also designed the interiors and their furnishings. Unfortunately Saarinen's successors in the president's chair at Cranbrook showed little interest in his work. The house deteriorated and the furnishings were dispersed—a trend happily reversed by current Cranbrook president Roy Slade, who has not only restored Saarinen House, as it is now called, but brought back some of its original furniture, including the handsome dining table and chairs made of holly wood inlaid with ebony that Eliel designed for it in 1929.

While chronologically Eliel Saarinen does not belong in this chapter, the impression his ideas made on his son Eero and Charles Eames, who were together at Cranbrook, must have been considerable. It was undoubtedly at Cranbrook—where metalsmiths, weavers, furniture makers, and other craftsmen worked much as they had at the Bauhaus—that Eames and the young Saarinen learned to appreciate furniture as an important element of architecture. It was at Cranbrook, in fact, that they designed their revolutionary prize-winning molded plywood chairs for the Museum of Modern Art's Organic Design competition in 1940. The object of the competition was to find furniture which could be machine produced at a reasonable cost. The furniture should, as the museum put it, "reflect today's social, economic, technological and aesthetic tendencies" and "provide adequately and handsomely for a typical American middle-income group family." Here, then, was a clear indication that technology was no longer an adolescent to be accepted or rejected but a full-fledged adult that must be dealt with in furniture as well as in almost everything else. In fact so much technology goes into a modern airport, shopping center, skyscraper, or whatever, it is remarkable that creative design is even possible. One is reminded of the words of Charles Greene when the public turned away from his architecture in the 1920s: "Artists don't have a chance. The educated public wants skill not soul." Now it wants technology and only the most brilliant architects can also supply soul.

In the 1920s architects were designing furniture to be mass produced, but by the 1940s this was imperative. Few could afford handcrafted furniture even if it were possible to produce enough to go around. In a little country like Finland Aalto might be able to mass produce his furniture in small quantities and thus retain something of both worlds, but that was not possible in most places, particularly a technology-minded country like the United States. Nevertheless such post-World War II architects as Eero Saarinen and Charles Eames managed to combine production-line methods with sensitive designs or, as Charles Greene would have it, with soul. It was Saarinen and Eames, moreover, who were responsible for making America a leader in technical innovation in furniture. The drive toward simplification that had started with Morris was now matched by technological know-how.

Saarinen put it well when he described the chair as "a three-dimensional object always seen within a room, which is essentially a box," and asked: "How do you best relate this object to the box? The cubists, the de Stijl designers, Mies van der Rohe, and Le Corbusier all saw this fundamental relationship and solved it by their light steel furniture—truly beautiful thinking and truly beautiful furniture. Somehow technology and taste have shifted. New materials and techniques have given us great opportunities with structural shells of plywood, plastic and metal."

EERO SAARINEN 1910–1961

I believe very strongly that the whole field of design is all one thing. Therefore my interest in furniture. EERO SAARINEN

As might be expected it was at Cranbrook before World War II that Saarinen first began designing chairs. He was not yet 20 when he designed the furniture for his father's Kingswood School for Girls (although at the time he didn't intend to be either an architect or furniture designer but a sculptor). And it wasn't long before his untimely death at 51 that he designed his famous pedestal chair. By that time, however, he was an architect of international standing who many considered, as Charles Jencks did, "the most versatile figure American architecture has produced" after Frank Lloyd Wright.

Eero Saarinen was born and lived in Finland until he was 13 years old. "I was a very lucky little boy," he told a *New York Times* reporter in January 1953. "My father had his architectural studio right in the house. The whole family would sit at one end of the studio. As a child, I would always draw and I happened to be good at it. Therefore, I got more attention from drawing than anything else. That made me draw more and more. . . . I was only praised if what I did was good, not the way children are praised today for anything they do." In that house, too, the young Saarinen met Sibelius, Gorky, Mahler, and many other members of the artistic world who were friends of his parents.

He was still a young boy when the family emigrated to the United States in 1923. In 1929 he went to Paris to study sculpture but soon returned to Cranbrook and entered the Yale School of Architecture in 1930. His initial interest in sculpture, however, was apparent in most of his later architecture as well as in his furniture. After graduating from Yale in 1934, he spent some time traveling in Europe before returning in 1936 to join his father in his architec-

tural firm and on the Cranbrook faculty. In 1940 when he and Charles Eames (who became a fellow at Cranbrook in 1936) won two first prizes in the Museum of Modern Art's furniture competition for their molded plywood chairs, the two young architects were already committed "to a structural aesthetic that owed more to the Bauhaus than to the gentle tradition of Eliel's Cranbrook," as Allan Temko put it. In addition to expressing physical structure, their molded plywood chair, in Temko's words, "carried the promise of assembly-line production. This was not craftsmanship but industrial design." They had taken the step from the Arts and Crafts tradition of Eliel's world to the machine esthetic of the modern movement. Saarinen, however, never rejected his father's world. He may have lived in a new world and it was for that world he designed. "I am a child of my period," he told a Dickinson College audience in 1959. "I am enthusiastic about the three common principles of modern architecture: function, structure, and being part of our time." Nevertheless he always freely admitted that his father and his ideas were a continuing influence. "Perhaps the most important thing I learned from my father," he said in 1958, "was that in any design problem one should seek the solution in terms of the next largest thing. If the problem is an ashtray, then the way it relates to a table will influence its design. If the problem is a chair, then its solution must be found in the way it relates to the room cube. If it is a building, the townscape will affect the solution."

It was from his father, too, and his father's generation that he learned that the "ideal interior," as he expressed it, "is one that grows

The shapely "womb" chair of molded plastic and foam rubber designed by Eero Saarinen in 1948 to replace the old overstuffed chair, or "dreadnought" as he called it. Matching ottoman shown on following page.

together with and out of the total concept of a building. In a sense, it grows the way chromosomes multiply out of the original sperm and the thinking of the total concept is carried down to the smallest detail. This organic unity is the ideal." But that he was designing for a different world in which the ideal is not always possible is implicit when he goes on to state: "Usually the problem of interior design is limited. It begins within the existing framework of an office, apartment, or ready-made house. The shells of these living and working units have to answer the needs of hundreds of thousands of people. They have become completely anonymous shells. . . . Likewise, furniture has moved from the handicraft era into a mass-production era and so, to a greater or lesser degree, have other items of the interior. The result is that the major equipment or furnishings of the interior have an impersonal character. As with the architectural shells, it is essential, in fact, that a mass-produced item must have this impersonal character. It must not be romantic, in the sense of answering a special problem or smacking of the artist's personality. It must be classic, in the sense of responding to an often recurring need, both practical and visual, in many different situations. . . ." But when an interior was really successful Saarinen found the compensations tremendous: "The clarity and serenity of a good interior give an absolutely marvelous feeling of strength with which to face our complicated and confused world. The fact that one has achieved this atmosphere with the form-world and technology of one's own era gives further satisfaction. And finally the psychological satisfaction of having expressed an identity is deeply rewarding. Especially in a world of standardization of people as well as things, this coherent, clear expression of one's own individuality is a necessary goal."

Saarinen approached each building as an individual problem, but he realized that since furniture had to be mass produced it was a different matter. "Though we use mass-produced parts in architecture, a building is custom-built to the extent it is a solution of a specific problem," he said in *Architectural Design* of August 1957. "In furniture design, the client is Everyman."

Top: The sculptural pedestal chair designed by Eero Saarinen in 1955–1957 has a cast aluminum stabilizing base which is indistinguishable from the light plastic upper portion—"all one thing," as Saarinen put it.

Above: Ottoman for the "womb" chair.

After the winning molded plywood chairs in the 1940 Museum of Modern Art competition, Saarinen's next chair was the famous womb chair—a molded plastic shell armchair upholstered in foam rubber with loose seat and back cushions—designed for Knoll Associates in 1948. When the late Hans Knoll asked Saarinen to give the chair a more conventional name, he replied: "I have been thinking and thinking about a printable name for that chair, but my mind keeps turning to those which are more

Saarinen House, as it is now called, was designed by Eliel Saarinen and completed in 1929. It was restored in the 1970s with some of Eliel's original furnishings filled in with furniture related to Cranbrook's history. In the area of the living room shown here Eliel's light fixtures shine on Breuer's Wassily chairs (see also page 169).

The Eames lounge chair (see also page 216),
with Eero's pedestal table beside it, faces the
Saarinen House dining room as it was restored with the handsome table and chairs
made of holly wood inlaid with ebony designed by Eliel.

biological, rather than less biological." Later Saarinen explained that he designed the womb chair to replace the old overstuffed chair—those "dreadnoughts," he called them, which disappeared from modern interiors, "partly because they were designed for an era which tried to impress by sheer mass, partly because their manufacture depended upon hundreds of hand-labor operations and costs became too high." But he realized that there was even more need to relax, and with the exception of Le Corbusier's cube chair, the architects of the modern movement hadn't really come up with a comfortable counterpart of the old upholstered chair. Among other modern needs prompting the design of the womb chair, Saarinen cited the fact that "people sit differently today than in the Victorian era. They want to sit lower and they like to slouch." He also noted that "a comfortable position, even if it were the most comfortable in the world, would not be so for very long." He pointed out that the "necessity of changing one's position is an important factor often forgotten in chair design. So, too, is the fact that an equal distribution of weight over a large surface of the body is important." The womb chair, he explained, "attempts to achieve psychological comfort by providing a great big cup-like shell into which you can curl up and pull up your legs (something which women seem especially to like to do). A chair is a background for a person sitting in it. Thus, the chair should not only look well as a piece of sculpture in the room when no one is in it, it should also be a flattering background when someone is in it—especially the female occupant." It can readily be seen that Saarinen's criteria for designing chairs was quite different from, say, Wright's or Rietveld's and many other designers of the modern movement who thought chiefly about how the chair worked with the architecture, and comfort had little to do with it. The person who was going to use Saarinen's chair was as important as the appearance of the chair itself. Its appearance in the room, moreover, was not neglected: "The scale of the chair was thought of as having architectural value. This larger form could make a transition to the loose furnishings." In 1950 Saarinen designed a really voluptuous easy chair for the General Motors Technical Center lobby that is not unlike Le Corbusier's cube chair. But it was probably Eames who best solved the problem of a comfortable modern chair with his famous lounge chair of 1956.

Saarinen's familiar sculptural molded plastic pedestal furniture of 1958, which is reinforced with fiberglass and supported on an aluminum pedestal base, is what he called "all one thing," noting that "the great furniture of the past from Tutankhamen's chair to Thomas Chippendale's have always been a structural total." Saarinen believed that the designers who had conceived the possibilities of the molded shell had treated legs as a thing apart. "Legs became a sort of metal plumbing," as he put it. "Modern chairs with shell shapes and cages over 'little sticks' below, mix different kinds of structures. The pedestal chair tries to bring unity of line."

In addition to doing away with the "metal plumbing" Saarinen objected to, his pedestal chairs are charming pieces of sculpture that blend well with the architectural spaces for which they were designed. He once described architecture as "something between earth and sky," and he obviously thought of his furniture as something between ceiling and floor, albeit the ceilings and floors designed by a post-World War II architect. In that sense Eames was probably right when he said that Saarinen treated furniture as "a miniature piece of architecture." Saarinen, who considered Wright "the greatest architect of his time," once reminded Temko that he "did not conceive structure separately; his structure, his funny decorations, his spaces, his lighting, were all one thing. Today we have all this 'icky' kind of architecture which is taken a little bit from here and a little from there." One is reminded of Wright's own words in his introduction to the Wasmuth portfolio of his work published in Berlin in 1910: "One thing instead of many things; a great thing instead of a collection of smaller ones." That Saarinen was also thinking of comfort—of the person who sits in his chairs—when he designed the pedestal chair is evident. Orthopedic surgeon Dr. Michael Lampert, when interviewed by *Progressive Architecture* in February 1975 about the comfort of various modern chairs, reported that Saarinen's pedestal chair felt secure. "The arms give support, helping you relieve some back loading by transmitting it to the shoulders. Your body is encased, with room to shift around without sliding or flopping over. I find it comfortable." And that is a great deal more than he found for Rietveld's Red and Blue chair, Breuer's Wassily chair, Aalto's scroll armchair, among others.

The father's work may have been steeped in humanism and the son's in technology, but the influence of the father ran like a gentle stream through everything the son did, including his interest in how people felt in his chairs. Eliel would have understood that, as some architects of the modern movement might not. In fact it sometimes seems as if Eero would have liked to accept his father's ways, but knowing he lived in an age of technology he thought he had to deny the older architect's emphasis on the more humane and personal work of the hand. The denial, however, was never total.

CHARLES EAMES 1907-1978

Now chairs have always been the forward-runners of design-change. They have for some mysterious reason the capacity of establishing a new sense of style almost overnight. PETER SMITHSON

Eames, who devoted far more time to designing furniture than architecture, once said: "If I feel guilty about chickening out of architecture, Eero was guilty about not giving architecture the careful detailing I could give furniture." Saarinen was worried about form, Eames was worried about how to produce, as Cesar Pelli put it. "When Eames had to sacrifice style to keep the technology coherent, he would; Eero would have no hesitation about sacrificing technology to keep the style and form clean." That was the difference between them, and as far as furniture was concerned it was great.

Ever since the turn of the century architects had tried to come to terms with the machine and to design furniture that could be mass produced and sold at a reasonable price but only with varying degrees of success. Eames seems to have been the first architect to design a collection of furniture that totally reconciles art and industry probably because he was the first architect to feel totally comfortable with technology. Eames, as Arthur Drexler has said, "tended to develop technical solutions first, and only later re-design the disparate parts to make them harmonious." No other architect had approached chair design in just that way. An Eames chair is informed by technical determinations which are the match of his esthetic convictions—a true partnership has been formed between art and technology. This is what Wright meant when he said, "genius must progressively dominate the work of the contrivance it has created." This is what C. R. Ashbee meant when he said, "Modern civilisation rests on machinery, and no system for the endowment, or the encouragement, or the teaching of art can be sound that does not recognize this." This is what Voysey meant when he

said, "When you design my tables and chairs you will think of the machine that is going to help in the making." And this is what Gropius meant when he said, "The Bauhaus believes the machine to be our modern medium of design and seeks to come to terms with it." Eames came to terms with the machine, but Eames, it should not be forgotten, was an artist.

Eames was born in St. Louis, Missouri, in 1907, where he attended Washington University on an architectural scholarship. In 1929 he went to Europe where he became familiar with the work of Gropius and Mies. In 1930 he opened his own office in St. Louis, but soon closed it because of lack of commissions in that depression year. In 1936 Eliel Saarinen offered him a fellowship at Cranbrook where he remained for several years teaching and helping to develop an experimental design department. It was at Cranbrook that he collaborated with Eero Saarinen on the molded plywood chair that won first prize in the Museum of Modern Art's 1940 furniture competition. It was also at Cranbrook that Eames met Ray Kaiser who was to become his wife and partner in all his future ventures.

The winning Eames-Saarinen chair was never manufactured because of the high cost of the molding process, and so after the Eameses moved to California in 1941 they spent their spare time trying to develop an inexpensive molding process. During World War II their research resulted in a commission from the U.S. Navy to produce plywood stretchers and splints. And by 1946 there was a new set of

Molded polyester armchair designed by Eames in 1971 is padded Naugahyde on an aluminum base—a sleek and comfortable 20th-century chair.

Eames-designed molded plywood chairs, which were not only exhibited in a one-man show at the Museum of Modern Art but produced by the furniture company Herman Miller using the tools the Eameses had developed in their workshop. Among the new group was the justly famed side chair of molded plywood with metal rod legs, which has been called one of the most compelling artifacts of its generation. Part of the elegance of its design, as Arthur Drexler has pointed out, must be attributed to the contours of the seat and back panel. Eames himself, Drexler tells us, cited the hundreds of studies he made for these two elements because their contours somehow attracted undue attention. Plainly his studies were a success. Reviewing the decade of the 1940s in *Interiors* 20th anniversary issue of November 1960, Olga Gueft called Eames its "biggest story" and goes on to explain that by inventing "processes for molding the laminated plywood into compound curves and electronically joining the plywood to other plywood or steel members with rubber disks between for resilience, he simultaneously produced exquisite forms and proportions and a new concept of completely separating a chair's back and seat within its supporting frame. At that time the technology of the Eames chair was what attracted attention. Today the nature of his forms seems the greater contribution."

There is, as Drexler has noted, something American about the "distinctive and memorable image contributed by what is now called simply 'the Eames chair,' " and that is because it "does not suppress necessary mechanical details but rather makes them plainly visible. Hardware is pragmatically designed to do a job, but not overdesigned in the romanticizing manner Americans often identify as European."

It is hardly surprising then that the "Eames chair" quickly became as essential a part of the modern post-World War II interior as the European tubular-steel chair had been an essential part of the modern post-World War I interior. The Eames chair, moreover, lent those post-World War II interiors a certain wit and elegance not often associated with the tubular-steel chair. It quickly became apparent that Eames had indeed achieved the integration between art and technology which the earlier architects had striven for.

Eames, of course, went on to design other chairs that are recognizable all over the world as both American and Eames. In 1948 an Eames entry prepared with a University of California team won second prize in another Museum of Modern Art Low-Cost Furniture Design competition. This time the exhibit chair was of molded stamped metal, but it became molded plastic when put into production by Herman Miller, with legs either of metal rods or a kind of cat's

Opposite page, top: The shell of this molded polyester armchair (left) was originally of stamped metal and won a second prize in the 1948 Museum of Modern Art International Competition for Low-Cost Furniture Design. When it was manufactured in 1950, Herman Miller Inc. set up economical production of molded plastic rather than metal. The same shape chair was also made of bent wire with an upholstered pad in fabric or leather (right).

Opposite page, bottom: Eames's molded plywood chairs are eminently at home in the dining area of the Eames's California house of 1949.

Above: This dining chair designed in 1946 of a single material—molded and bent birch plywood—is one of many versions of the familiar Eames chair.

Right: This world-famous side chair of 1946, made in both dining and lounge heights, is of molded walnut plywood with steel rods and rubber shock mounts. It was first produced in Eames's studio and later taken over by Herman Miller Inc.

cradle metal wire composition. A version of this chair without arms was developed as a stacking chair, and the same shape was also made of bent wire with an upholstered pad in fabric or leather.

In 1956 Eames designed the lounge chair and ottoman that not only has become familiar in modern offices and living rooms but through numerous advertisements, that for one reason or another, give the impression that the man sitting in it is an important executive or exclusive club man. Many architects including Wright, Le Corbusier, Breuer, Mies, and Saarinen tried to design a chair that would replace the old over-stuffed wing chair or leather club chair, but Eames was the first to successfully produce a really comfortable chair in an entirely new form. Made of laminated rosewood "petals" padded with leather cushions and joined with aluminum connections, the chair is mounted on a metal swivel base.

In the 1960s Eames designed furniture of cast aluminum as well as tandem seating for use in airports. He also designed many storage cabinets and tables, but Eames' chairs are his most revolutionary creations. In fact Eames' molded plywood chair and Mies's Barcelona chair would have little difficulty winning the honors as the great chair designs of the 20th century—chairs that gave the whole world a new way of seeing as well as sitting.

Eames understood craft as anyone who had been at Eliel Saarinen's Cranbrook would have to, and he understood technology. One might say that he justified Gropius's theory stated in 1923 that "it would be senseless to launch a gifted apprentice straight into industry without preparation in a craft. . . . He would be stifled by the materialistic and one-sided outlook predominant in factories today. A craft, however, cannot conflict with the feeling for workmanship which, as an artist, he inevitably has, and it is therefore the best opportunity for practical training."

As he had done in furniture Eames did in the house he designed and built for himself in 1949 in Santa Monica, California: he achieved an al-

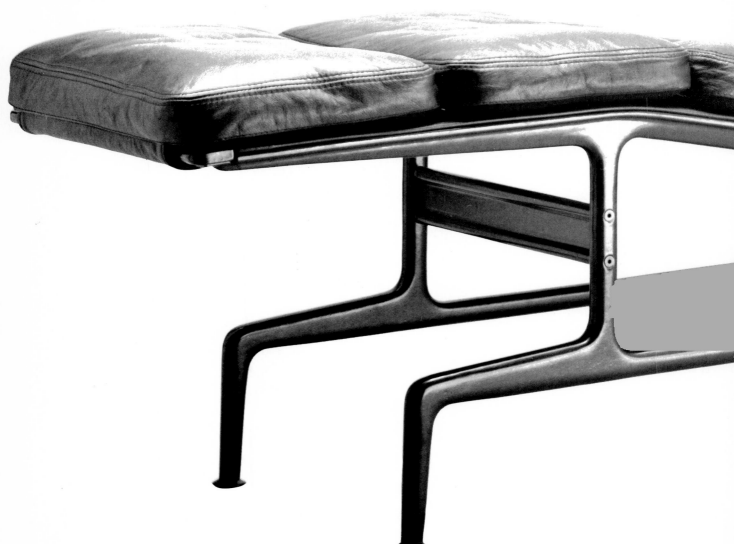

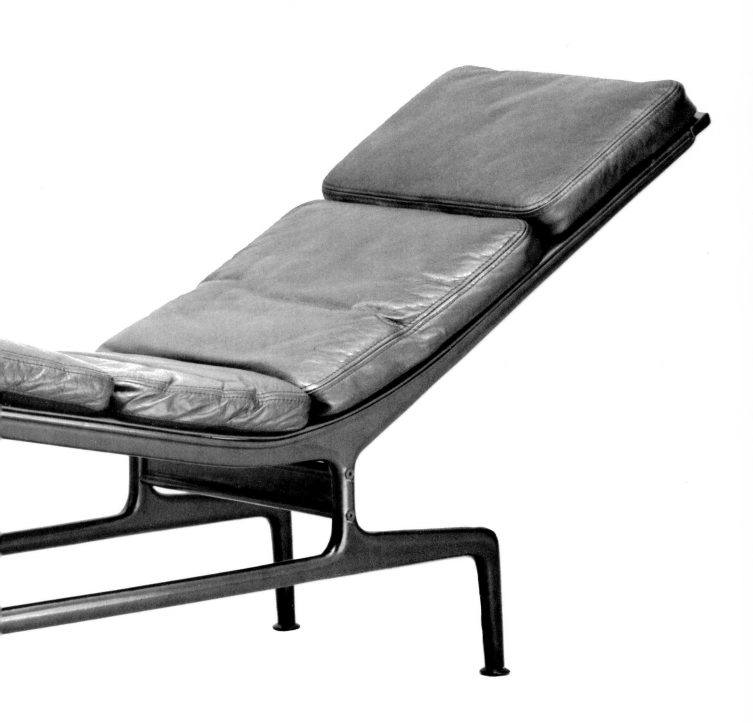

Chaise designed by Eames in 1968, is of nylon-coated aluminum made comfortable with foam-padded black leather cushions.

most perfect synthesis among art, craft, and technology. To use industrial materials for an esthetic end, in fact, was the reason for designing it. The Eames house, however, was not designed self-consciously as a showcase of industrial products. Here again the technician and the artist worked in equal partnership. "I think of myself officially as an architect," Eames once said and then added, "I can't help but look at the problems around us as problems of structure—and structure is architecture." And for Eames technology was part of structure. It wasn't as it had been for those earlier architects who found it necessary to expend so many words on achieving a unity of art and technology. For Eames there really was no conflict between them. He considered the use of mass-produced industrial materials a perfectly valid means of achieving the art of architecture. The Eames house was almost entirely constructed of standard, factory-made, mass-produced parts—windows, doors, and steel beams combined with glass and stucco—but it doesn't look like a factory. It looks like architecture as a work of art. The art, of course, derives partly from the fact that it was designed by one who understood the esthetics as well as the function of architecture and partly from the lively collections and furniture that stamp it so peculiarly as an Eames house. Those who hailed it as a harbinger of prefabrication missed the point. If it ever was that, it is certainly much more. It is the synthesis, in creation as well as theory, of all those words about a machine art.

This is what the Bauhaus was all about. But Bauhaus-inspired architecture is often of forbidding simplicity, more suggestive of a factory than a place in which artists might live and work. The prefabricated house in Santa Monica provided the ideal neutral background for the Eames' way of life and the highly individual and colorful objects they collected. Light streaming through factory-made windows picks up the colors of an Indian bowl, the texture of a Mexican doll, or the contours of an Eames chair. This is surely what Le Corbusier meant by a "machine for living." No one can see where the machine begins or the living ends. It is all one. Reyner Banham, trying to account for the "profound effect" the Eames house had on many English and European architects of his generation, came to the conclusion that the inherent style of both the house and the molded plywood chair "answered exactly to an emerging taste for that kind of fine-drawn design in many parts of the world."

Eames was part of the California tradition that included Maybeck, the Greene brothers, Gill, Schindler, Neutra, and others. Maybeck, in fact, used factory parts in his Christian Science Church in Berkeley some 30 years before Eames built his house in Santa Monica. All these architects respected materials, they respected craft, and with the possible exception of the Greenes they respected the machine. They all produced houses that harmonized with their landscape and all maintained a sense of human-

Above: The interior of Eames's house in Venice, California, of 1949 has been aptly described as a changing, evolving space. This view shows the famous Eames lounge chair in the two-story living room.

Opposite page: Eames's famous lounge chair and ottoman of 1956, of molded plywood with black leather cushions, is the modern designer's answer to the traditional club chair.

ity in everything they did. They were experimenters, they were individualists, and they were somehow peculiarly American.

William Morris started it all, as Nikolaus Pevsner says in his *Pioneers of Modern Design*, by reviving handicraft as an art worthy of the best person's efforts. The pioneers around 1900 went further by discovering the immense untried possibilities of machine art. But the balance stayed on the side of craft through the Arts and Crafts, Prairie school, and Art Nouveau movements. The Bauhaus and De Stijl shifted it to the side of the machine. This is even more true of furniture than of architecture. To look at a chair by Gaudi, Guimard, Mackintosh, Voysey, or even Wright, one senses more craft than machine. But Rietveld's Zigzag chair or Breuer's tubular-steel chair weigh the scales on the side of the machine. Eames, with his house and his chairs, pointed the way to righting the balance. At last art and technology began working together, and Morris's romantic protest against machine production was stilled. No other architect had approached chair design as Eames did—developing sophisticated technical solutions first. It is an American way, but it took the sensitivity and genius of an Eames to make it an art. "Art and Technics, a New Unity," the title of the first exhibition of the Bauhaus workshops in 1923, had finally come into its own. In a sense, wrote Peter Smithson in *Architectural Design* of September 1966, "both the machine-aesthetic and the Eames-aesthetic are art-forms of ordinary life and ordinary objects seen with an eye that sees the ordinary as also magical."

Thus in the hands of Charles Eames and Eero Saarinen with their arts and crafts background, the machine was no longer a threat but an obedient servant. In their different ways, these two post-World War II architects showed that technology need not exclude art any more than art need exclude technology.

SELECTED BIBLIOGRAPHY

GENERAL

Aslin, Elizabeth. *Nineteenth Century English Furniture*. London: Faber and Faber, 1962.

Banham, Reyner. *Age of the Masters: A Personal View of Modern Architecture*. New York: Harper & Row, 1962.

————. *The Architecture of the Well-Tempered Environment*. Chicago: University of Chicago Press.1969.

————. *Theory and Design in the First Machine Age*. London, 1960.

Benton, Tim and Charlotte, with Dennis Sharp, eds. *Architecture and Design 1890–1939: An International Anthology of Original Articles*. New York: Whitney Library of Design, 1975.

Blake, Peter. *Form Follows Fiasco: Why Modern Architecture Hasn't Worked*. Boston: Little, Brown and Co.,1977.

————. *The Master Builders*. New York: W.W. Norton, 1976.

Boger, Louise Ade. *Furniture Past & Present*. New York: Doubleday & Company, Inc., 1966.

Burchard, John, and Bush-Brown, Albert. *The Architecture of America*. Boston: Little, Brown & Co., 1961.

Collins, Peter. *Changing Ideals in Modern Architecture 1750–1950*. Montreal: McGill-Queen's University Press, 1965.

Giedion, Seigfried. *Mechanization Takes Command*. New York: Oxford University Press, 1970.

————. *Space, Time and Architecture*. Cambridge, Mass.: Harvard University Press, 1976.

Gloag, John. *A Social History of Furniture Design from B.C. 1300 to A.D. 1960*. New York: Crown Publishers, Inc., 1966.

Gowans, Alan. *Images of American Living*. Philadelphia and New York: J.B. Lippincott Company, 1964.

Heyer, Paul. *Architects on Architecture*. New York: Walker & Company, 1966.

Hitchcock, Henry-Russell. *Architecture: Nineteenth and Twentieth Centuries*. 3rd ed. Baltimore: Penguin, 1969.

Jencks, Charles. *Modern Movements in Architecture*. Garden City, N.Y.: Anchor Books, 1973.

Jordan, Robert Furneaux. *Victorian Architecture*. Baltimore: Penguin, 1966.

Jordy, William H. *American Buildings and Their Architects: Progressive and Academic Ideals at the Turn of the Twentieth Century*. Garden City, N.Y. : Anchor Books, 1976.

Logie, Gordon. *Furniture from Machines*. London: George Allen and Unwin Ltd., 1947.

Meadmore, Clement. *The Modern Chair, Classics in Production*. New York: Van Nostrand, 1975.

Mumford, Lewis. *Roots of Contemporary American Architecture*. New York: Grove Press, Inc., 1959.

19th-Century American Furniture and Other Decorative Arts. New York: The Metropolitan Museum of Art,1970.

Pevsner, Nikolaus. *Pioneers of Modern Design*. Harmondsworth, England: Penguin, 1964.

————. *The Sources of Modern Architecture and Design*. New York: Frederick A. Praeger, 1968.

————. *Studies in Art, Architecture and Design*. Vol. 2. New York: Walker & Company, 1968.

————, and Richards, J.M., eds. *The Anti-Rationalists*. Toronto: University of Toronto Press, 1973.

Scully, Vincent, Jr. *Modern Architecture*. New York: George Braziller, Inc., 1975.

18th-CENTURY ENGLAND AND FEDERAL AMERICA

Adam, Robert. *The Works in Architecture of Robert and James Adam*. Vols. 1,2. London, 1773–1779.

Clunie, Margaret Burke. "Joseph True and the Piecework System in Salem." *Antiques*, May 1977.

Fastnedge, Ralph. *English Furniture Styles 1500–1830*. Baltimore: Penguin, 1962.

Harris, Eileen. *The Furniture of Robert Adam*. New York: St. Martin's Press, 1973.

Jourdain, Margaret. *English Decoration and Furniture of the Late XVIII Century*. London: 1922.

————. *The Work of Willaim Kent*. London: Country Life Ltd., 1948.

Kimball, Fiske. *Mr. Samuel McIntire: The Architect of Salem*. Salem, Mass.: The Essex Institute, 1940.

Lees-Milne, James. *The Age of Adam*. London: B.T. Batsford, Ltd., 1947.

————. *Earls of Creation*. New York, London: House & Maxwell, 1963.

Parker, James. "Croome Court: The Architecture and Furniture." *The Metropolitan Museum of Art Bulletin* 18 (November 1959).

Samuel McIntire: A Bicentennial Symposium 1757-1957. Salem, Mass.: The Essex Institute, 1957.

Stillman, Damie. *The Decorative Work of Robert Adam*. London: Alec Tiranti, 1966.

Tomlin, Maurice. "Back to Adam at Osterly." *Country Life*, June 18, 1970.

————. "Osterly in the 18th Century." *Country Life*, June 25, 1970.

TWO GOTHIC REVIVAL ARCHITECTS

Andrews, Wayne. *American Gothic: Its Origins, Its Triumphs*. New York: Random House, 1975.

Cantor, Jay E. *The Public Architecture of James Renwick, Jr.: An Investigation of the Concept of an American National Style during the Nineteenth Century*. Unpublished M.A. thesis, University of Delaware, 1967.

Clark, Kenneth. *The Gothic Revival*. Harmondsworth, England: Penguin, 1962.
New York: Penguin, 1962.

Davies, Jane B. "Gothic Revival Furniture Designs of Alexander Jackson Davis." *Antiques*, May 1977.

Donnell, Edna. "A.J. Davis and the Gothic Revival." *Metropolitan Museum Studies*, 5, part 2.

Downing, A.J. *The Architecture of Country Houses*. New York: Dover Publications, Inc., 1969.

Dunlap, William. *A History of the Rise and Progress of the Arts of Design in the United States*. Vol. 3. Boston: C.E. Goodspeed & Company, 1918.

Goode, James M. "A View of the Castle." *Museum News*, July-August, 1976.

Newton, R.H. *Town & Davis Architects*. New York: Columbia University Press, 1942.

Pearce, John. "Changing Taste and the Evolution of the Furnishings at Lyndhurst." *Historic Preservation*. 17 (March-April 1965).

Pugin, A. Welby. *The Principles and Revival of Christian Architecture*. London: Henry G. Bohn, 1853.

Stanton, Phoebe. *Pugin*. New York: Viking Press, 1972.

THE ARTS AND CRAFTS TRADITION

Ball, A.H.R., ed. *Selections from the Prose of William Morris.* Cambridge: Cambridge University Press, 1931.

Brandon-Jones, John, et al. *C.F.A. Voysey Architect and Designer 1857–1941* (including section on furniture by Duncan Simpson). London: Lund Humphries Publishers, Ltd., in association with the Art Gallery and Museum and the Royal Pavilion, Brighton, England, 1978.

Clark, Robert Judson, ed. *The Arts and Crafts Movement in America 1876–1916.* Princeton, N.J.: Princeton University Press, 1972.

Farnam, Anne. "A.H. Davenport and Company, Boston Furniture Maker." *Antiques,* May 1978.

Ferguson, Robert. "Castles: Notes towards a Reading of the Architecture of Harvey Ellis." *Vital Statistics,* May 1978.

France, Jean R. "A Rediscovery: Harvey Ellis, Artist, Architect." A joint exhibition of the Memorial Art Gallery of the University of Rochester and Margaret Woodbury Strong Museum, 1972–1973.

Gebhard, David. "C.F.A. Voysey: To and From America." *Journal of the Society of Architectural Historians,* September 1971.

————. *Charles F.A. Voysey.* Los Angeles: Hennessey & Engels, Inc., 1975.

Hanks, David, and Talbott, Page. "Daniel Pabst: Philadelphia Cabinetmaker." *Philadelphia Museum of Art Bulletin,* April 1977.

Hitchcock, Henry-Russell. *The Architecture of H.H. Richardson and His Times.* Hamden, Conn.: Archon Books, 1961.

Kennedy, Roger G. "The Long Shadow of Harvey Ellis." *Minnesota History.* Fall, 1966.

————. "Long Dark Corridors: Harvey Ellis." *Prairie School Review* 5 (First and Second Quarter, 1968).

O'Gorman, James F. *The Architecture of Frank Furness.* Philadelphia: Philadelphia Museum of Art, 1973.

————. *H.G. Richardson and His Office: A Centennial of His Move to Boston 1874.* Cambridge, Mass.: Department of Printing and Graphic Arts, Harvard College Library, 1974.

Philadelphia: Three Centuries of American Art, Bicentennial Exhibition. Philadelphia: Philadelphia Museum of Art, 1976.

Randall, Richard H., Jr. *The Furniture of H.H. Richardson.* Boston: Museum of Fine Arts, 1962.

Scheyer, Ernest. "Henry Adams and Henry Hobson Richardson." *Journal of the Society of Architectural Historians,* March 1953.

Thompson, E.P. *William Morris: Romantic to Revolutionary.* New York: Pantheon Books, 1977.

Thompson, Paul. *The Work of William Morris.* New York: The Viking Press, 1967.

Van Rensselaer, Marian Griswold. *Henry Hobson Richardson and His Works.* Boston and New York, 1888.

THREE ARCHITECTS OF THE PRAIRIE SCHOOL

Brooks, H. Allen. "The Early Work of the Prairie Architects." *Journal of the Society of Architectural Historians,* March 1960.

————. *The Prairie School: Frank Lloyd Wright and His Midwest Contemporaries.* New York: W.W. Norton & Company, Inc., 1976.

Condit, Carl W. *The Chicago School of Architecture.* Chicago: The University of Chicago Press, 1964.

David, Arthur C. "The Architecture of Ideas." *The Architectural Record,* April 1904.

Gebhard, David. "Purcell and Elmslie, Architects." Catalog of Walker Art Center exhibition, March 1953.

————. *The Architecture of Purcell and Elmslie.* Park Forest, Ill.: Prairie School Press, 1965.

————. "Louis Sullivan and George Grant Elmslie." *Journal of the Society of Architectural Historians,* May 1960.

"George W. Maher: A Democrat in Architecture." *Western Architect,* March 1914.

Gutheim, Frederick, ed. *In the Cause of Architecture, Frank Lloyd Wright.* (Wright's Historic Essays for *Architectural Record,* 1908–1952).

Hanks, David A. *The Decorative Designs of Frank Lloyd Wright.* New York: E.P. Dutton, 1979.

Historic Preservation (special issue on Pope-Leighey House), April-September 1969.

Hitchcock, Henry-Russell. *In the Nature of Materials 1887–1941: The Buildings of Frank Lloyd Wright.* New York: Duell, Sloan and Pearce, 1942.

Hoffmann, Donald. *Frank Lloyd Wright's Fallingwater.* With Introduction by Edgar Kaufmann, Jr. New York: Dover Publications, Inc., 1978.

Jacobs, Herbert, with Jacobs, Katherine. *Building with Frank Lloyd Wright.* San Francisco: Chronicle Books, 1978.

Kalec, Donald. "The Prairie School Furniture." *Prairie School Redview,* 1 (Fourth Quarter, 1964).

Kaufmann, Edgar, and Raeburn, Ben. *Frank Lloyd Wright: Writings and Buildings.* New York: Horizon Press, 1960.

Maher, George W. "An Architecture of Ideas." *Arts and Decoration* 1 (June 1911).

Morrison, Hugh. *Louis Sullivan: Prophet of Modern Architecture.* New York: W.W. Norton, 1935.

Rudd, J. William. "George W. Maher: Architect of the Prairie School." *Prairie School Review* 1 (First Quarter, 1964).

Twombly, Robert C. *Frank Lloyd Wright: An Interpretive Biography.* New York: Harper & Row, 1973.

Wright, Frank Lloyd. *An Autobiography.* New York: Duell, Sloan and Pearce, 1943.

————. *The Future of Architecture.* New York: Horizon Press, 1953.

————. *The Natural House.* New York: New American Library, 1970.

FOUR CALIFORNIA ARCHITECTS

"Architecture in California 1868–1968." An exhibition organized by David Gebhard and Harriette von Breton to celebrate the Centennial of the University of California, 1968.

Bangs, J.M. "Bernard Ralph Maybeck, Architect, Comes into His Own." *Architectural Record,* January 1948.

Banham, Reyner. *Los Angeles: The Architecture of Four Ecologies.* New York: Pelican Book, 1976.

Cardwell, Kenneth H. *Bernard Maybeck, Artisan, Architect, Artist.* Santa Barbara and Salt Lake City: Peregrine Smith, Inc., 1977.

Gebhard, David. *R.M. Schindler,* New York: The Viking Press, 1972.

————, and Von Breton, Harriette. *Los Angeles in the Thirties 1931–1941.* Santa Barbara and Salt Lake City: Peregrine Smith, Inc., 1975.

"Greene & Greene." *American Preservation,* April-May 1978.

"Greene and Greene: The Architecture and Related Designs of Charles Sumner Greene and

Henry Mather Greene, 1894–1934." Exhibition at Los Angeles Museum Art Gallery, 1977.

Harris, Jean. "Bernard Ralph Maybeck." *Journal of the American Institute of Architects,* May 1951.

Lancaster, Clay. "My Interviews with Greene and Greene." *Journal of the American Institute of Architects,* July 1957.

McCoy, Esther. *Five California Architects.* New York: Reinhold Publishing Company, 1960.

Makinson, Randell L. *Greene & Greene: Architecture as a Fine Art.* Salt Lake City and Santa Barbara: Peregrine Smith, Inc., 1977.

———. *Greene & Greene: Furniture and Related Designs.* Layton, Utah: Peregrine Smith, Inc., 1979.

Marks, Alan. "Greene and Greene: A Study in Functional Design." *Fine Woodworking,* September 1978.

Schindler, R.M. "Furniture and the Modern House: A Theory of Interior Design." *The Architect and Engineer.* December 1935 and March 1936.

———. *Collected Papers* (1 volume mimeographed in the library of the New York Historical Society).

Winter, Robert W. "American Sheaves from 'C.R.A.' and Janet Ashbee." *Journal of the Society of Architectural Historians,* December 1971.

THREE ART NOUVEAU ARCHITECT-DESIGNERS

Alison, Filippo. *Charles Rennie Mackintosh as a Designer of Chairs.* Woodbury, N.Y.: Barron's, 1977.

Amaya, Mario. *Art Nouveau.* New York: Dutton Vista Paperback, 1966.

Barnes, H. Jefferson. *Charles Rennie Mackintosh: Furniture.* Glasgow: Glasgow School of Art, 1978.

Binney, Marcus. "An Architect of Unfulfilled Promise: Charles Rennie Mackintosh." *Country Life,* Nov. 7, 1968.

Cirlot, Juan-Eduardo. *The Genesis of Gaudian Architecture.* New York: George Wittenborn, Inc.

Collins, George R. *Antonio Gaudi.* New York: George Braziller Inc., 1960.

———. "The Organic Art of Antonio Gaudi." *Lithopion* 25 (Spring, 1972).

Descharnes, Robert, and Prevost, Clovis. *Gaudi: The Visionary.* New York: The Viking Press, 1969.

Graham, Lanier. " Hector Guimard."

Museum of Modern Art exhibition catalog, 1970.

Hitchcock, Henry-Russell. *Gaudi.* New York: Museum of Modern Art, 1957.

Howarth, Thomas. *Charles Rennie Mackintosh and the Modern Movement.* London, 1968.

MacLeod, Robert. *Charles Rennie Mackintosh.* London: Country Life Book, 1978.

Madsen, S. Tschudi. *Art Nouveau.* New York: McGraw-Hill Book Company, 1967.

Schmutzler, Robert. *Art Nouveau.* New York: Harry N. Abrams, Inc., 1962.

Sert, Jose-Luis. "Gaudi from Nature to Geometry." *The Selective Eye.* Edited by Georges and Rosamond Bernier. New York: Random House, 1955.

THE MODERN MOVEMENT

"Aalto: Architecture and Furniture." New York: Museum of Modern Art, 1938.

"Alvar Aalto." *Progressive Architecture,* April 1977.

Alvar Aalto 1898 –1976. Catalog of exhibition at The Museum of Finnish Architecture, Helsinki, 1978.

Baroni, Daniele. *The Furniture of Gerrit Thomas Rietveld.* Woodbury, N.Y.: Barron's, 1978.

Blake, Peter. *Marcel Breuer: Architect and Designer.* New York: Architectural Record and The Museum of Modern Art, 1949.

———. *Marcel Breuer: Sun and Shadow, The Philosophy of the Architect.* New York: Dodd Mead & Co., 1955.

Brown, Theodore M. *The Work of G. Rietveld, Architect.* Cambridge, Mass.: The MIT Press, 1958.

———. "Rietveld's Egocentric Vision." *Journal of the Society of Architectural Historians.* December 1965.

Burchard, John E. "Finland and Architect Aalto." *Architectural Record,* January 1959.

Choay, Francoise. *Le Corbusier.* New York: George Braziller, Inc., 1960.

De Fusco, Renato. *Le Corbusier Designer: Furniture, 1929.* Woodbury, N.Y.: Barron's, 1977.

Drexler, Arthur. *Mies van der Rohe.* New York: George Braziller, 1960.

Fleig, Karl. *Alvar Aalto.* New York: Praeger Publishers, 1971.

Gardiner, Stephen. *Le Corbusier.* New York: The Viking Press, 1974.

Giedon, Siegfried. "Alvar Aalto." *Architectural Review,* February 1950.

Glaeser, Ludwig. *Ludwig Mies van der Rohe Furniture and Drawings from the Design Collection and the Mies van der Rohe Archive.* New York: The Museum of Modern Art, 1977.

Gutheim, Frederick. *Alvar Aalto.* New York: George Braziller, 1960.

Hitchcock, Henry-Russell, Jr. *Exhibition by Marcel Breuer, Harvard University, Department of Architecture.* Cambridge, Mass., 1938.

Jencks, Charles. *Le Corbusier and the Tragic View of Architecture.* Cambridge, Mass.: Harvard University Press, 1973.

Kaufmann, Edgar. "Modern Rooms of the Last 50 Years Assembled for a Circulating Exhibition of the Museum of Modern Art." *Interiors,* February 1947.

Le Corbusier. *Towards a New Architecture.* London, 1927.

Papachristou, Tician. *Marcel Breuer: New Buildings and Projects.* New York: Praeger Publishers, 1970.

Pearson, Paul David. *Alvar Aalto and the International Style.* New York: Whitney Library of Design, 1978.

Schildt, Goran. "Aalto and Architecture." *Zodiac,* no. 3 (1958).

———. *Alvar Aalto Sketches.* Cambridge, Mass.: The MIT Press, 1978.

Von Eckardt, Wolf. "The Architect." In catalog of Marcel Breuer exhibition at the Metropolitan Museum of Art, New York, 1972.

TWO POST-WORLD WAR II ARCHITECTS

Christ-Janer, Albert. *Eliel Saarinen.* Chicago: The University of Chicago Press, 1947.

Drexler, Arthur. *Charles Eames Furniture from the Design Collection.* New York: The Museum of Modern Art, 1973.

McCoy, Esther. "Charles and Ray Eames." *Design Quarterly* 98/99 (1975).

McQuade, Walter. "Eero Saarinen: A Complete Architect." *Architectural Forum,* April 1962.

Saarinen, Aline B., ed. *Eero Saarinen on His Work.* New Haven, Conn.: Yale University Press, 1962.

Temko, Allan. *Eero Saarinen.* New York: George Braziller, 1962.

———. "Eero Saarinen: '. . .something between earth and sky. . .' " *Horizon,* July 1960.

CREDITS

Photographs and drawings have been reproduced courtesy of the following individuals and institutions:

Albright-Knox Art Gallery, Buffalo, New York. Gift of Darwin D. Martin: 93, 94 (left)
American Art & Antiques: 67
The Art Institute of Chicago: 111, 113 (left), 114 (bottom)
The Art Museum, Princeton University: 88
Artek: 198 (top), 200
Atelier International, Ltd.: 153 (bottom), 155, 163 (right), 166, 188 (top)
Avery Library, Columbia University: 43
The Bohemian Club: 126
Marcel Breuer & Associates Architects, New York: 170, 171, 173, 174, 175, 176, 177
Cátedra Gaudi: 145, 146 (top right, bottom), 147, 148–149
The Cooper-Hewitt Museum of Design, Smithsonian Institution: 29 (top), 100 (top), 138, 139 (bottom)
Cranbrook Academy of Art/Museum: 207, 208
Charles Eames, Venice, California: 212 (bottom), 217
Essex Institute, Salem, Massachusetts: 32; Photo by Richard Merrill: 29 (bottom)
Photo by Louis H. Frohman: 40–41
The Glasgow School of Art: 152, 153 (top)
HABS photo, Library of Congress: 97; by Cervin Robinson: 109, 110
Photo by Thomas A. Heinz: 94 (right), 95, 101
Houghton Library, Harvard University: 64, 65
ICF, Inc., New York: 193, 194, 196, 197, 199
Jordan-Volpe Gallery, New York: 85, 87
Knoll International: 205, 206
The Metropolitan Museum of Art, New York: 98, 99; Gift of Mrs. D. Chester Noyes: 48
The Museum of the City of New York: 38 (top)
Museum of Fine Arts, Boston: 63, 68, 69; M. & M. Karolik Collection: 27, 28, 30–31
The Museum of Modern Art, New York: 137, 139 (top), 140, 141, 142, 143, 146 (top left), 198 (bottom), 211, 212 (top), 213, 214–215, 216; Gift of Herbert Bayer: 169; Gift of the Glasgow School of Art: 157 (left); Gift of Philip Johnson: 163 (left); Gift of Edgar Kaufmann, Jr.: 96, 195; Gift of Knoll International: 181 (right); Phyllis B. Lambert Fund: 164, 165; Gift of Phylis B. Lambert: 185; The Mies van der Rohe Archives: 180 (left), 182, 183; The Mies van der Rohe Archives, Gift of Knoll International: 179; Gift of Thonet Industries, Inc.: 188–189, 190
National Monuments Record, London: 15
The National Trust, London. Photo by John Bethell: 20, 21, 24, 25
The National Trust for Historic Preservation: 37, 38 (bottom), 39, 42, 44, 106 (bottom); Photo by Jack Boucher: 106 (top)
New York State Court of Appeals: 66
Northwestern Architectural Archives, University of Minnesota: 113 (right), 114 (top), 115
The Philadelphia Museum of Art: 14; Gift of George Wood Furness: 72–73, 74
Marvin Rand photo: 119, 120, 121, 122
Photograph by Cervin Robinson: 71
The Royal Commission of the Ancient & Historical Monuments of Scotland. Photo by Bedford Lemere: 154, 158
Smithsonian Institution: 47, 50–51
Sir John Soane's Museum, London: 18, 19
Sotheby's Belgravia, London: 156
The Margaret Woodbury Strong Museum, Rochester, New York: 86
Thonet Industries, Inc.: 172, 180 (right), 181 (left)
Documents Collection, College of Environmental Design, University of California, Berkeley: 125
Architectural Drawing Collection, UCSB Art Museum, University of California, Santa Barbara: 78, 79, 82, 129, 130, 132
Property of the Western Pennsylvania Conservancy: 103
Frank Lloyd Wright Memorial Foundation: 100 (bottom), 102, 105
The Victoria and Albert Museum, London: 17, 22–23, 55, 56, 57, 59, 60, 61, 77, 80, 151, 157 (right), 186

INDEX

Italicized page numbers indicate illustrations.